bor Seki

Tonari no Seki-kun

5

Takuma Morishige

Schedule

My
Neighbor
Seki

5

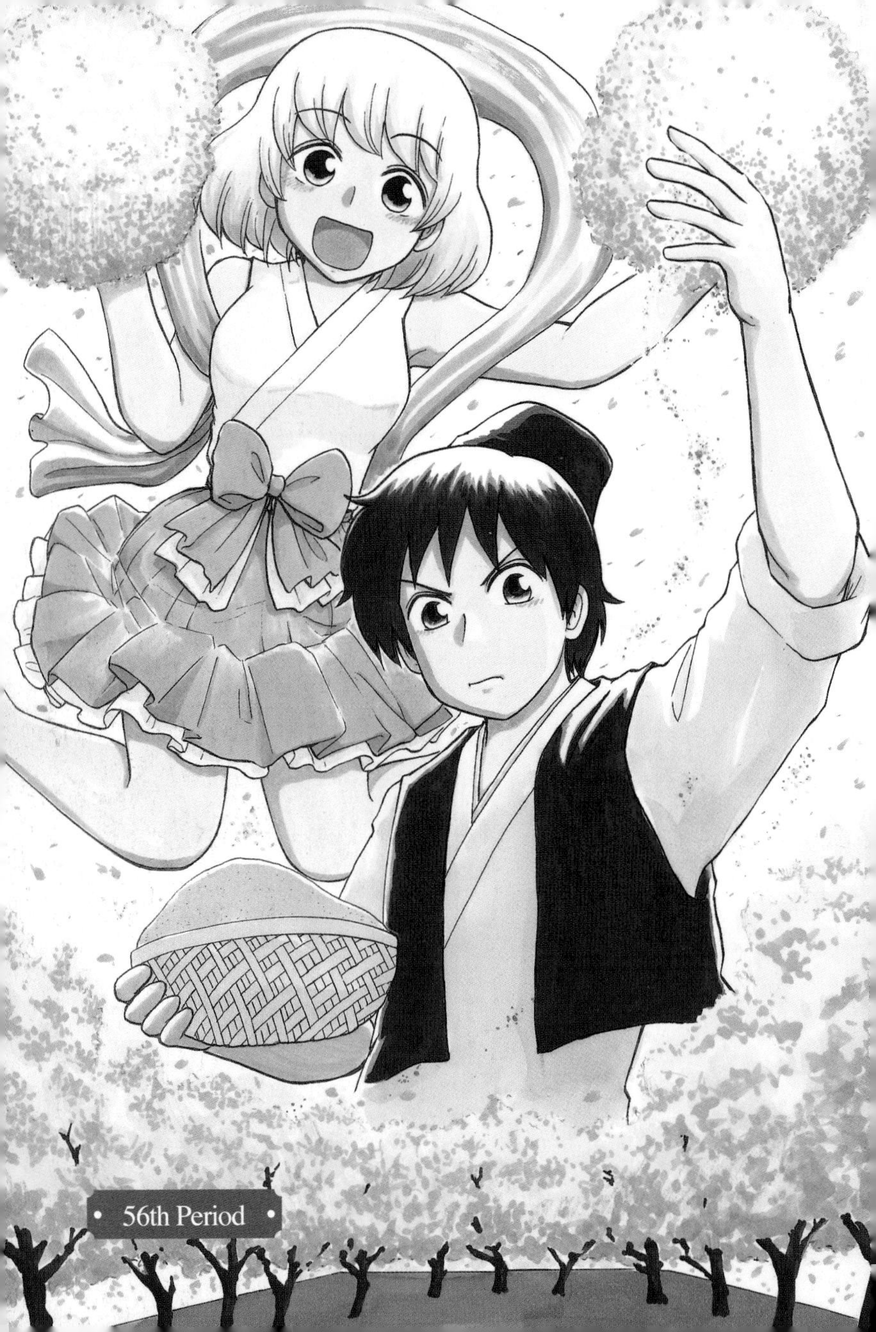
56th Period

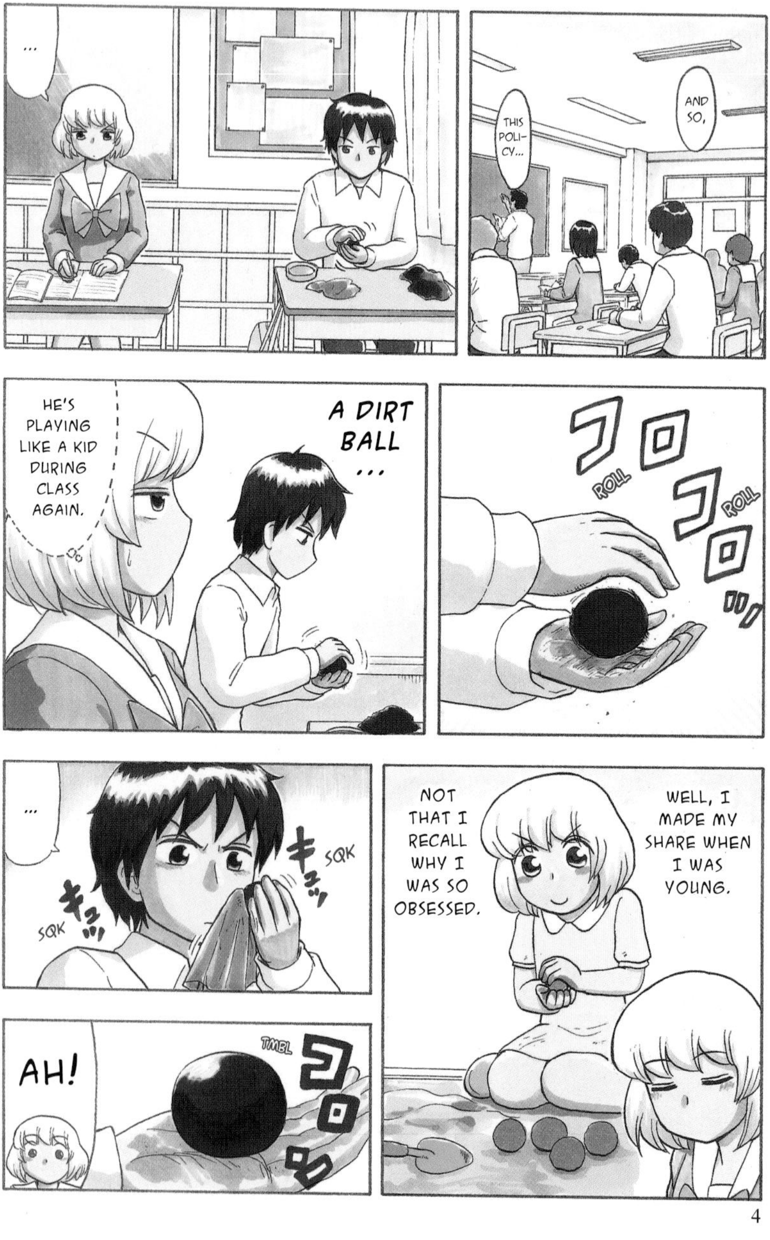
AND SO,
THIS POLICY...
...
ROLL
ROLL
A DIRT BALL...
HE'S PLAYING LIKE A KID DURING CLASS AGAIN.
WELL, I MADE MY SHARE WHEN I WAS YOUNG.
NOT THAT I RECALL WHY I WAS SO OBSESSED.
...
SQK
SQK
AH!
TMBL

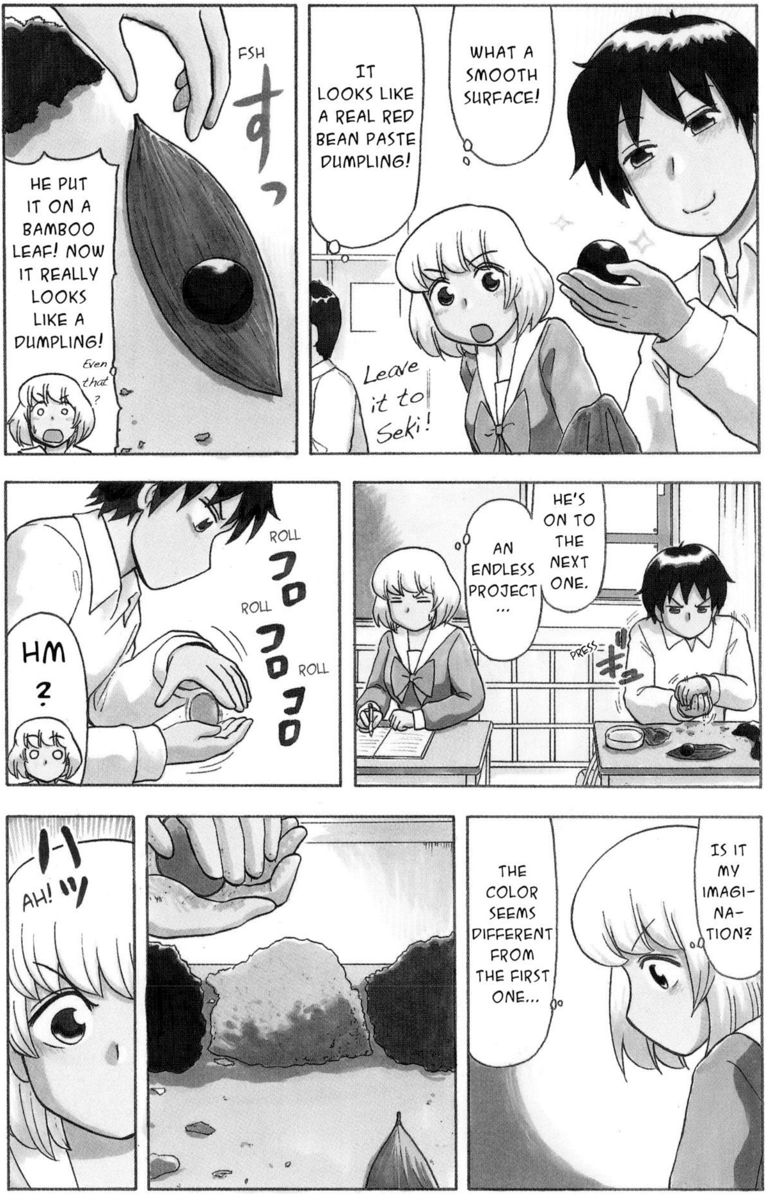
WHAT A SMOOTH SURFACE!
IT LOOKS LIKE A REAL RED BEAN PASTE DUMPLING!
Leave it to Seki!
FSH すっ
HE PUT IT ON A BAMBOO LEAF! NOW IT REALLY LOOKS LIKE A DUMPLING!
Even that?
HE'S ON TO THE NEXT ONE.
AN ENDLESS PROJECT...
PRESS ギュ
ROLL コロ
ROLL コロ
ROLL コロ
HM?
IS IT MY IMAGINATION?
THE COLOR SEEMS DIFFERENT FROM THE FIRST ONE...
AH! ハッ

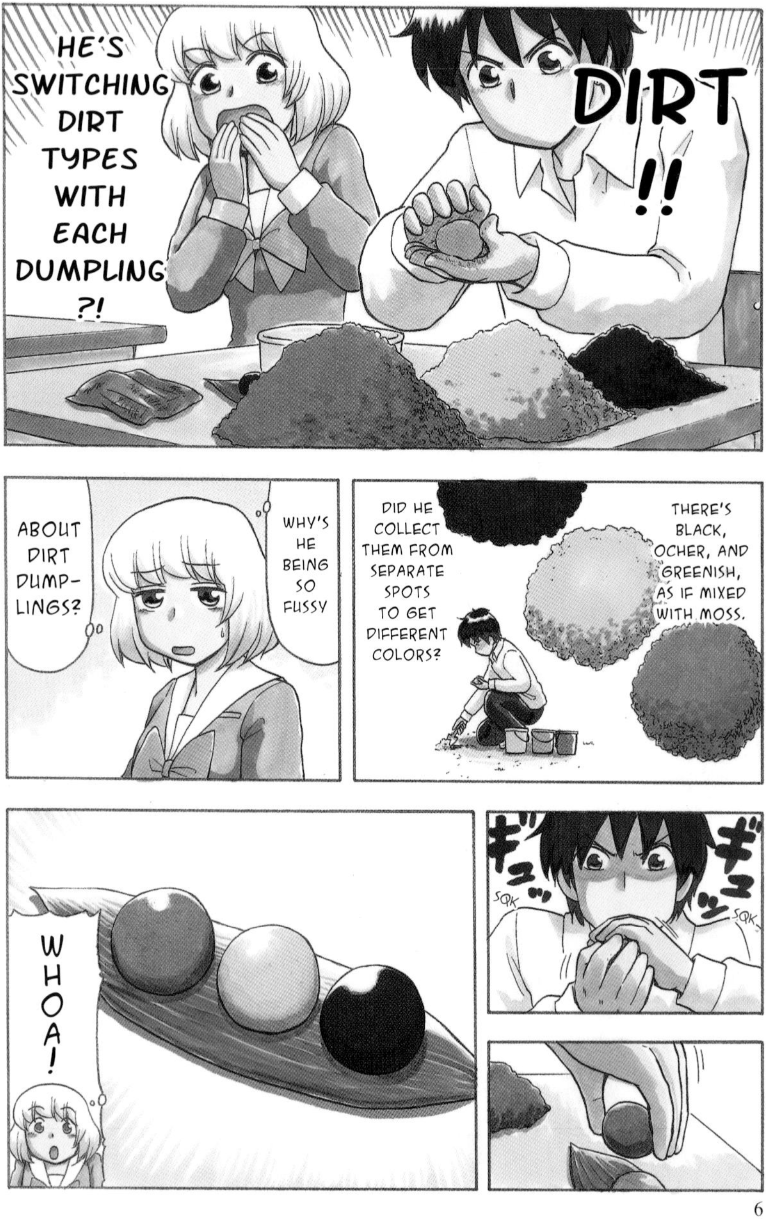
DIRT!!
HE'S SWITCHING DIRT TYPES WITH EACH DUMPLING?!
THERE'S BLACK, OCHER, AND GREENISH, AS IF MIXED WITH MOSS.
DID HE COLLECT THEM FROM SEPARATE SPOTS TO GET DIFFERENT COLORS?
WHY'S HE BEING SO FUSSY
ABOUT DIRT DUMP-LINGS?
ギュッ
SQK
ギュッ
SQK
WHOA!

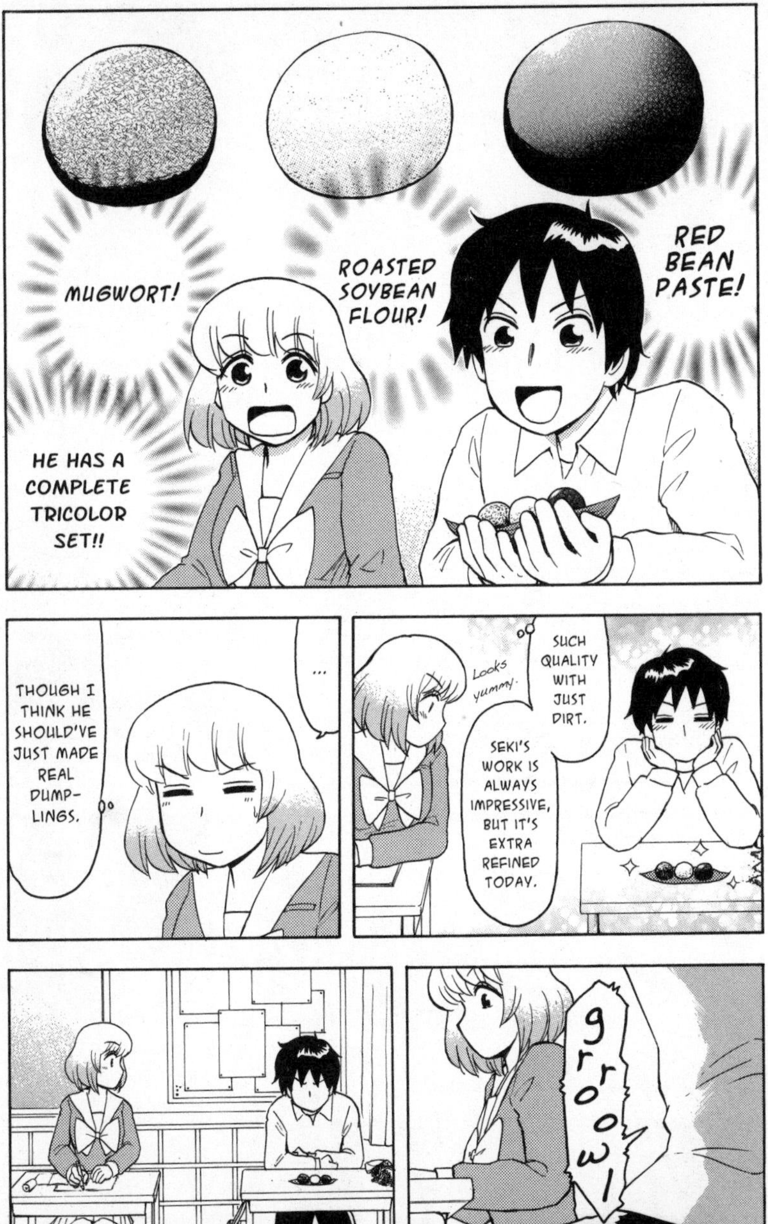
RED BEAN PASTE!
ROASTED SOYBEAN FLOUR!
MUGWORT!
HE HAS A COMPLETE TRICOLOR SET!!
SUCH QUALITY WITH JUST DIRT.
Looks yummy.
SEKI'S WORK IS ALWAYS IMPRESSIVE, BUT IT'S EXTRA REFINED TODAY.
...
THOUGH I THINK HE SHOULD'VE JUST MADE REAL DUMP-LINGS.
grroowl

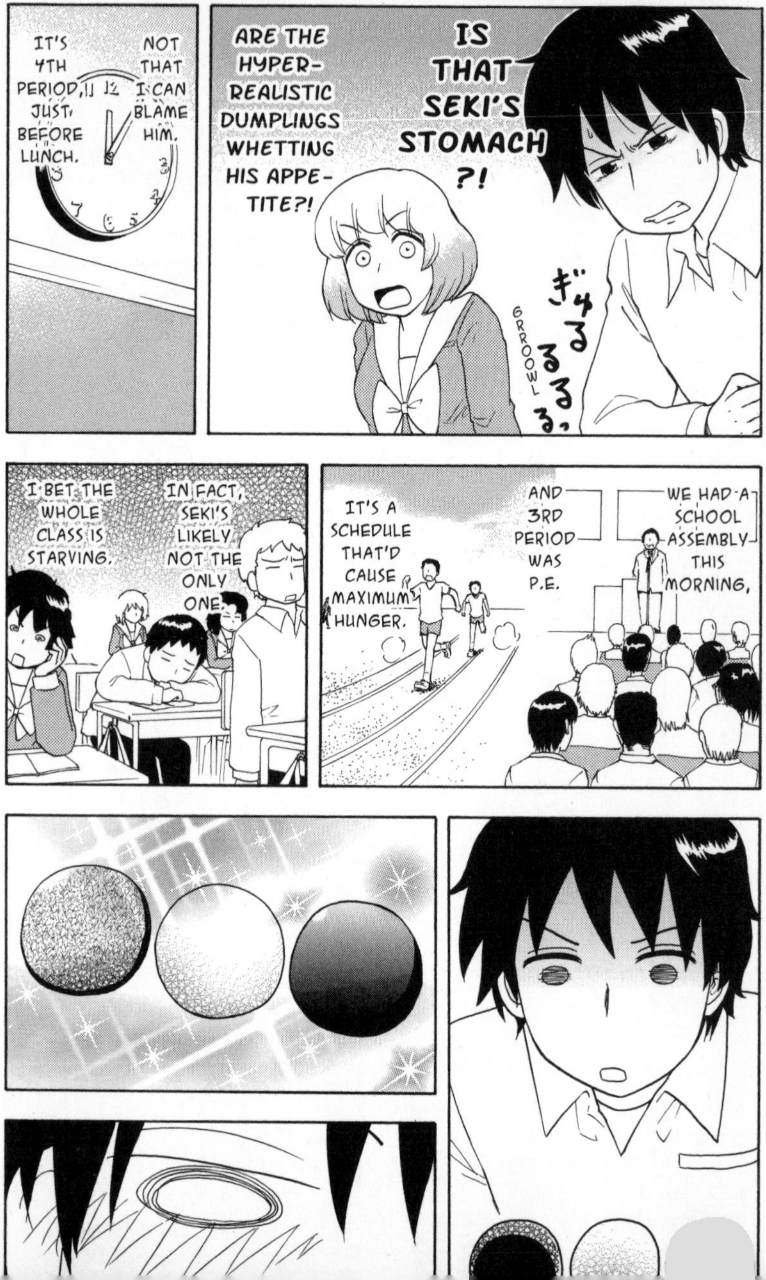
IS THAT SEKI'S STOMACH?!
ARE THE HYPER-REALISTIC DUMPLINGS WHETTING HIS APPETITE?!
ぎゅるるるるっ
GRROOWL
NOT THAT I CAN BLAME HIM.
IT'S 4TH PERIOD, JUST BEFORE LUNCH.
WE HAD A SCHOOL ASSEMBLY THIS MORNING,
AND 3RD PERIOD WAS P.E.
IT'S A SCHEDULE THAT'D CAUSE MAXIMUM HUNGER.
IN FACT, SEKI'S LIKELY NOT THE ONLY ONE.
I BET THE WHOLE CLASS IS STARVING.

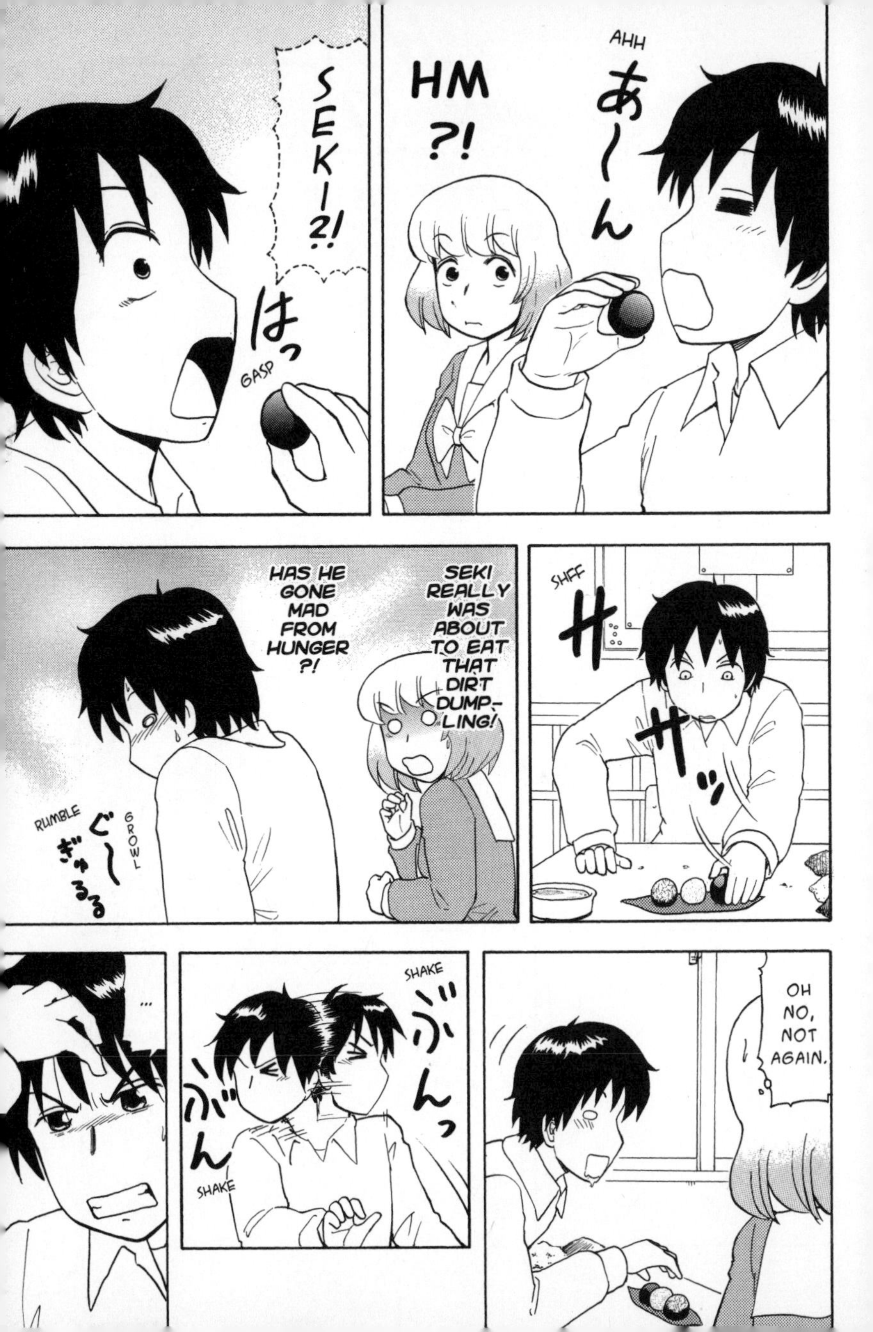
AHH
あ〜ん
HM?!
SEKI?!
はっ
GASP
SHFF
ササッ
SEKI REALLY WAS ABOUT TO EAT THAT DIRT DUMP-LING!
HAS HE GONE MAD FROM HUNGER?!
RUMBLE
ぐ〜
ぎゅるる
GROWL
OH NO, NOT AGAIN.
SHAKE
ぶんっ
ぶん
SHAKE
...

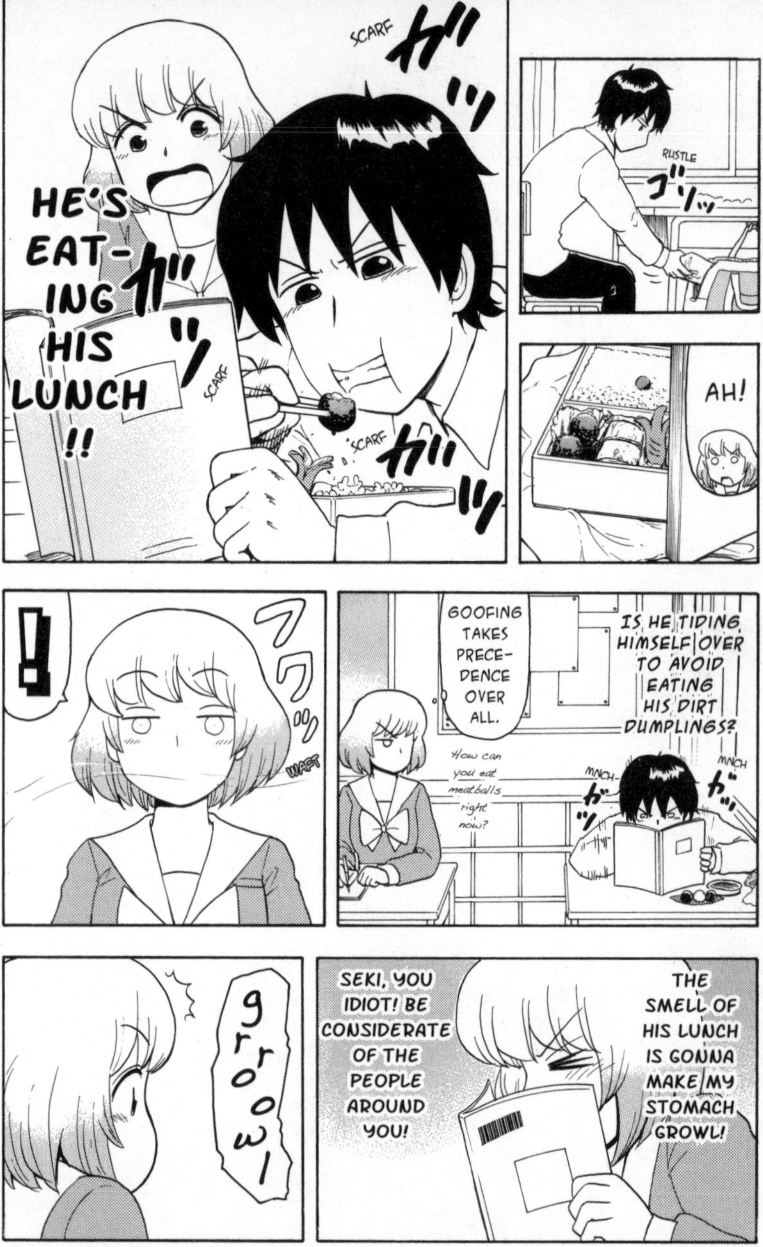
RUSTLE
AH!
SCARF
HE'S EAT-ING HIS LUNCH!!
SCARF
SCARF
IS HE TIDING HIMSELF OVER TO AVOID EATING HIS DIRT DUMPLINGS?
GOOFING TAKES PRECE-DENCE OVER ALL.
MNCH
How can you eat meatballs right now?
MNCH
!
WAFT
THE SMELL OF HIS LUNCH IS GONNA MAKE MY STOMACH GROWL!
SEKI, YOU IDIOT! BE CONSIDERATE OF THE PEOPLE AROUND YOU!
groowl

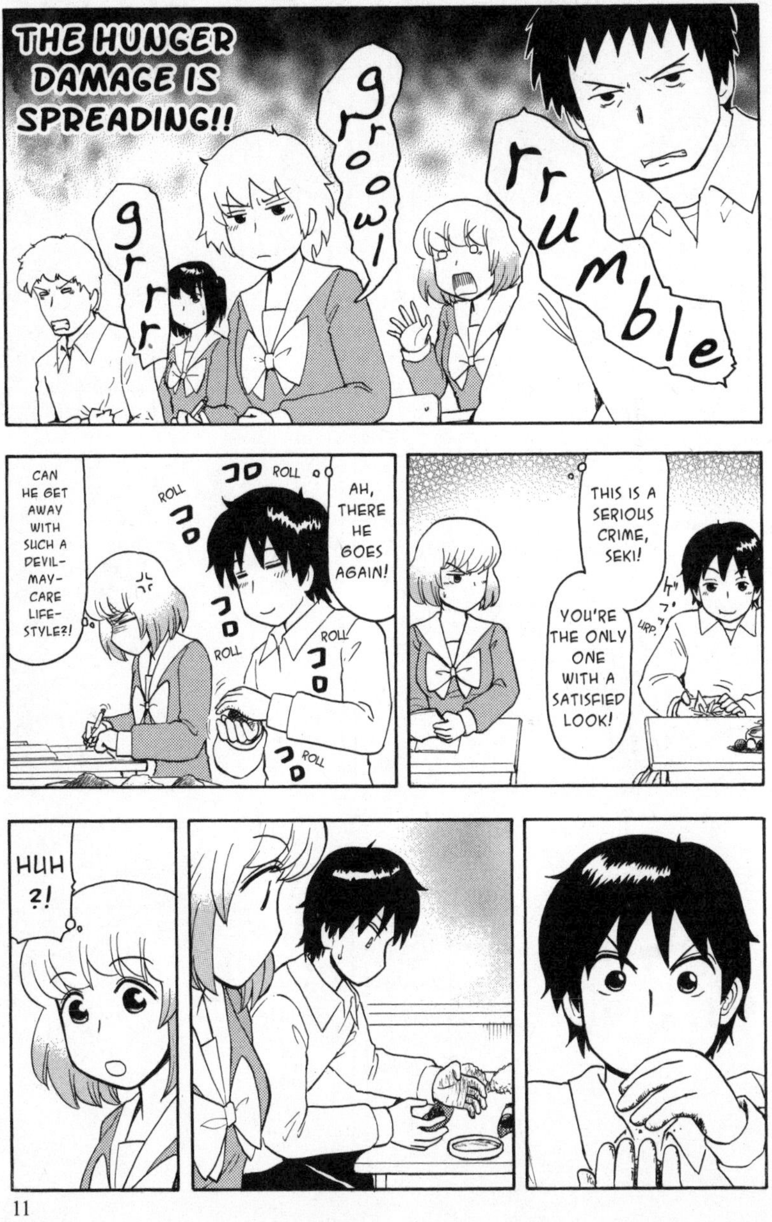
rrumble
groowl
THE HUNGER DAMAGE IS SPREADING!!
grrr
THIS IS A SERIOUS CRIME, SEKI!
YOU'RE THE ONLY ONE WITH A SATISFIED LOOK!
URP
AH, THERE HE GOES AGAIN!
コロ ROLL
コロ ROLL
コロ ROLL
コロ ROLL
コロ ROLL
CAN HE GET AWAY WITH SUCH A DEVIL-MAY-CARE LIFE-STYLE?!
HUH ?!

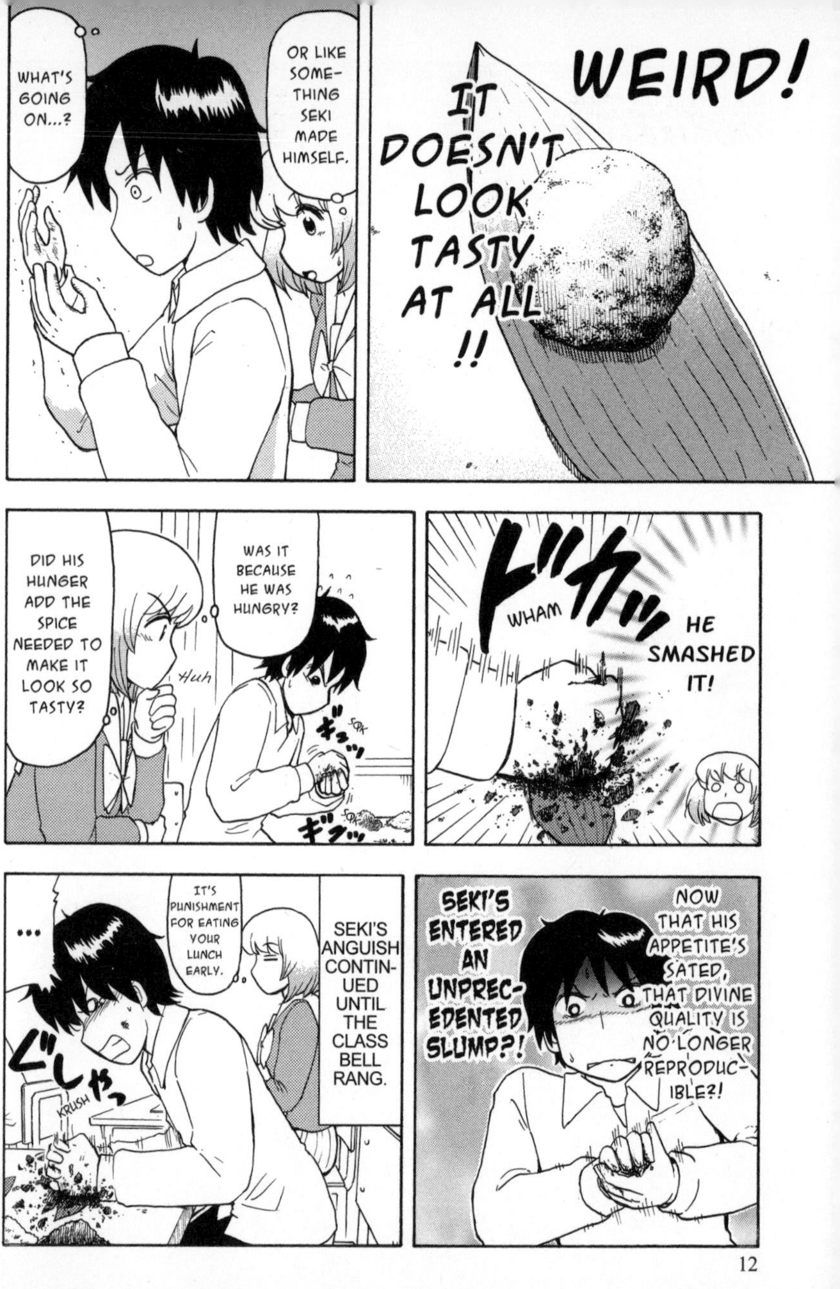
WEIRD!
IT DOESN'T LOOK TASTY AT ALL!!
OR LIKE SOMETHING SEKI MADE HIMSELF.
WHAT'S GOING ON...?
ドカッ
WHAM
HE SMASHED IT!
WAS IT BECAUSE HE WAS HUNGRY?
DID HIS HUNGER ADD THE SPICE NEEDED TO MAKE IT LOOK SO TASTY?
Huh
ギュッ
SQK
ギュッ
SQK
NOW THAT HIS APPETITE'S SATED, THAT DIVINE QUALITY IS NO LONGER REPRODUCIBLE?!
SEKI'S ENTERED AN UNPRECEDENTED SLUMP?!
SEKI'S ANGUISH CONTINUED UNTIL THE CLASS BELL RANG.
IT'S PUNISHMENT FOR EATING YOUR LUNCH EARLY.
...
ぐしゃっ
KRUSH

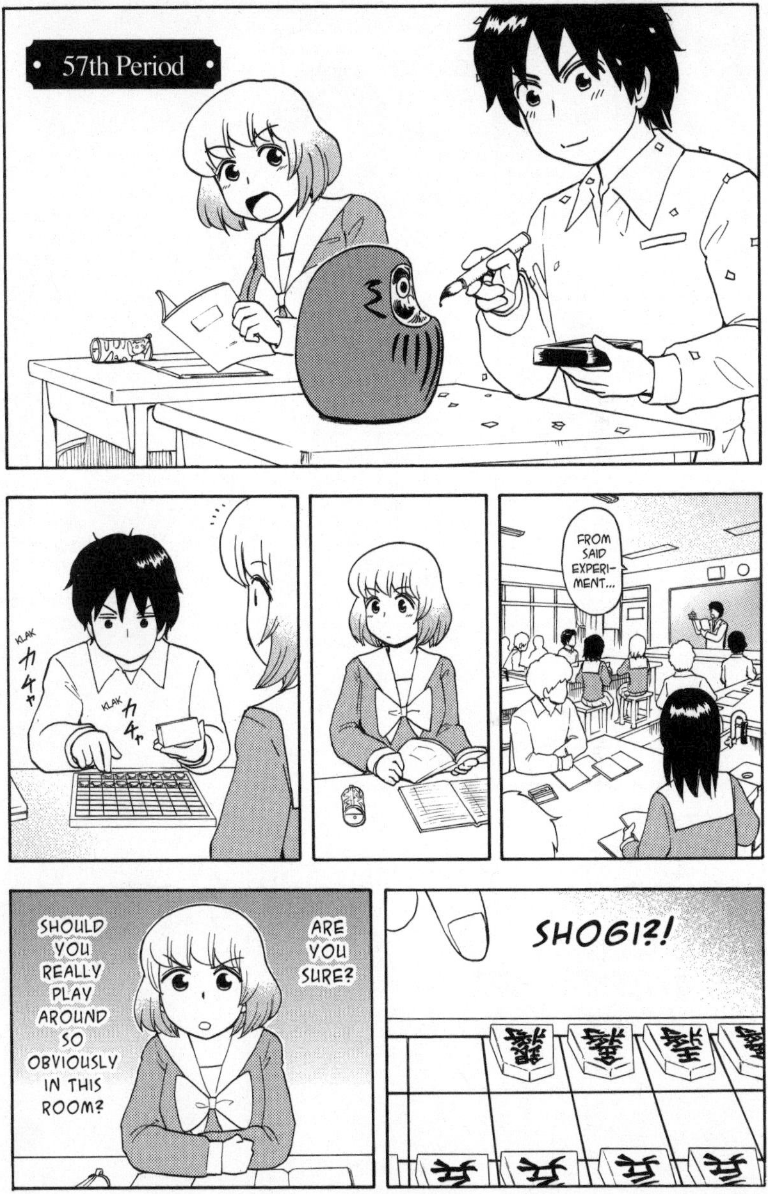
57th Period
FROM SAID EXPERIMENT...
KLAK カチャ
KLAK カチャ
SHOGI?!
ARE YOU SURE?
SHOULD YOU REALLY PLAY AROUND SO OBVIOUSLY IN THIS ROOM?

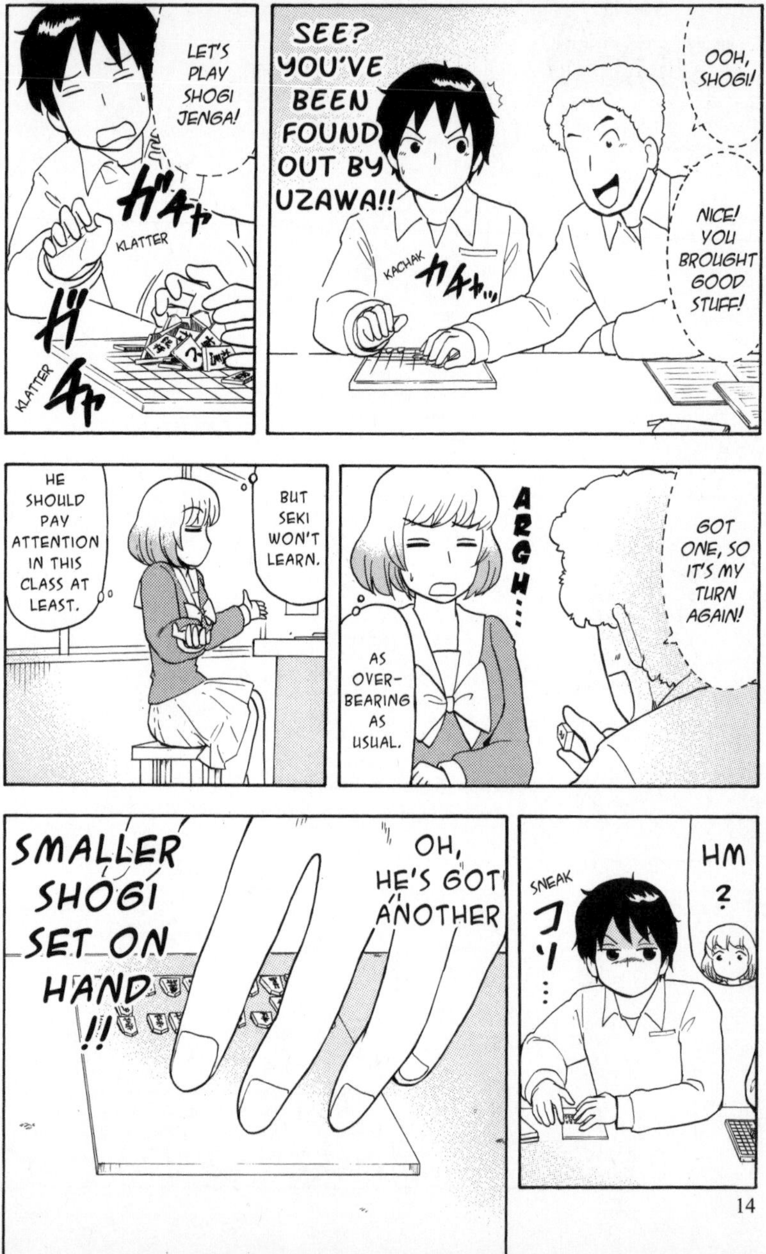
OOH, SHOGI!
NICE! YOU BROUGHT GOOD STUFF!
SEE? YOU'VE BEEN FOUND OUT BY UZAWA!!
KACHAK
LET'S PLAY SHOGI JENGA!
KLATTER
KLATTER
GOT ONE, SO IT'S MY TURN AGAIN!
ARGH...
AS OVER-BEARING AS USUAL.
BUT SEKI WON'T LEARN.
HE SHOULD PAY ATTENTION IN THIS CLASS AT LEAST.
HM?
SNEAK
OH, HE'S GOT ANOTHER
SMALLER SHOGI SET ON HAND!!

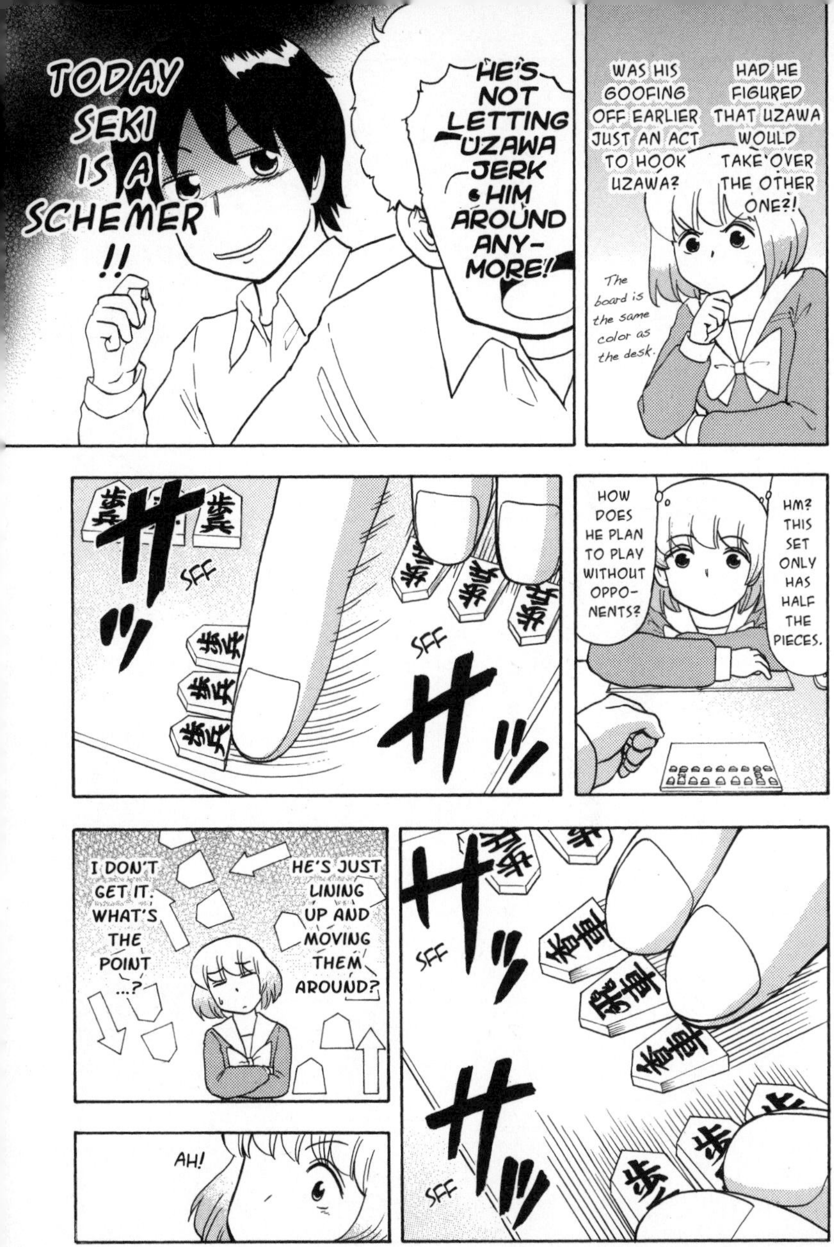
HAD HE FIGURED THAT UZAWA WOULD TAKE OVER THE OTHER ONE?!
WAS HIS GOOFING OFF EARLIER JUST AN ACT TO HOOK UZAWA?
The board is the same color as the desk.
HE'S NOT LETTING UZAWA JERK HIM AROUND ANYMORE!
TODAY SEKI IS A SCHEMER!!
HM? THIS SET ONLY HAS HALF THE PIECES.
HOW DOES HE PLAN TO PLAY WITHOUT OPPONENTS?
SFF
SFF
SFF
SFF
HE'S JUST LINING UP AND MOVING THEM AROUND?
I DON'T GET IT. WHAT'S THE POINT ...?
AH!

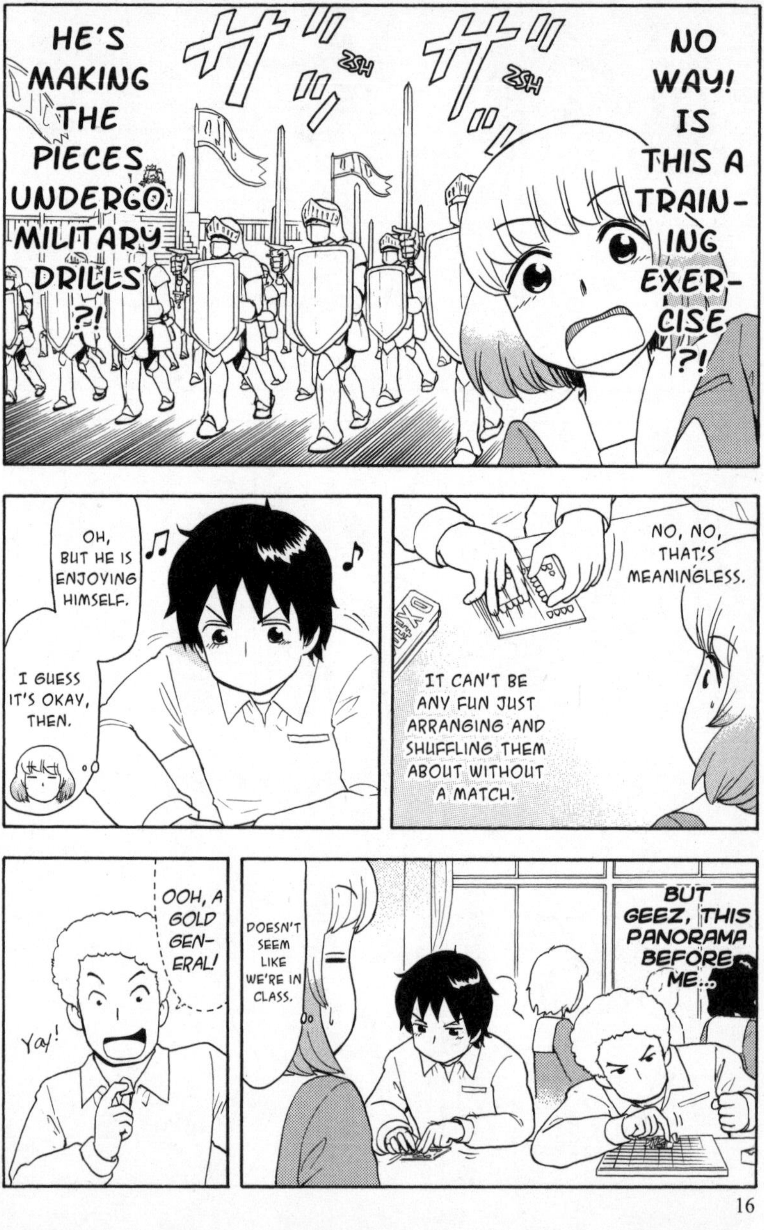

NO WAY! IS THIS A TRAINING EXERCISE?!
ZSH
ZSH
HE'S MAKING THE PIECES UNDERGO MILITARY DRILLS?!
NO, NO, THAT'S MEANINGLESS.
IT CAN'T BE ANY FUN JUST ARRANGING AND SHUFFLING THEM ABOUT WITHOUT A MATCH.
OH, BUT HE IS ENJOYING HIMSELF.
I GUESS IT'S OKAY, THEN.
BUT GEEZ, THIS PANORAMA BEFORE ME...
DOESN'T SEEM LIKE WE'RE IN CLASS.
OOH, A GOLD GENERAL!
Yay!

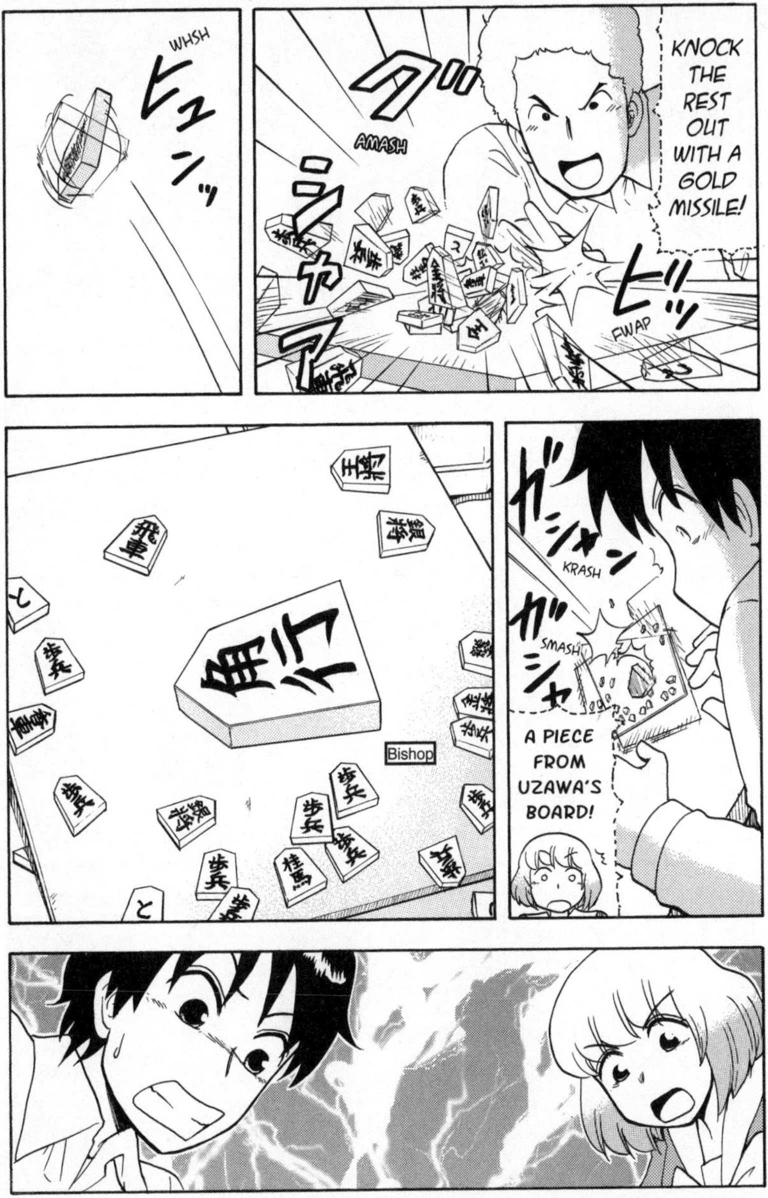
KNOCK THE REST OUT WITH A GOLD MISSILE!
AMASH
FWAP
WHSH
KRASH
SMASH
A PIECE FROM UZAWA'S BOARD!
Bishop

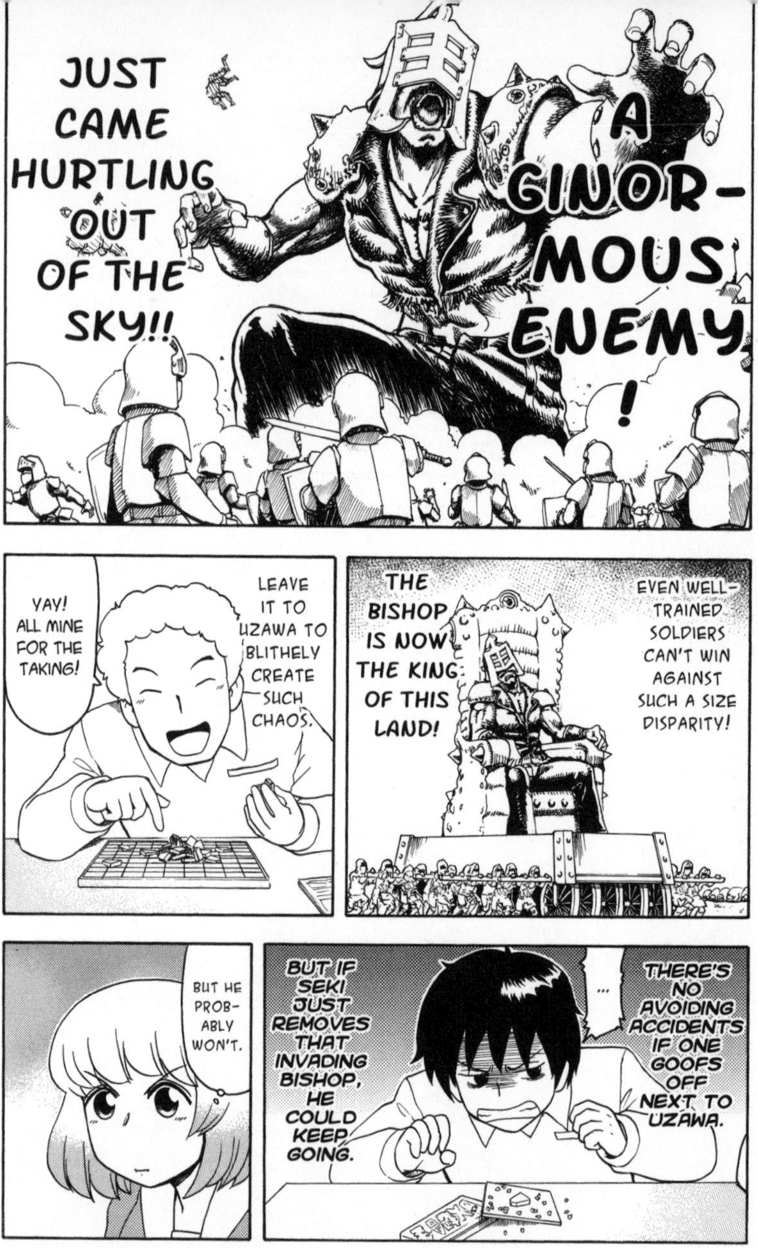
A GINORMOUS ENEMY!
JUST CAME HURTLING OUT OF THE SKY!!
EVEN WELL-TRAINED SOLDIERS CAN'T WIN AGAINST SUCH A SIZE DISPARITY!
THE BISHOP IS NOW THE KING OF THIS LAND!
LEAVE IT TO UZAWA TO BLITHELY CREATE SUCH CHAOS.
YAY! ALL MINE FOR THE TAKING!
THERE'S NO AVOIDING ACCIDENTS IF ONE GOOFS OFF NEXT TO UZAWA.
...
BUT IF SEKI JUST REMOVES THAT INVADING BISHOP, HE COULD KEEP GOING.
BUT HE PROBABLY WON'T.

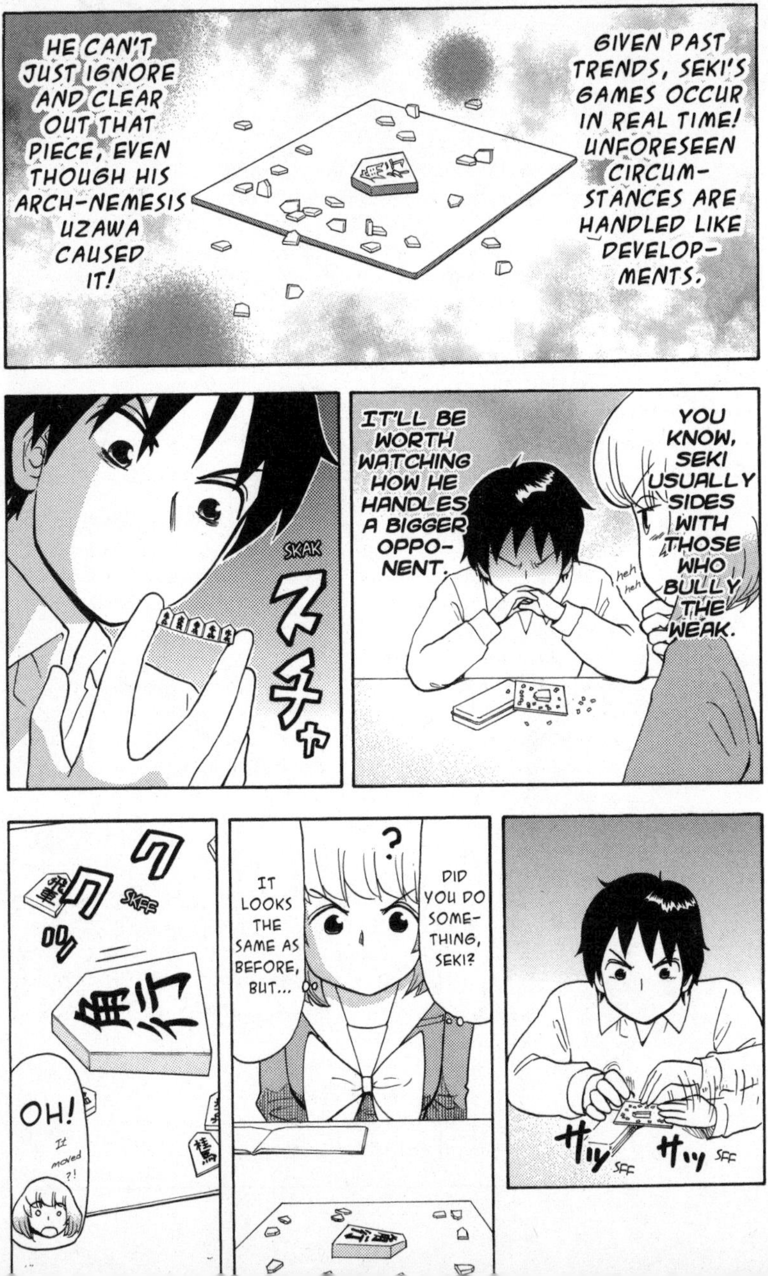
GIVEN PAST TRENDS, SEKI'S GAMES OCCUR IN REAL TIME! UNFORESEEN CIRCUM-STANCES ARE HANDLED LIKE DEVELOP-MENTS.
HE CAN'T JUST IGNORE AND CLEAR OUT THAT PIECE, EVEN THOUGH HIS ARCH-NEMESIS UZAWA CAUSED IT!
YOU KNOW, SEKI USUALLY SIDES WITH THOSE WHO BULLY THE WEAK.
IT'LL BE WORTH WATCHING HOW HE HANDLES A BIGGER OPPO-NENT.
heh heh
SKAK
スチャ
サッ
SFF
サッ
SFF
?
DID YOU DO SOME-THING, SEKI?
IT LOOKS THE SAME AS BEFORE, BUT...
クク
SKFF
ッ
OH!
It moved ?!

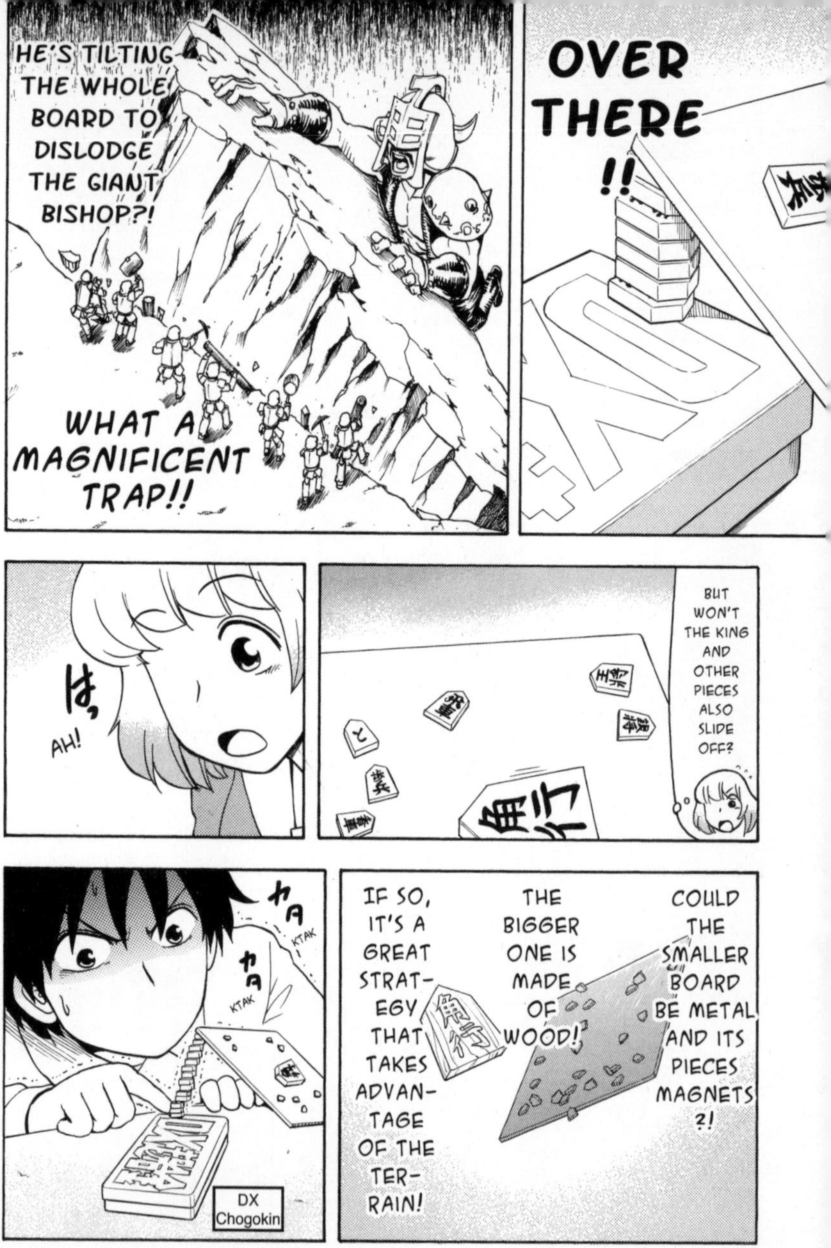

OVER THERE!!
HE'S TILTING THE WHOLE BOARD TO DISLODGE THE GIANT BISHOP?!
WHAT A MAGNIFICENT TRAP!!
BUT WON'T THE KING AND OTHER PIECES ALSO SLIDE OFF?
は,
AH!
COULD THE SMALLER BOARD BE METAL AND ITS PIECES MAGNETS?!
THE BIGGER ONE IS MADE OF WOOD!
IF SO, IT'S A GREAT STRAT-EGY THAT TAKES ADVAN-TAGE OF THE TER-RAIN!
カタ
KTAK
カタ
KTAK
DX Chogokin

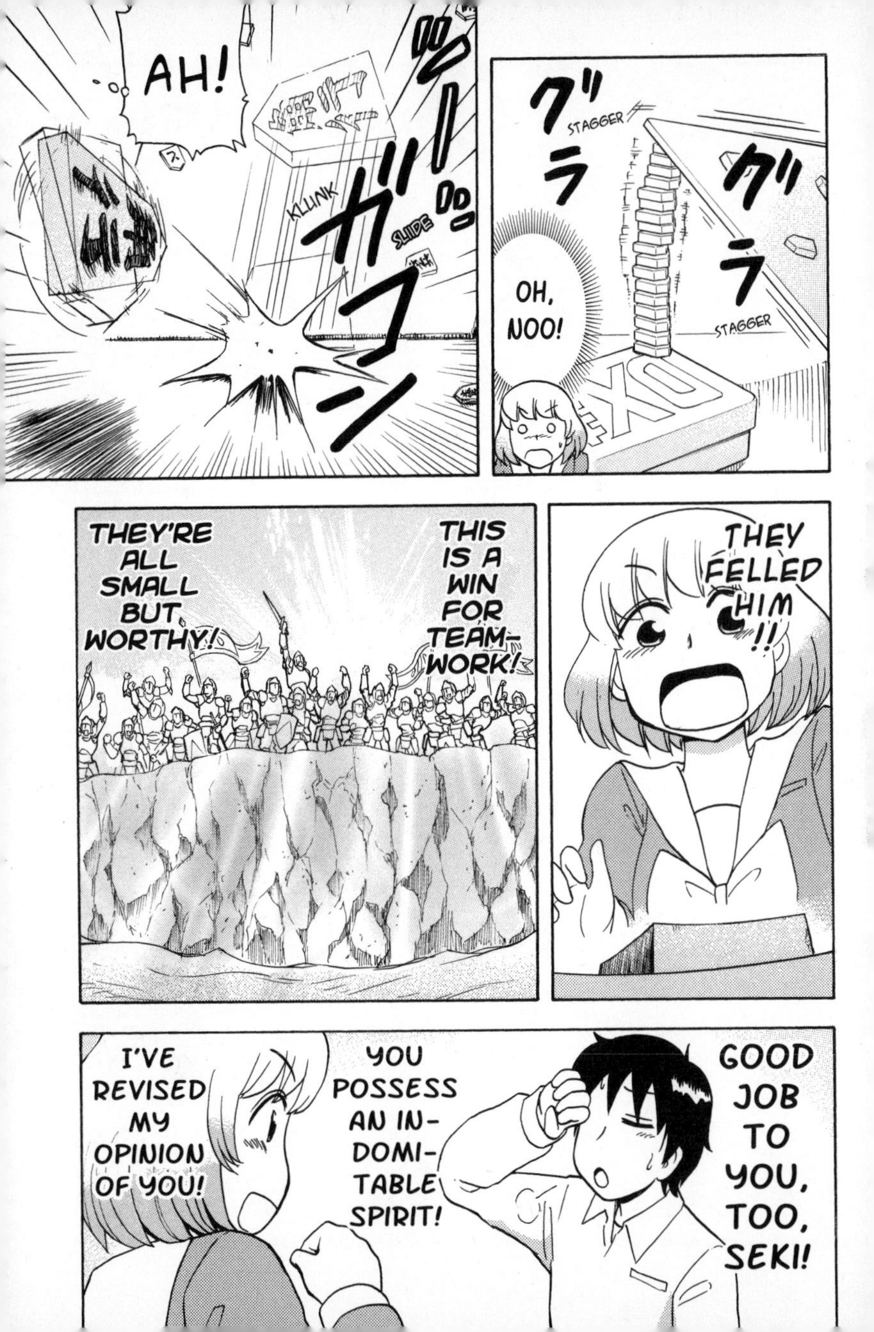
グラ
STAGGER
グラ
STAGGER
OH, NOO!
AH!
KLUNK
SLIDE
ガコン
THEY FELLED HIM!!
THIS IS A WIN FOR TEAM-WORK!
THEY'RE ALL SMALL BUT WORTHY!
GOOD JOB TO YOU, TOO, SEKI!
YOU POSSESS AN IN-DOMI-TABLE SPIRIT!
I'VE REVISED MY OPINION OF YOU!

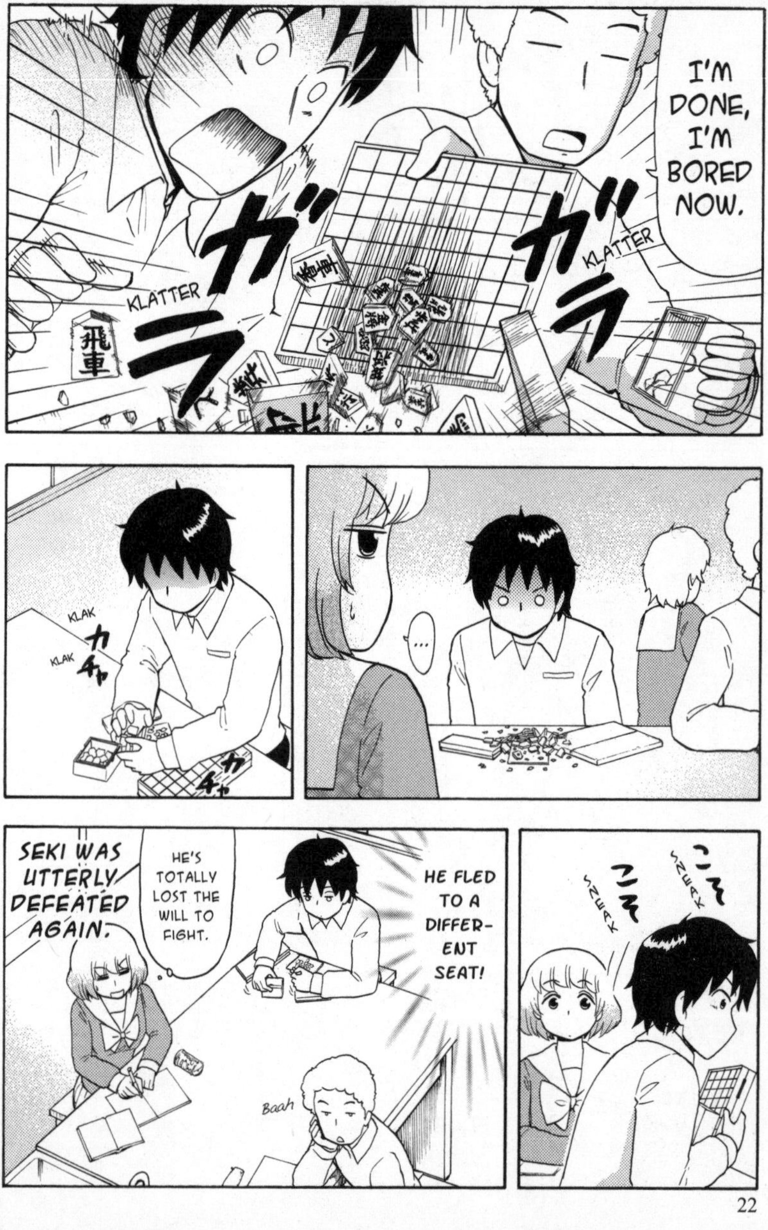
I'M DONE, I'M BORED NOW.
KLATTER
ガラ
KLATTER
ガラ
…
KLAK
カチャ
KLAK
カチャ
こそ
SNEAK
こそ
SNEAK
HE FLED TO A DIFFER-ENT SEAT!
HE'S TOTALLY LOST THE WILL TO FIGHT.
SEKI WAS UTTERLY DEFEATED AGAIN.
Baah

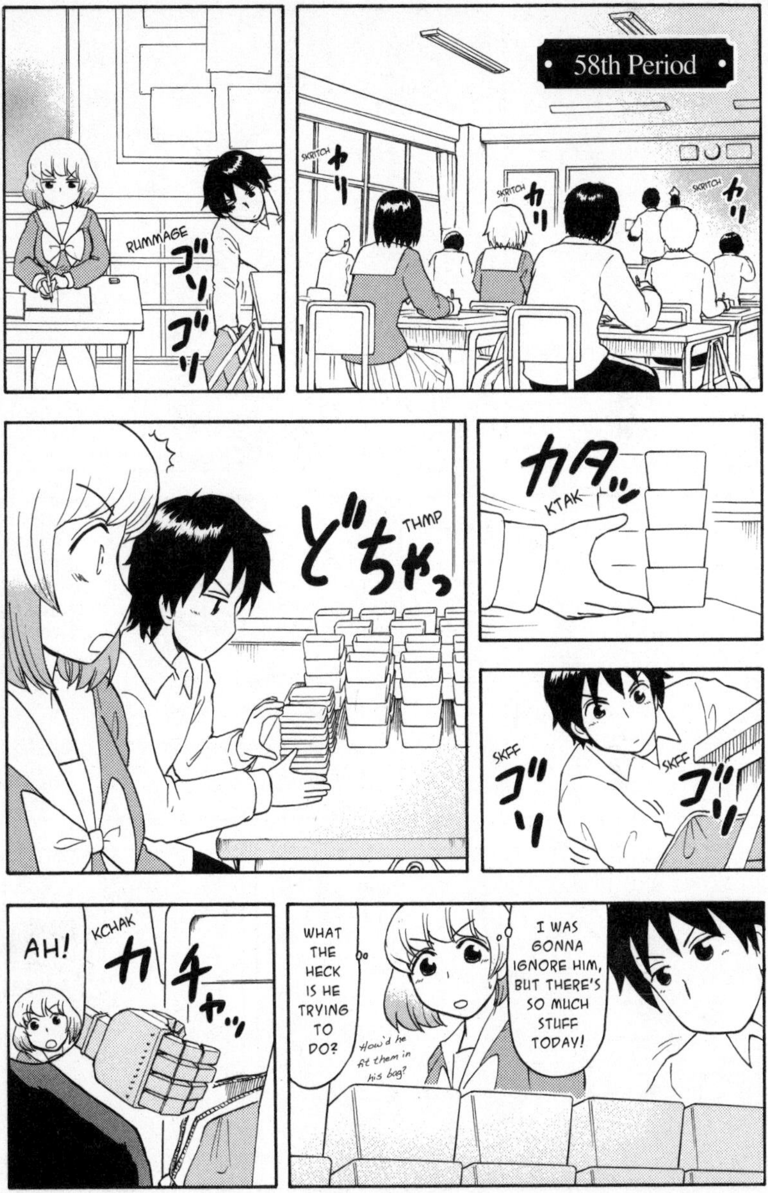

58th Period
SKRITCH ヤリ
SKRITCH カリ
SKRITCH ヤリ
RUMMAGE ゴソゴソ
KTAK カタッ
SKFF ゴソ
SKFF ゴソ
THMP どちゃっ
I WAS GONNA IGNORE HIM, BUT THERE'S SO MUCH STUFF TODAY!
WHAT THE HECK IS HE TRYING TO DO?
How'd he fit them in his bag?
KCHAK カチャッ
AH!

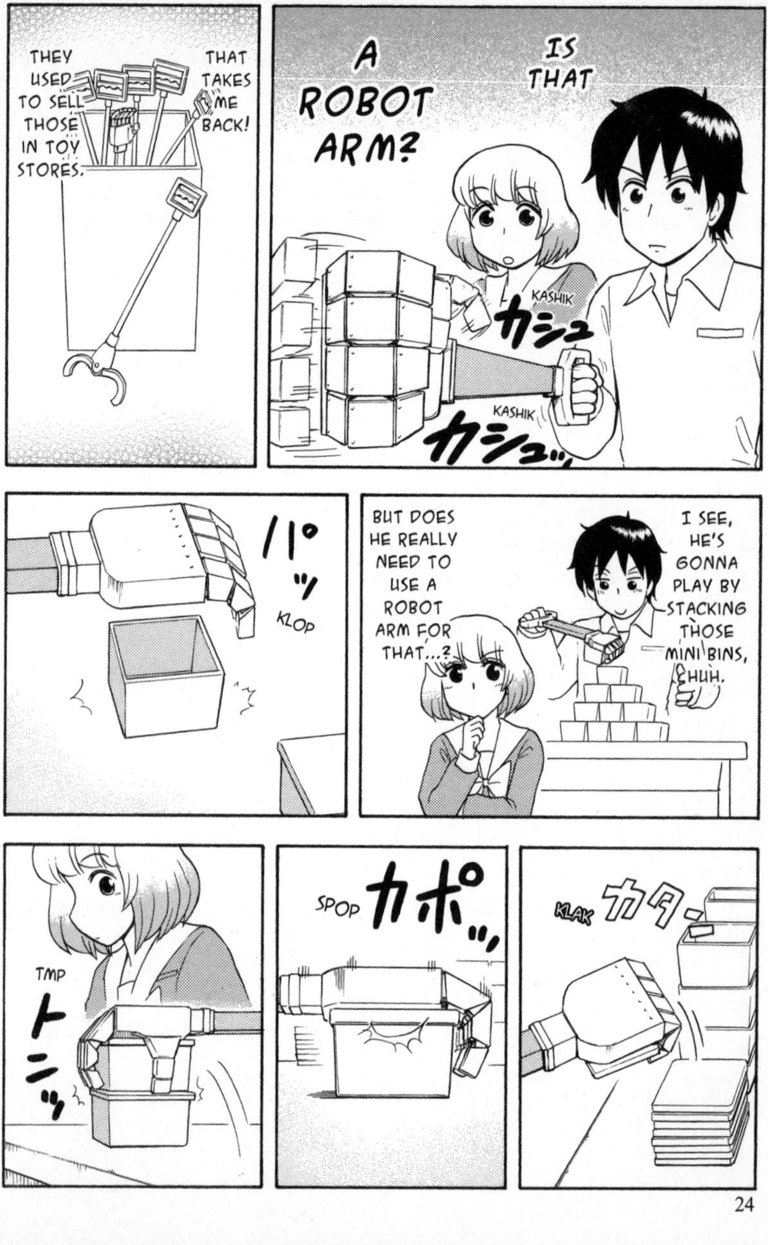
IS THAT
A ROBOT ARM?
KASHIK
カシュ
KASHIK
カシュッ
THAT TAKES ME BACK!
THEY USED TO SELL THOSE IN TOY STORES.
I SEE, HE'S GONNA PLAY BY STACKING THOSE MINI BINS, HUH.
BUT DOES HE REALLY NEED TO USE A ROBOT ARM FOR THAT...?
パッ
KLOP
KLAK
カター
SPOP
カポッ
TMP
トンッ

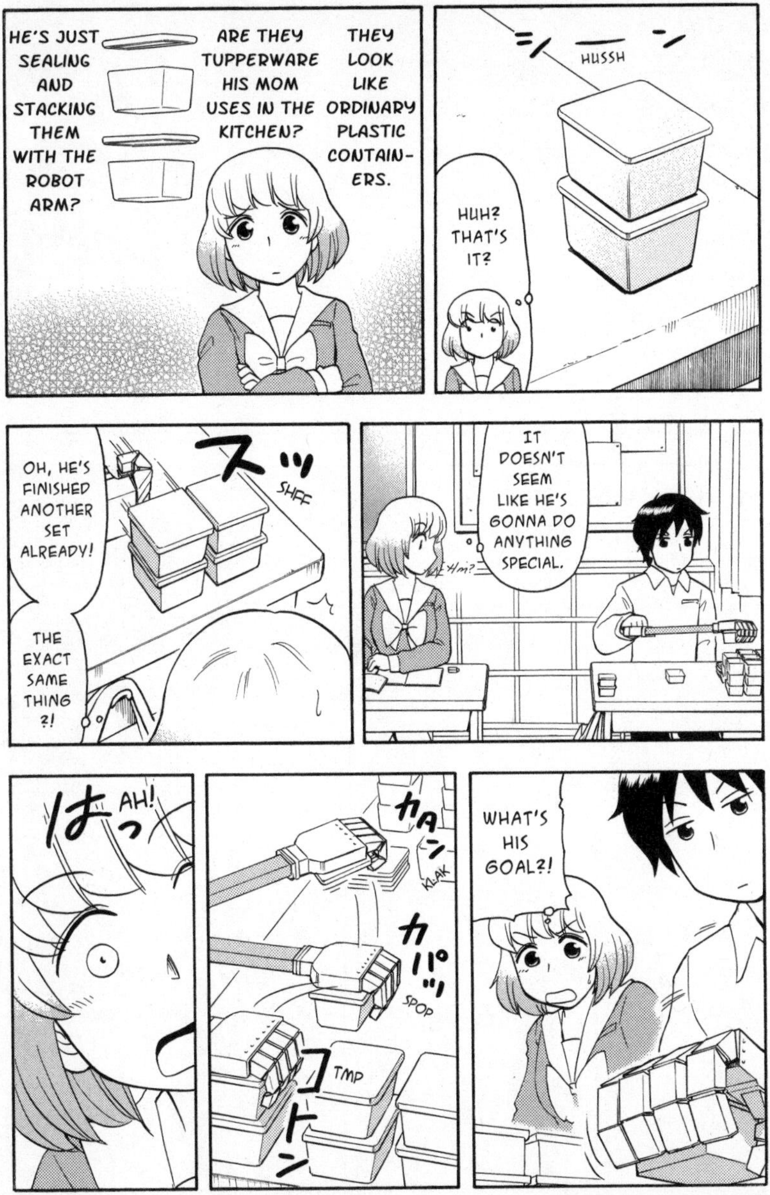
HUSSH
HUH? THAT'S IT?
THEY LOOK LIKE ORDINARY PLASTIC CONTAIN-ERS.
ARE THEY TUPPERWARE HIS MOM USES IN THE KITCHEN?
HE'S JUST SEALING AND STACKING THEM WITH THE ROBOT ARM?
IT DOESN'T SEEM LIKE HE'S GONNA DO ANYTHING SPECIAL.
Hm?
SHFF
OH, HE'S FINISHED ANOTHER SET ALREADY!
THE EXACT SAME THING?!
WHAT'S HIS GOAL?!
KLAK
SPOP
TMP
AH!

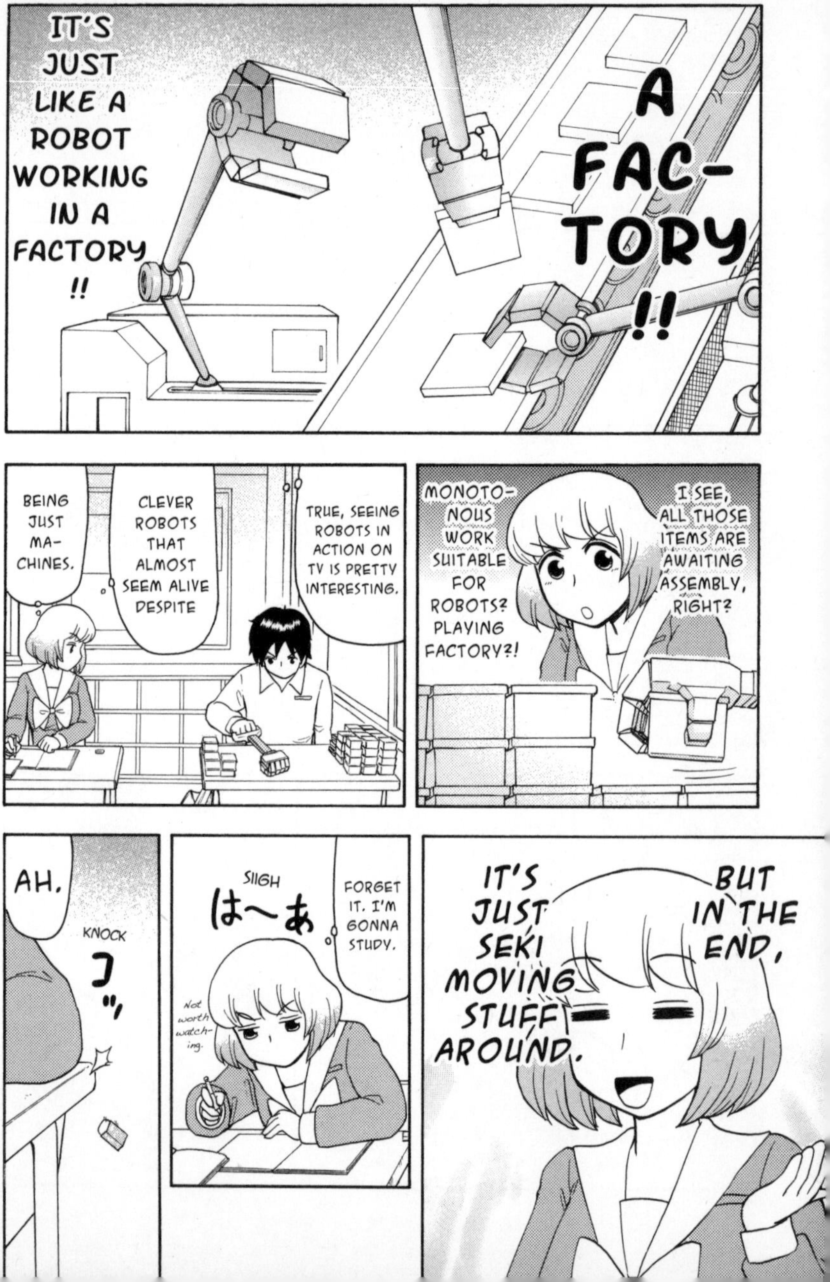
A FAC-TORY!!
IT'S JUST LIKE A ROBOT WORKING IN A FACTORY!!
I SEE, ALL THOSE ITEMS ARE AWAITING ASSEMBLY, RIGHT?
MONOTO-NOUS WORK SUITABLE FOR ROBOTS? PLAYING FACTORY?!
TRUE, SEEING ROBOTS IN ACTION ON TV IS PRETTY INTERESTING.
CLEVER ROBOTS THAT ALMOST SEEM ALIVE DESPITE
BEING JUST MA-CHINES.
BUT IN THE END,
IT'S JUST SEKI MOVING STUFF AROUND.
FORGET IT. I'M GONNA STUDY.
SIIGH
は～あ
Not worth watch-ing.
KNOCK
コッ
AH.

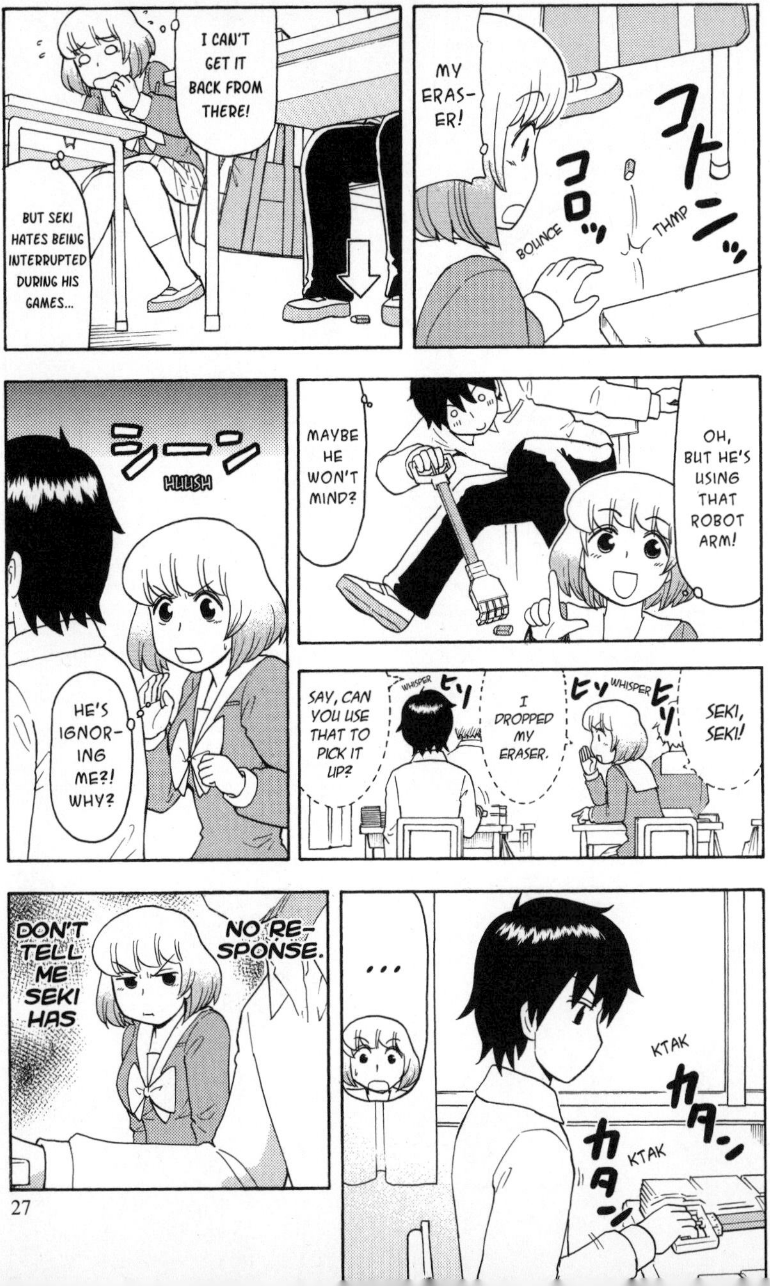

MY ERAS-ER!
コトンッ
THMP
コロッ
BOUNCE
I CAN'T GET IT BACK FROM THERE!
BUT SEKI HATES BEING INTERRUPTED DURING HIS GAMES...
OH, BUT HE'S USING THAT ROBOT ARM!
MAYBE HE WON'T MIND?
SEKI, SEKI!
ヒソ
WHISPER
ヒソ
I DROPPED MY ERASER.
ヒソ
WHISPER
SAY, CAN YOU USE THAT TO PICK IT UP?
シーン
HUSH
HE'S IGNORING-ING ME?! WHY?
KTAK
カタン
KTAK
カタン
...
NO RE-SPONSE.
DON'T TELL ME SEKI HAS

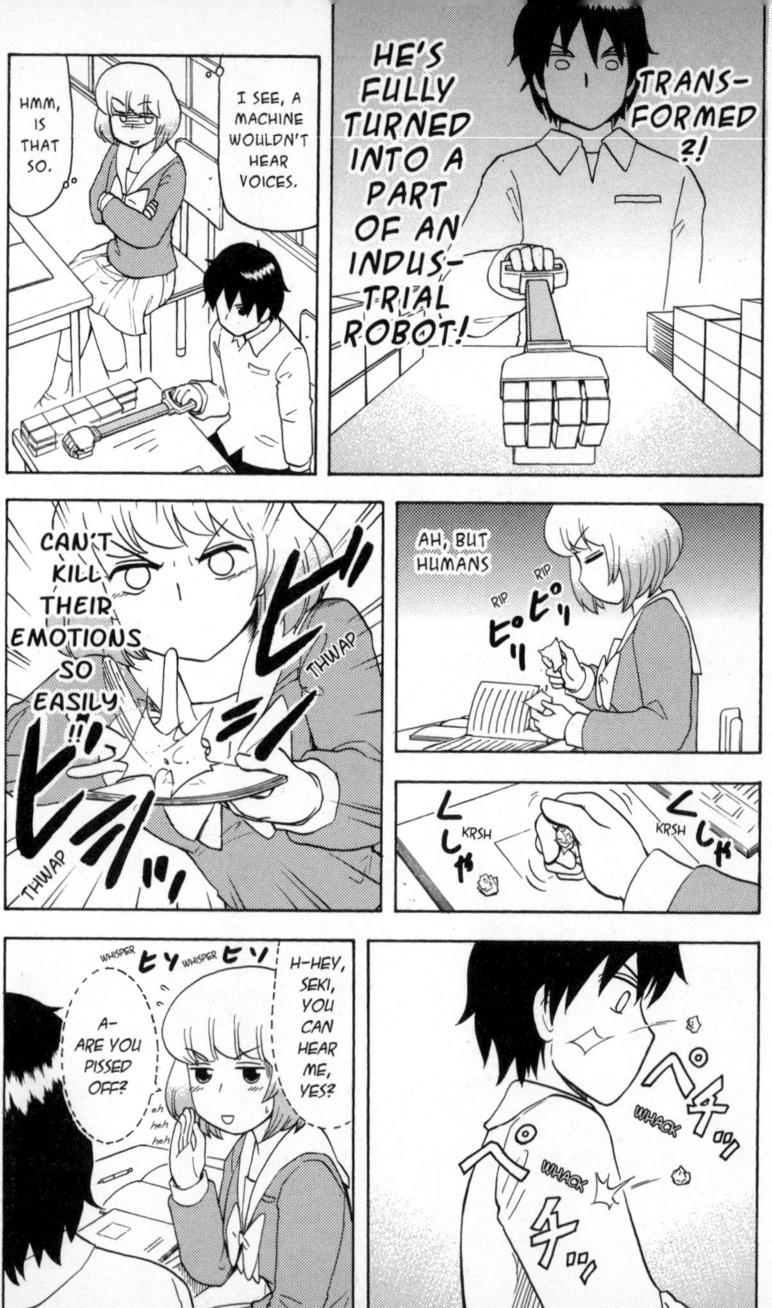
TRANS-FORMED?!
HE'S FULLY TURNED INTO A PART OF AN INDUS-TRIAL ROBOT!
I SEE, A MACHINE WOULDN'T HEAR VOICES.
HMM, IS THAT SO.
AH, BUT HUMANS
RIP RIP
KRSH
KRSH
CAN'T KILL THEIR EMOTIONS SO EASILY!!
THWAP
THWAP
WHACK
WHACK
H-HEY, SEKI, YOU CAN HEAR ME, YES?
WHISPER WHISPER
A-ARE YOU PISSED OFF?
eh heh heh

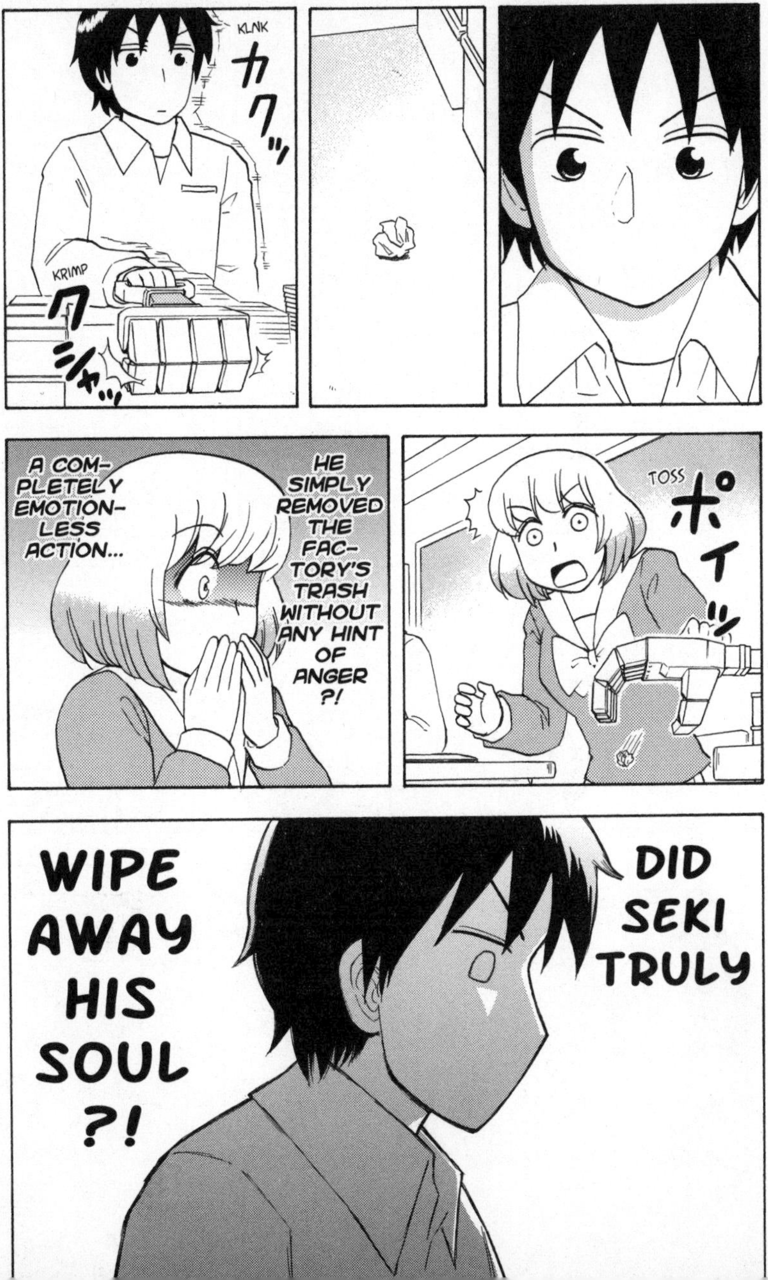

KLNK
カクッ
KRIMP
クシャッ
TOSS
ポイッ
HE SIMPLY REMOVED THE FACTORY'S TRASH WITHOUT ANY HINT OF ANGER ?!
A COMPLETELY EMOTIONLESS ACTION...
DID SEKI TRULY
WIPE AWAY HIS SOUL ?!

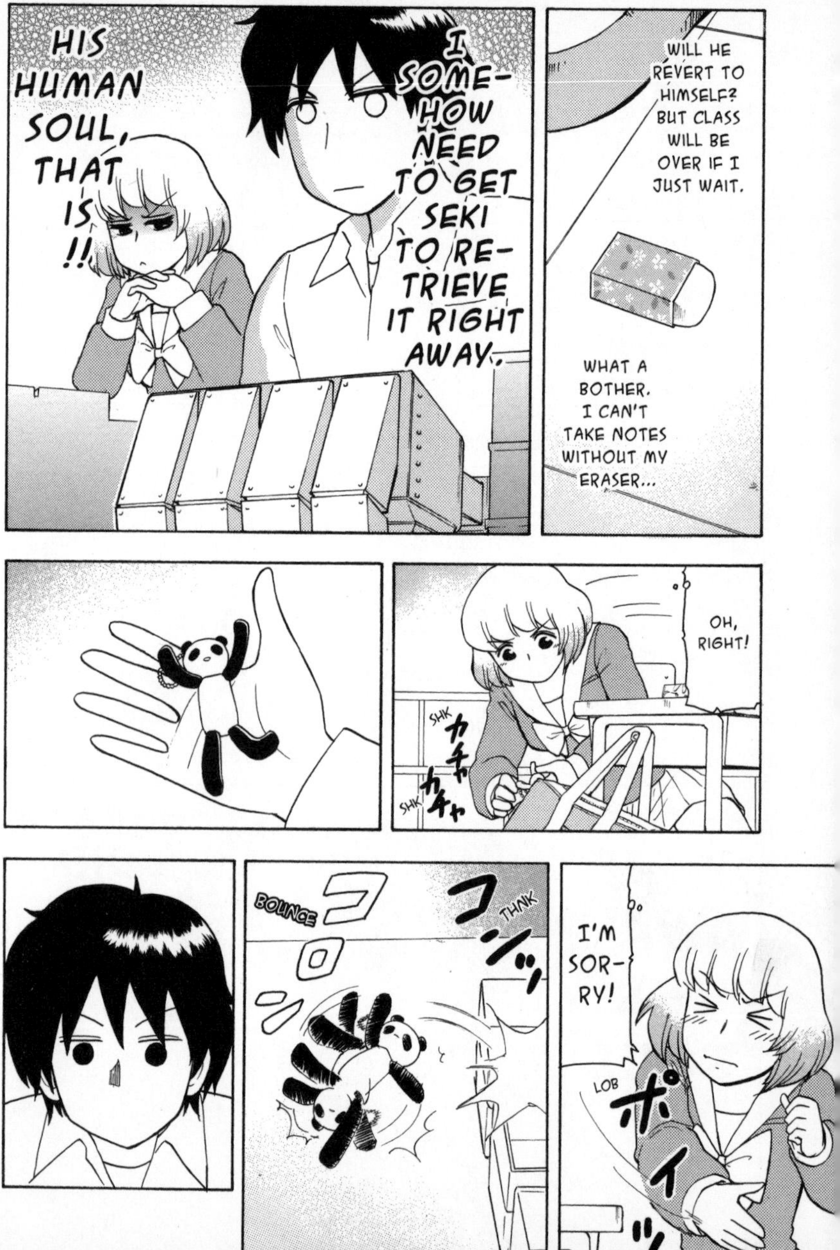
WILL HE REVERT TO HIMSELF? BUT CLASS WILL BE OVER IF I JUST WAIT.
WHAT A BOTHER. I CAN'T TAKE NOTES WITHOUT MY ERASER...
I SOMEHOW NEED TO GET SEKI TO RETRIEVE IT RIGHT AWAY.
HIS HUMAN SOUL, THAT IS!!
OH, RIGHT!
カチャ SHK
カチャ SHK
I'M SORRY!
ポイッ LOB
コンッ THNK
コロン BOUNCE

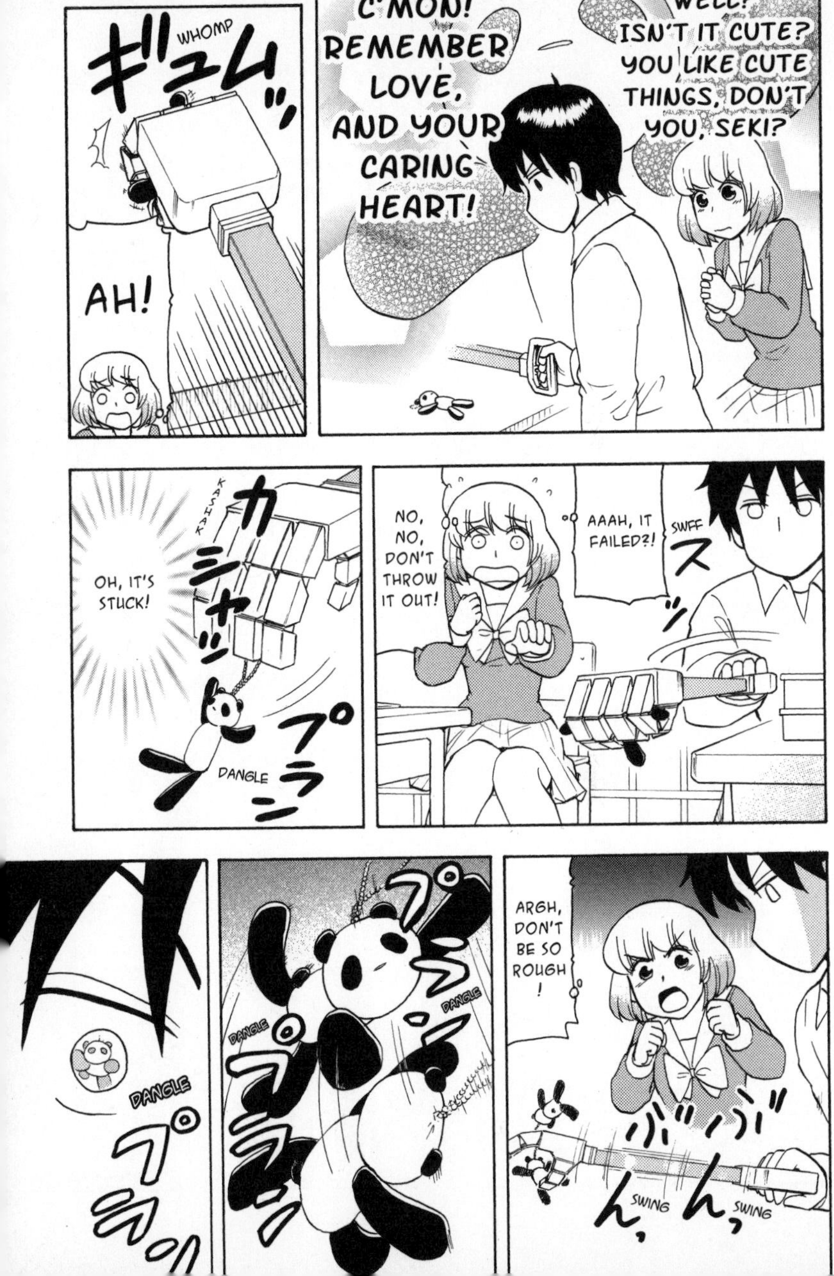
WELL? ISN'T IT CUTE? YOU LIKE CUTE THINGS, DON'T YOU, SEKI?
C'MON! REMEMBER LOVE, AND YOUR CARING HEART!
ギュムッ
WHOMP
AH!
ス
SWFF
AAAH, IT FAILED?!
NO, NO, DON'T THROW IT OUT!
カシャッ
KASHAK
OH, IT'S STUCK!
プラン
DANGLE
ARGH, DON'T BE SO ROUGH!
ぶんぶん
SWING
SWING
プラプラ
DANGLE
DANGLE
DANGLE
プラ

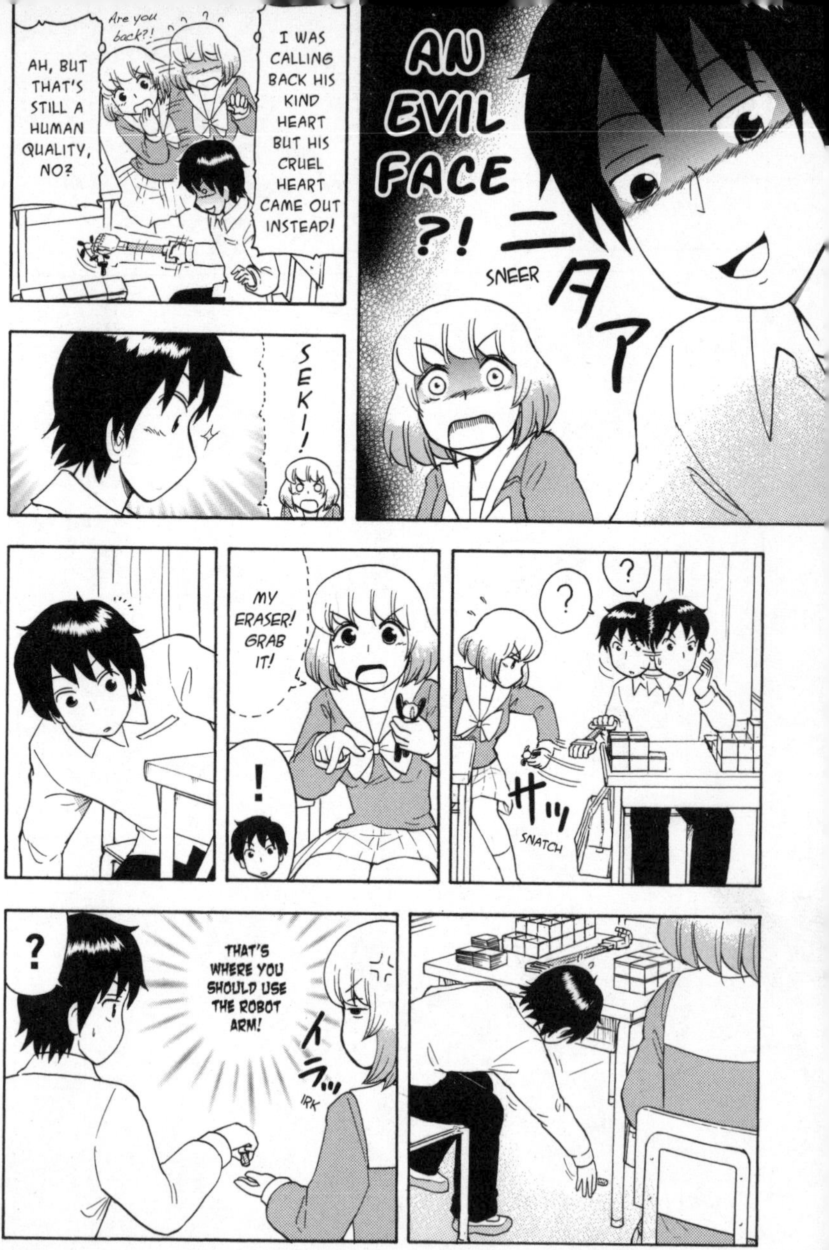
AN EVIL FACE ?!
ニタア
SNEER
I WAS CALLING BACK HIS KIND HEART BUT HIS CRUEL HEART CAME OUT INSTEAD!
Are you back?!
AH, BUT THAT'S STILL A HUMAN QUALITY, NO?
SEKI!
?
?
サッ
SNATCH
MY ERASER! GRAB IT!
!
THAT'S WHERE YOU SHOULD USE THE ROBOT ARM!
イラッ
IRK
?

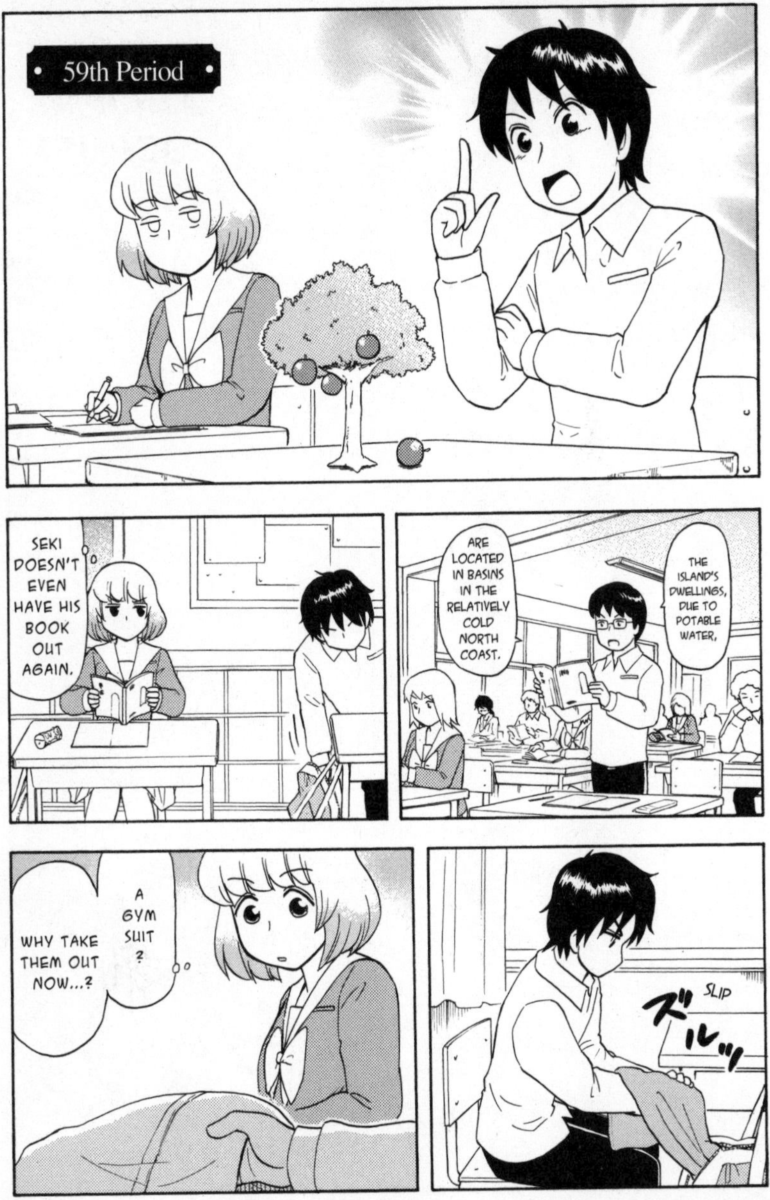
59th Period
THE ISLAND'S DWELLINGS, DUE TO POTABLE WATER,
ARE LOCATED IN BASINS IN THE RELATIVELY COLD NORTH COAST.
SEKI DOESN'T EVEN HAVE HIS BOOK OUT AGAIN.
SLIP
A GYM SUIT?
WHY TAKE THEM OUT NOW...?

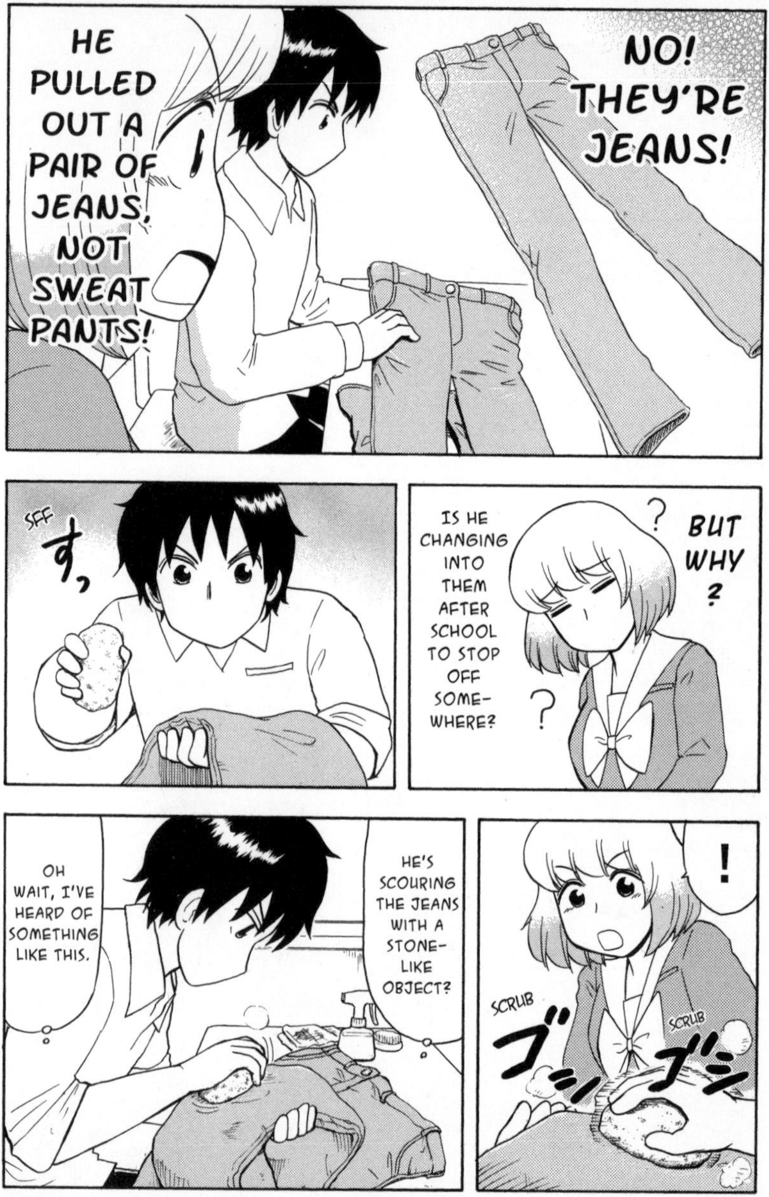
NO! THEY'RE JEANS!
HE PULLED OUT A PAIR OF JEANS, NOT SWEAT PANTS!
BUT WHY?
IS HE CHANGING INTO THEM AFTER SCHOOL TO STOP OFF SOME-WHERE?
SFF
すっ
!
SCRUB
ゴシ
SCRUB
ゴシ
HE'S SCOURING THE JEANS WITH A STONE-LIKE OBJECT?
OH WAIT, I'VE HEARD OF SOMETHING LIKE THIS.

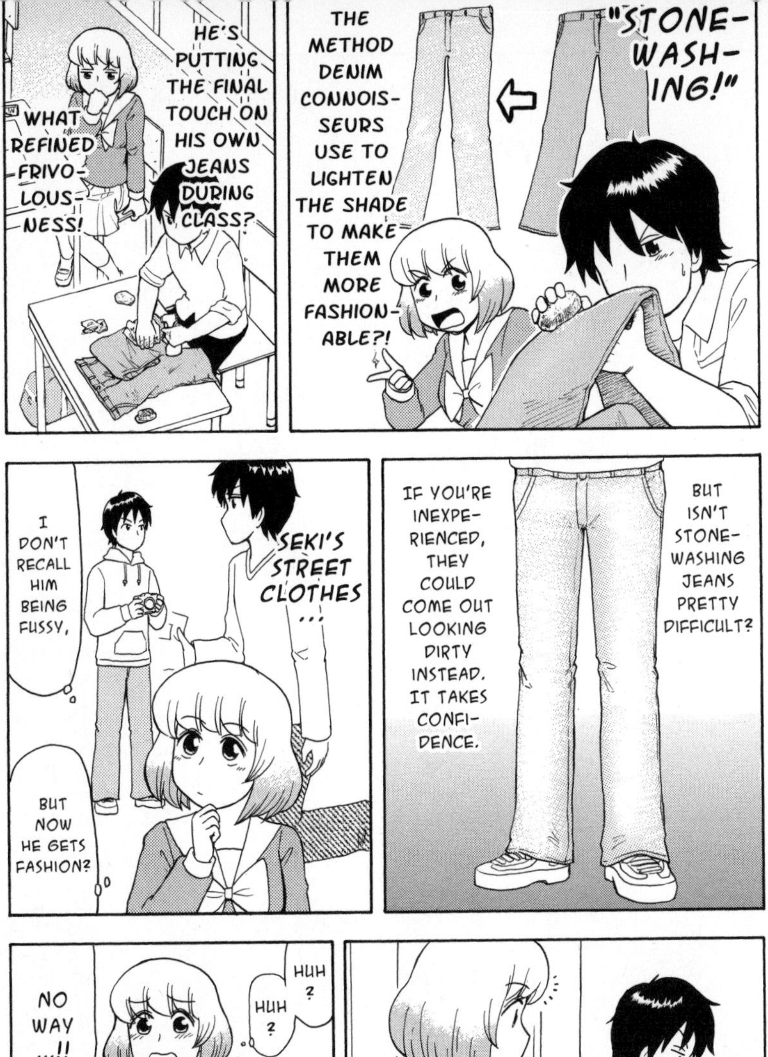
"STONE-WASHING!"
THE METHOD DENIM CONNOISSEURS USE TO LIGHTEN THE SHADE TO MAKE THEM MORE FASHIONABLE?!
HE'S PUTTING THE FINAL TOUCH ON HIS OWN JEANS DURING CLASS?
WHAT REFINED FRIVOLOUSNESS!
BUT ISN'T STONE-WASHING JEANS PRETTY DIFFICULT?
IF YOU'RE INEXPERIENCED, THEY COULD COME OUT LOOKING DIRTY INSTEAD. IT TAKES CONFIDENCE.
SEKI'S STREET CLOTHES...
I DON'T RECALL HIM BEING FUSSY,
BUT NOW HE GETS FASHION?
CHAK
HUH?
HUH?
NO WAY...!!

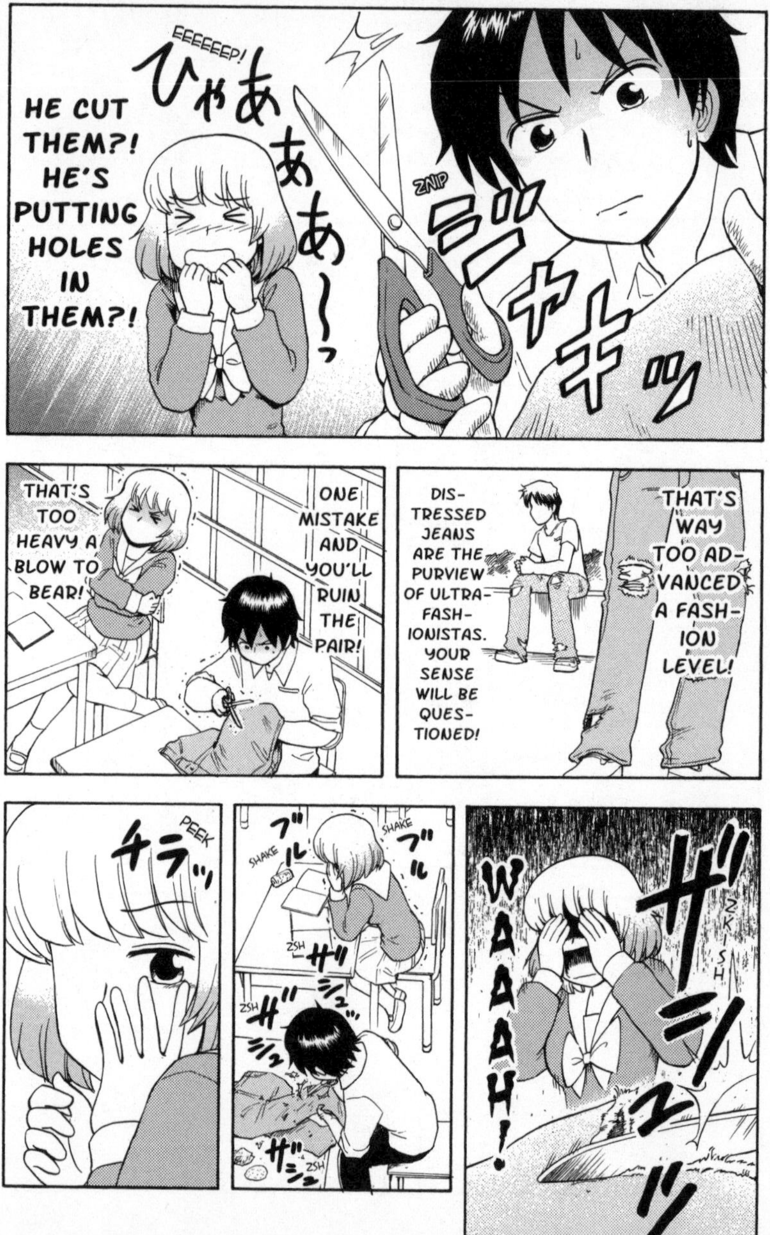
ジャキッ
ZNIP
ひゃあああ～～っ
EEEEEEP!
HE CUT THEM?! HE'S PUTTING HOLES IN THEM?!
THAT'S WAY TOO ADVANCED A FASHION LEVEL!
DISTRESSED JEANS ARE THE PURVIEW OF ULTRA-FASHIONISTAS. YOUR SENSE WILL BE QUESTIONED!
ONE MISTAKE AND YOU'LL RUIN THE PAIR!
THAT'S TOO HEAVY A BLOW TO BEAR!
ザシュッ
ZKISH
WAAAAH!
ブル
SHAKE
ブル
SHAKE
ザシュ
ZSH
ザシュ
ZSH
ザシュ
ZSH
チラッ
PEEK

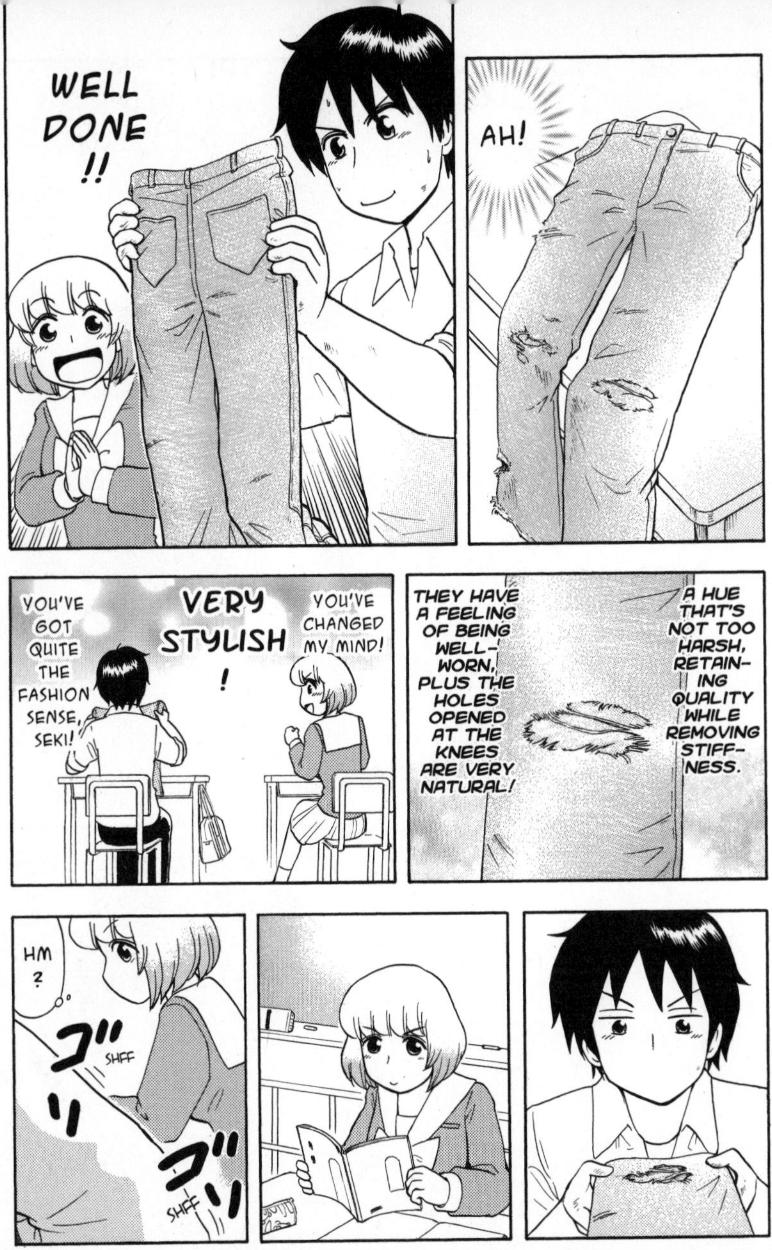
AH!
WELL DONE !!
A HUE THAT'S NOT TOO HARSH, RETAINING QUALITY WHILE REMOVING STIFFNESS.
THEY HAVE A FEELING OF BEING WELL-WORN, PLUS THE HOLES OPENED AT THE KNEES ARE VERY NATURAL!
YOU'VE CHANGED MY MIND!
VERY STYLISH !
YOU'VE GOT QUITE THE FASHION SENSE, SEKI!
HM ?
ゴソ
SHFF
ゴソ
SHFF

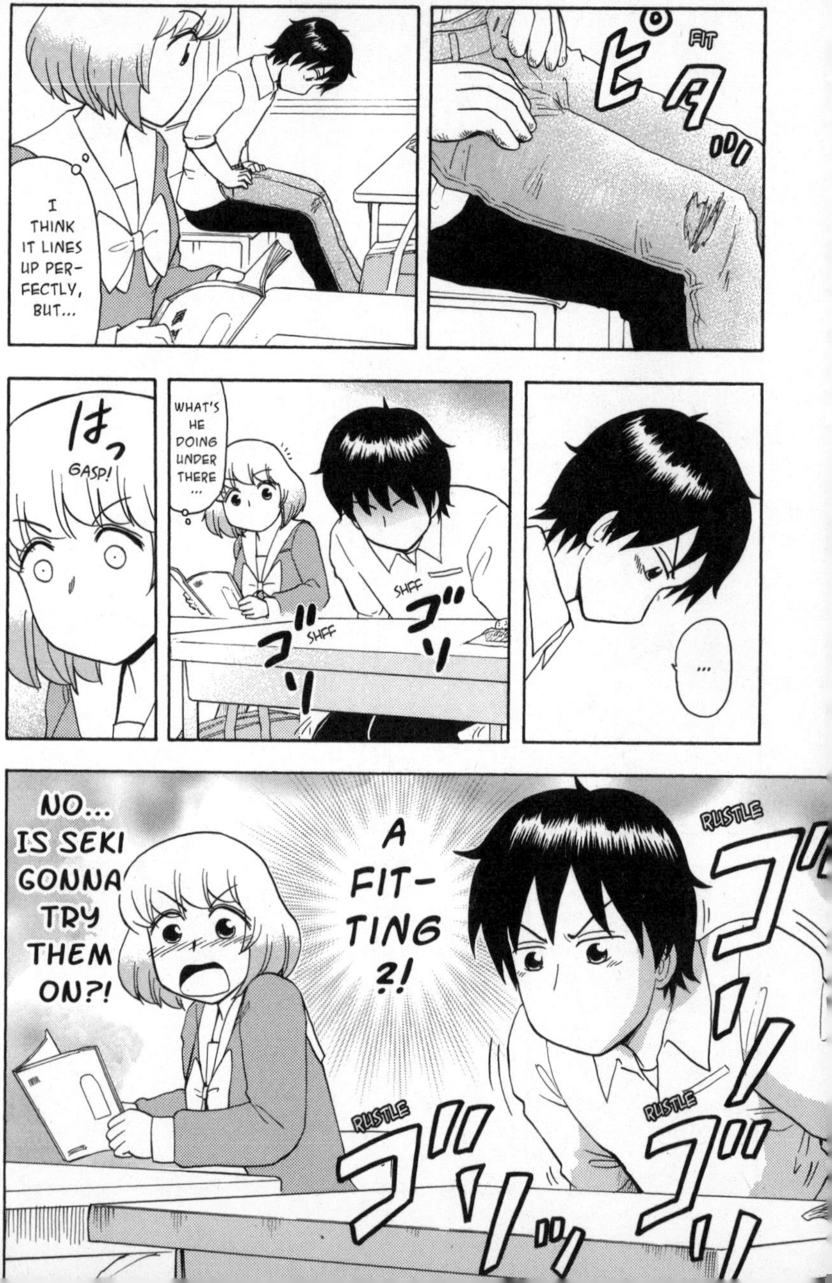
ピタ
FIT
I THINK IT LINES UP PER- FECTLY, BUT...
...
WHAT'S HE DOING UNDER THERE ...
ゴソ
SHFF
ゴソ
SHFF
はっ
GASP!
RUSTLE
ゴソ
A FIT- TING?!
NO... IS SEKI GONNA TRY THEM ON?!
RUSTLE
ゴソ
RUSTLE
ゴソッ

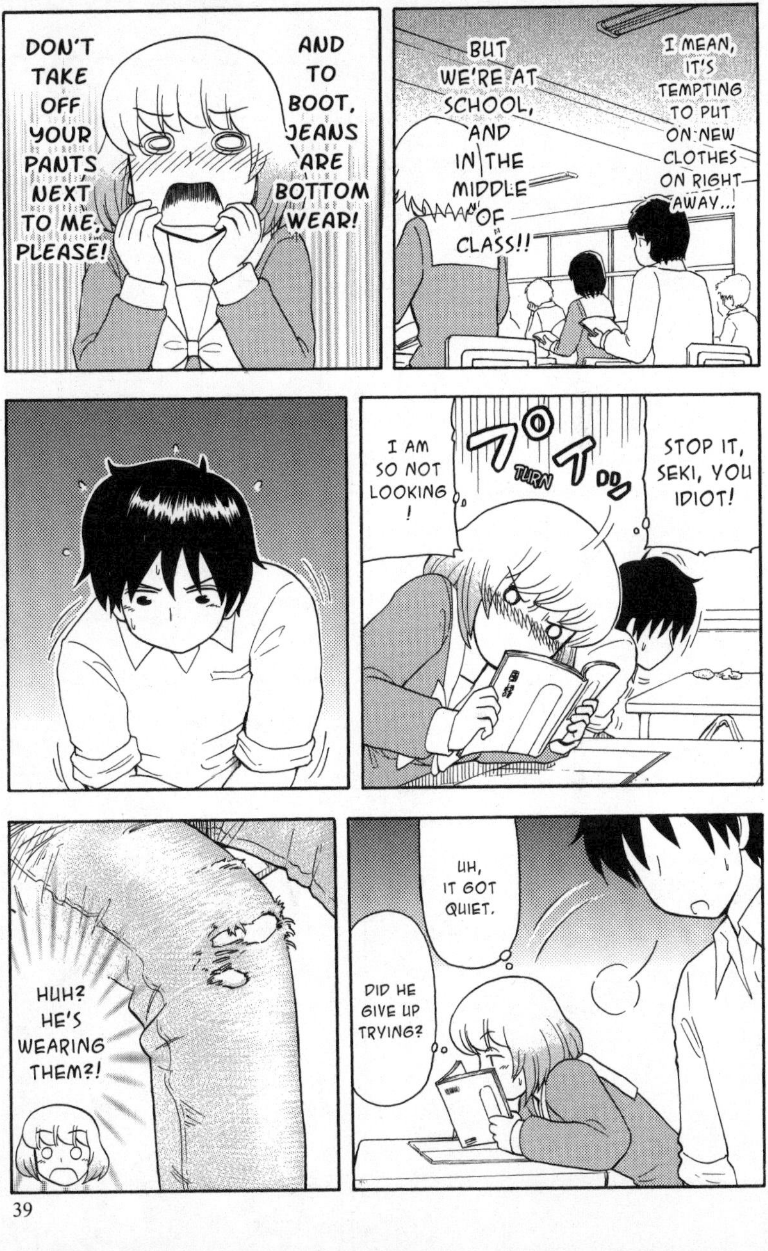
I MEAN, IT'S TEMPTING TO PUT ON NEW CLOTHES ON RIGHT AWAY...
BUT WE'RE AT SCHOOL, AND IN THE MIDDLE OF CLASS!!
AND TO BOOT, JEANS ARE BOTTOM WEAR!
DON'T TAKE OFF YOUR PANTS NEXT TO ME, PLEASE!
STOP IT, SEKI, YOU IDIOT!
TURN
I AM SO NOT LOOKING!
UH, IT GOT QUIET.
DID HE GIVE UP TRYING?
HUH? HE'S WEARING THEM?!

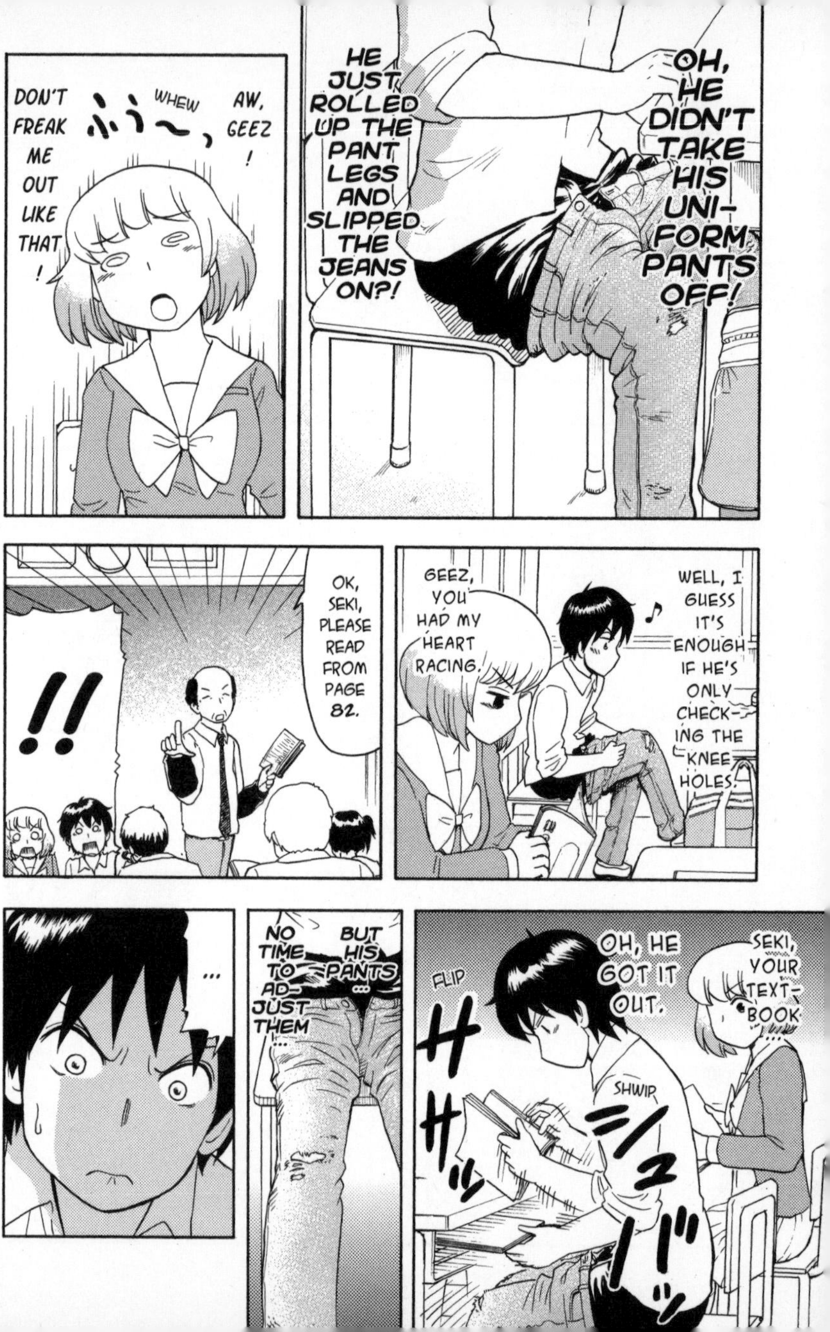
OH, HE DIDN'T TAKE HIS UNI-FORM PANTS OFF!
HE JUST ROLLED UP THE PANT LEGS AND SLIPPED THE JEANS ON?!
AW, GEEZ!
ふぅ～,
WHEW
DON'T FREAK ME OUT LIKE THAT!
WELL, I GUESS IT'S ENOUGH IF HE'S ONLY CHECKING THE KNEE HOLES.
GEEZ, YOU HAD MY HEART RACING.
OK, SEKI, PLEASE READ FROM PAGE 82.
!!
SEKI, YOUR TEXT-BOOK...
OH, HE GOT IT OUT.
FLIP
ハッ
SHWIP
シュ
BUT HIS PANTS...
NO TIME TO AD-JUST THEM...
...

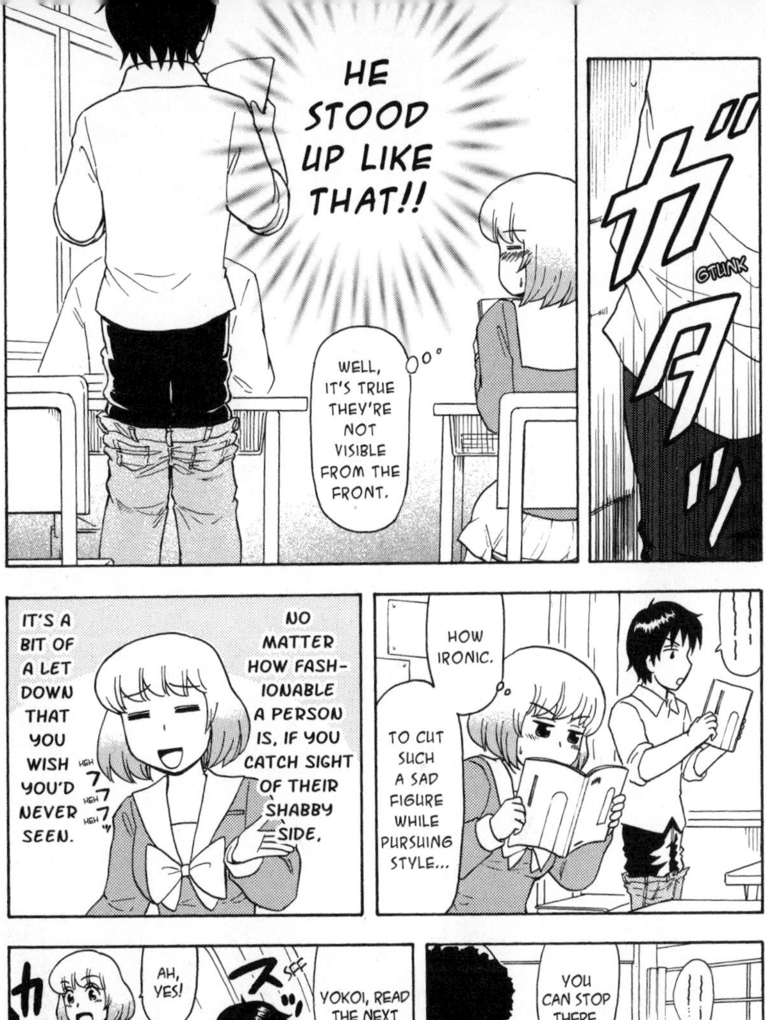
GTUNK
HE STOOD UP LIKE THAT!!
WELL, IT'S TRUE THEY'RE NOT VISIBLE FROM THE FRONT.
HOW IRONIC.
TO CUT SUCH A SAD FIGURE WHILE PURSUING STYLE...
NO MATTER HOW FASHIONABLE A PERSON IS, IF YOU CATCH SIGHT OF THEIR SHABBY SIDE,
IT'S A BIT OF A LET DOWN THAT YOU WISH YOU'D NEVER SEEN.
HEH HEH HEH
YOU CAN STOP THERE.
YOKOI, READ THE NEXT PARAGRAPH.
SFF
AH, YES!
KLATTER

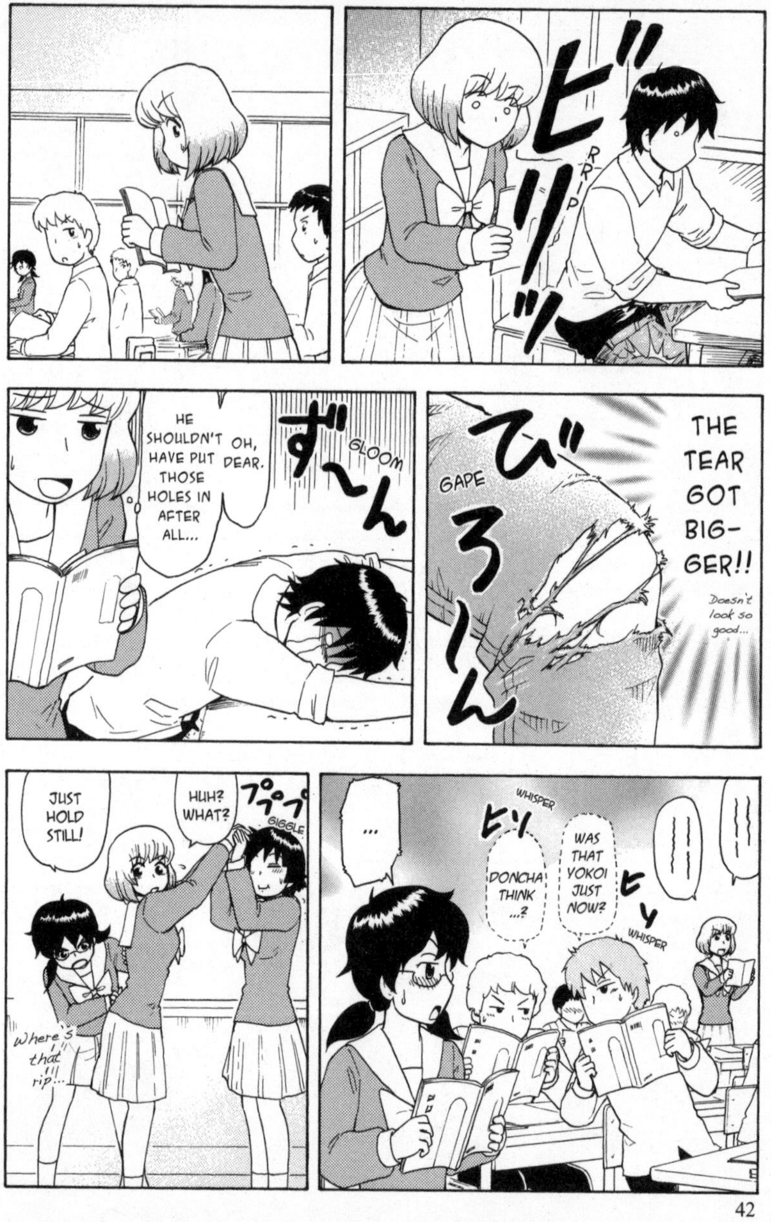
ビリッ
RRIP
THE TEAR GOT BIG-GER!!
びろーん
GAPE
Doesn't look so good...
ずーん
GLOOM
OH, DEAR.
HE SHOULDN'T HAVE PUT THOSE HOLES IN AFTER ALL...
ヒソ
WHISPER
WAS THAT YOKOI JUST NOW?
ヒソ
WHISPER
DONCHA THINK ...?
...
プププ
GIGGLE
HUH? WHAT?
JUST HOLD STILL!
Where's that rip...

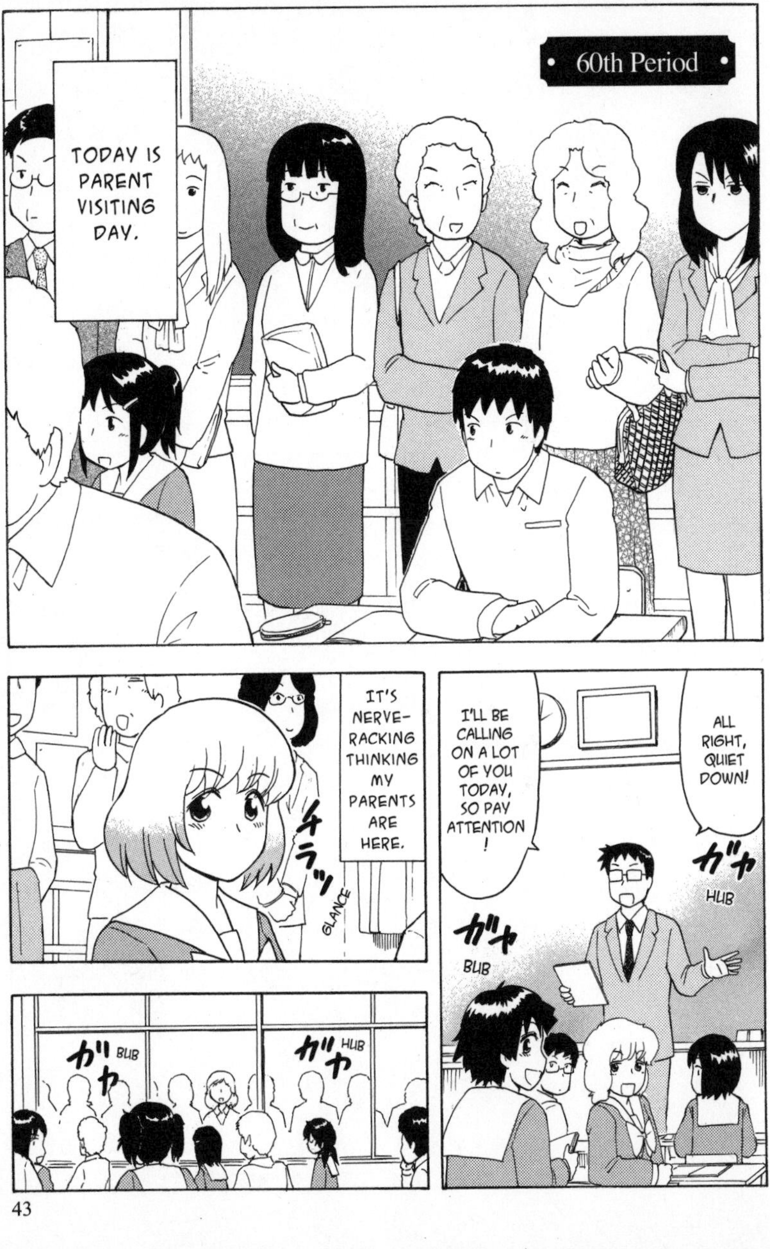

60th Period
TODAY IS PARENT VISITING DAY.
ALL RIGHT, QUIET DOWN!
ガヤ
HUB
I'LL BE CALLING ON A LOT OF YOU TODAY, SO PAY ATTENTION!
ガヤ
BUB
IT'S NERVE-RACKING THINKING MY PARENTS ARE HERE.
チラッ
GLANCE
ガヤ
HUB
ガヤ
BUB

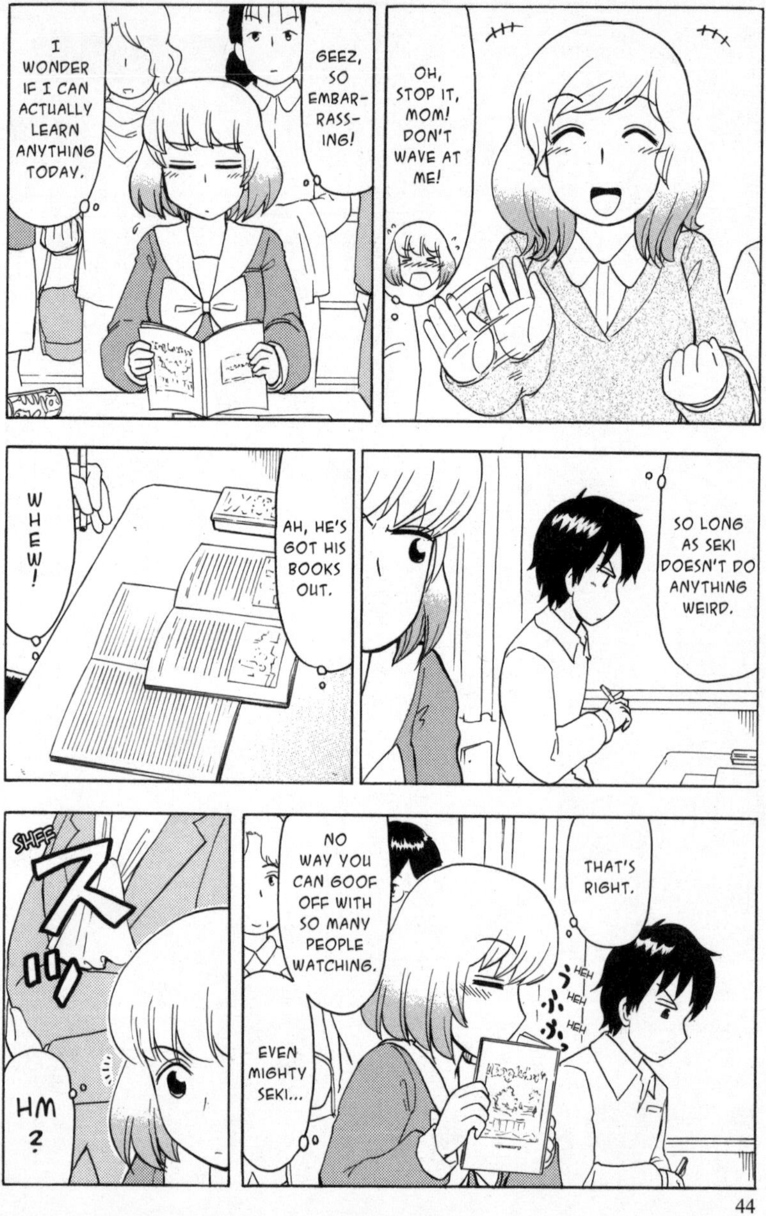
OH, STOP IT, MOM! DON'T WAVE AT ME!
GEEZ, SO EMBARRASSING!
I WONDER IF I CAN ACTUALLY LEARN ANYTHING TODAY.
SO LONG AS SEKI DOESN'T DO ANYTHING WEIRD.
AH, HE'S GOT HIS BOOKS OUT.
WHEW!
THAT'S RIGHT.
NO WAY YOU CAN GOOF OFF WITH SO MANY PEOPLE WATCHING.
HEH HEH HEH
EVEN MIGHTY SEKI...
SHFF
HM?

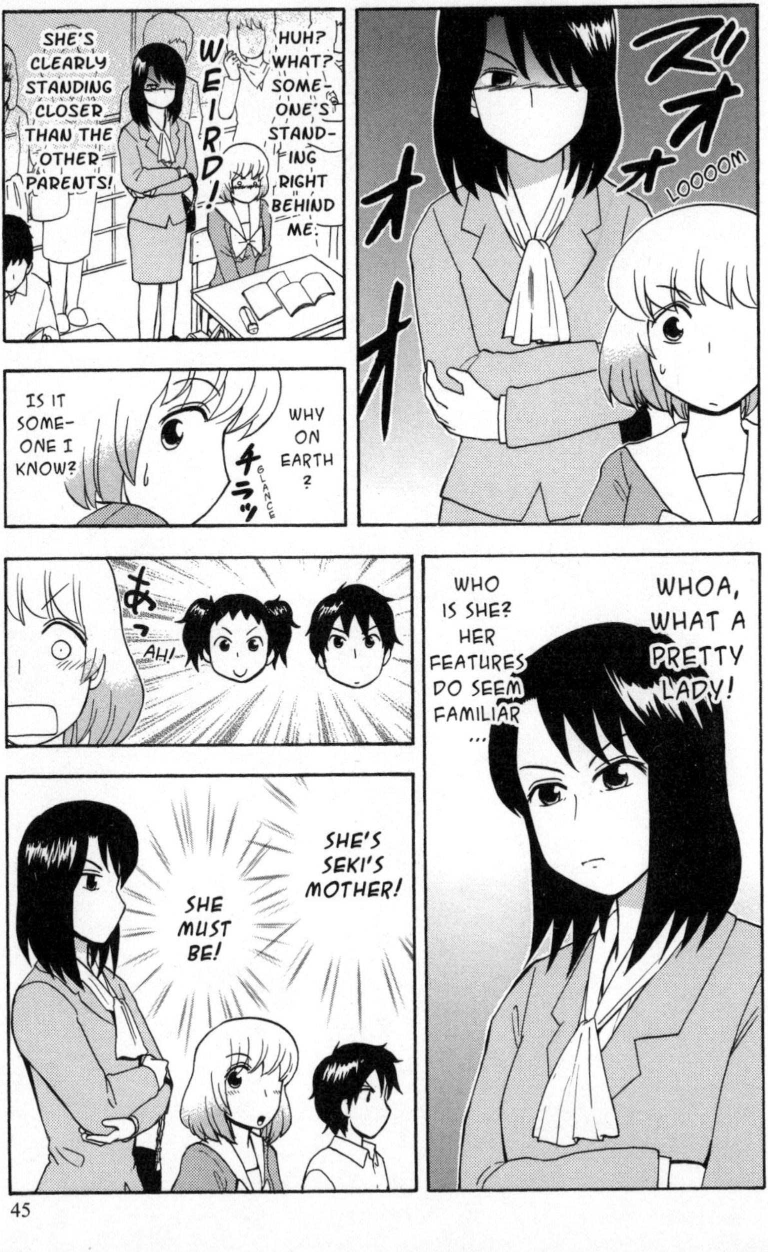
ズオオオ
LOOOOM
HUH? WHAT? SOME-ONE'S STAND-ING RIGHT BEHIND ME.
WEIRD!
SHE'S CLEARLY STANDING CLOSER THAN THE OTHER PARENTS!
WHY ON EARTH?
チラッ
GLANCE
IS IT SOME-ONE I KNOW?
WHOA, WHAT A PRETTY LADY!
WHO IS SHE? HER FEATURES DO SEEM FAMILIAR ...
あっ
AH!
SHE'S SEKI'S MOTHER!
SHE MUST BE!

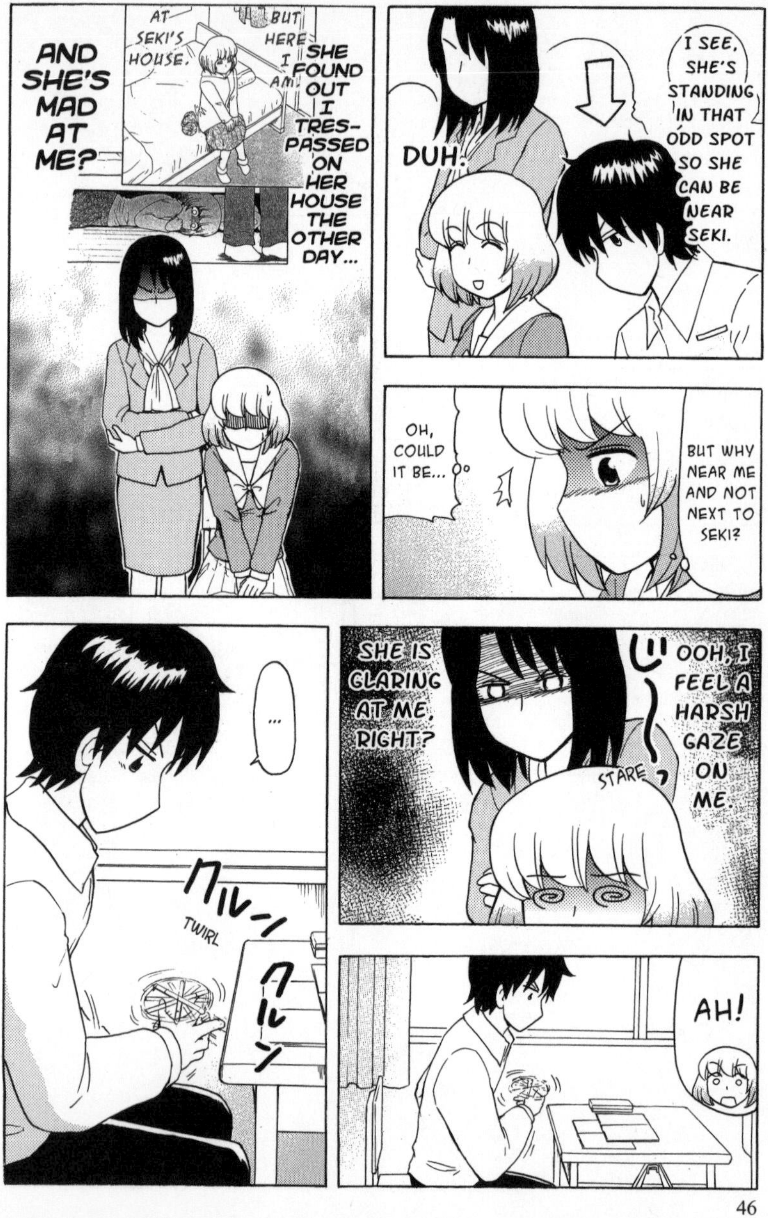
I SEE, SHE'S STANDING IN THAT ODD SPOT SO SHE CAN BE NEAR SEKI.
DUH.
BUT WHY NEAR ME AND NOT NEXT TO SEKI?
OH, COULD IT BE...
SHE FOUND OUT I TRESPASSED ON HER HOUSE THE OTHER DAY...
BUT HERE I AM
AT SEKI'S HOUSE.
AND SHE'S MAD AT ME?
OOH, I FEEL A HARSH GAZE ON ME.
じー
STARE
SHE IS GLARING AT ME, RIGHT?
AH!
...
クルーン
TWIRL
クルーン

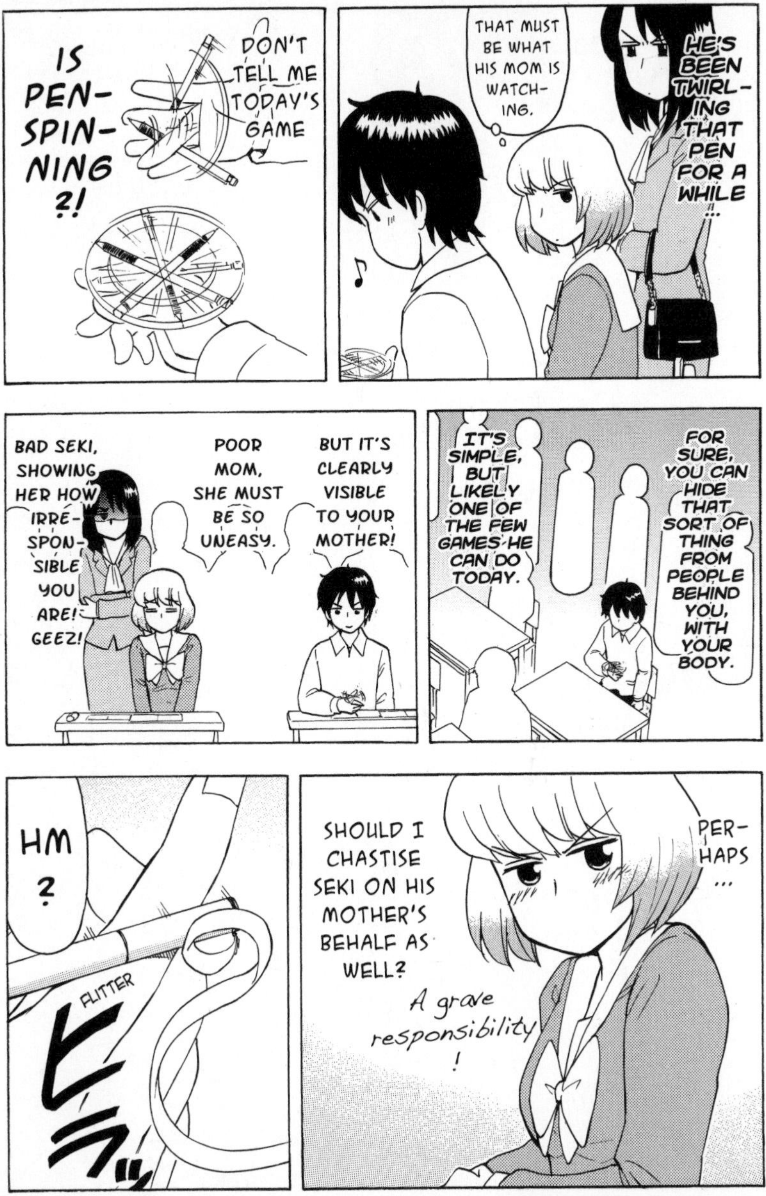
HE'S BEEN TWIRLING THAT PEN FOR A WHILE...
THAT MUST BE WHAT HIS MOM IS WATCHING.
DON'T TELL ME TODAY'S GAME
IS PEN-SPINNING?!
FOR SURE, YOU CAN HIDE THAT SORT OF THING FROM PEOPLE BEHIND YOU, WITH YOUR BODY.
IT'S SIMPLE, BUT LIKELY ONE OF THE FEW GAMES HE CAN DO TODAY.
BUT IT'S CLEARLY VISIBLE TO YOUR MOTHER!
POOR MOM, SHE MUST BE SO UNEASY.
BAD SEKI, SHOWING HER HOW IRRESPONSIBLE YOU ARE! GEEZ!
PERHAPS...
SHOULD I CHASTISE SEKI ON HIS MOTHER'S BEHALF AS WELL?
A grave responsibility!
HM?
FLITTER
ヒラッ

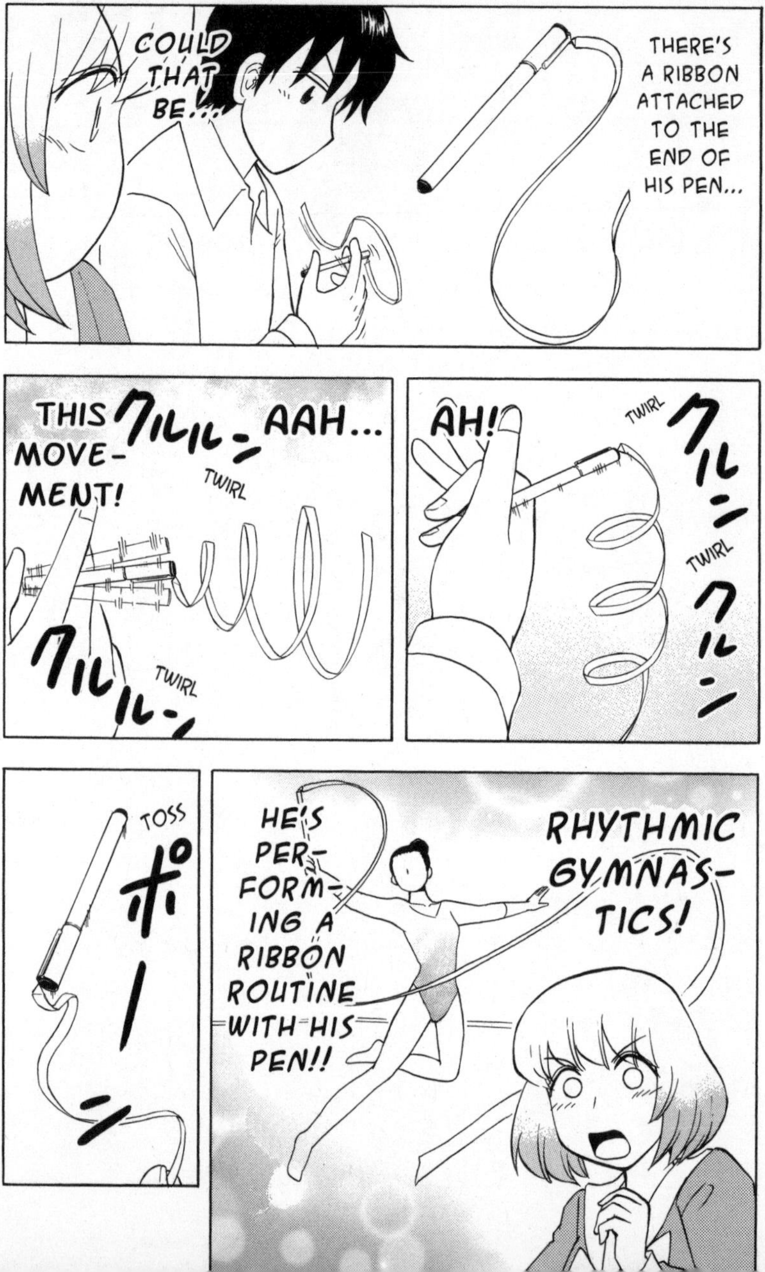
THERE'S A RIBBON ATTACHED TO THE END OF HIS PEN...
COULD THAT BE...?
AH!
TWIRL
クルン
TWIRL
クルン
AAH...
THIS MOVE-MENT!
クルルーン
TWIRL
クルルーン
TWIRL
RHYTHMIC GYMNAS-TICS!
HE'S PER-FORM-ING A RIBBON ROUTINE WITH HIS PEN!!
TOSS
ポーン

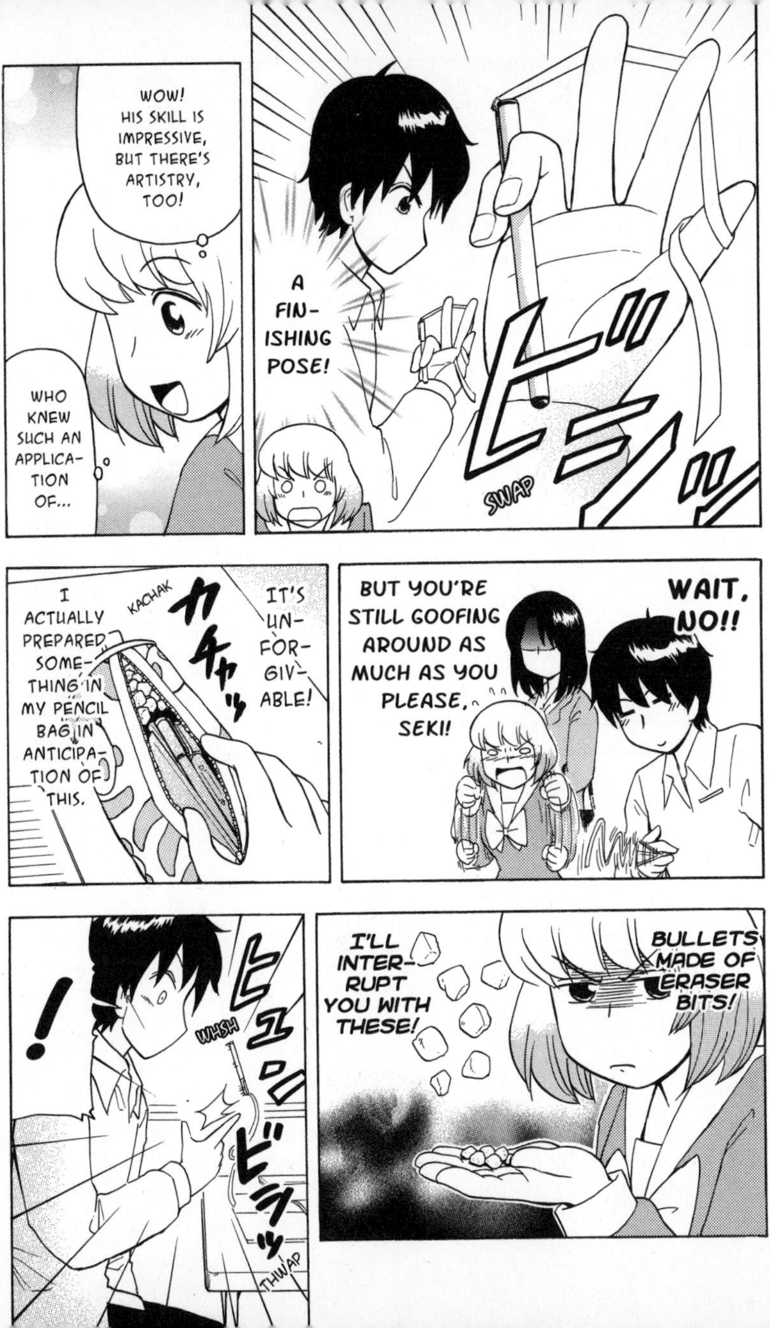
A FIN-ISHING POSE!
SWAP
WOW! HIS SKILL IS IMPRESSIVE, BUT THERE'S ARTISTRY, TOO!
WHO KNEW SUCH AN APPLICA-TION OF...
WAIT, NO!!
BUT YOU'RE STILL GOOFING AROUND AS MUCH AS YOU PLEASE, SEKI!
IT'S UN-FOR-GIV-ABLE!
KACHAK
I ACTUALLY PREPARED SOME-THING IN MY PENCIL BAG IN ANTICIPA-TION OF THIS.
BULLETS MADE OF ERASER BITS!
I'LL INTER-RUPT YOU WITH THESE!
WHSH
!
THWAP

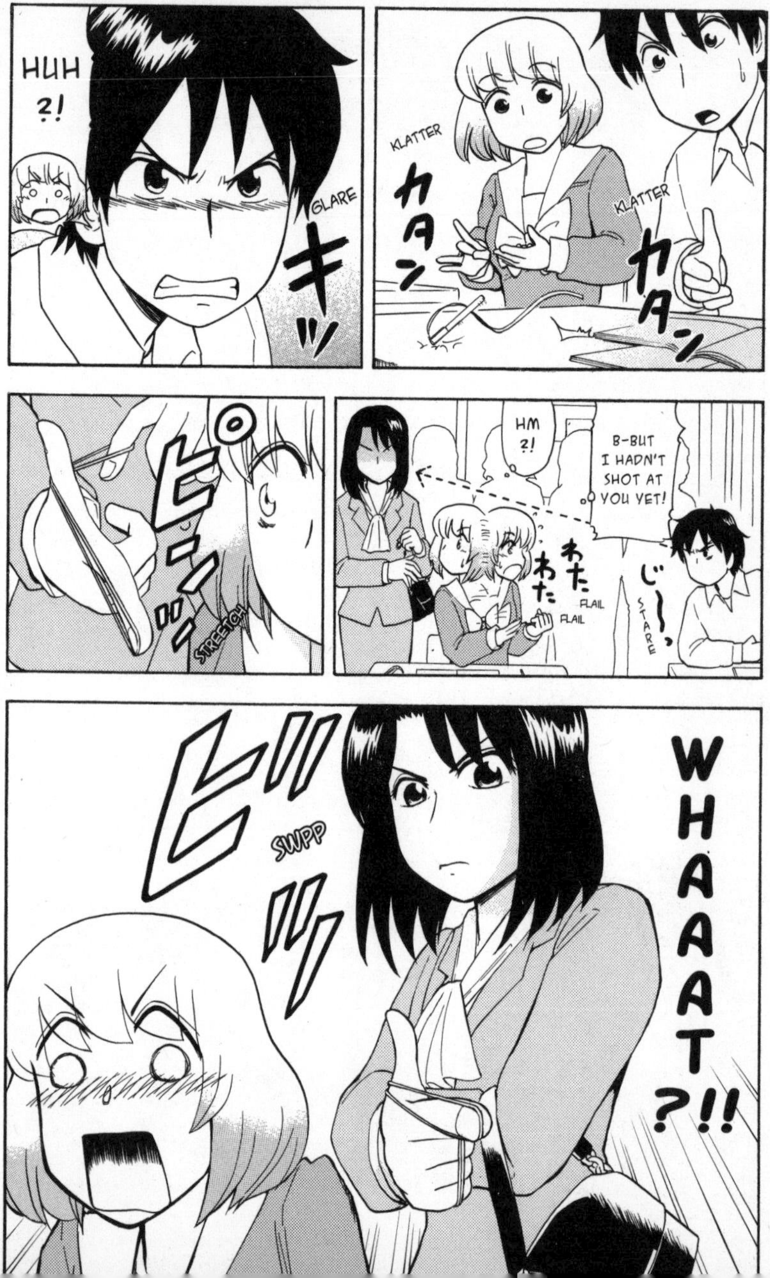
KLATTER
カタン
KLATTER
カタン
HUH ?!
GLARE
キッ
B-BUT I HADN'T SHOT AT YOU YET!
HM ?!
わたわた
FLAIL
FLAIL
じ～っ
STARE
ピーン
STREETCH
WHAAAT ?!!
ピシッ
SWPP

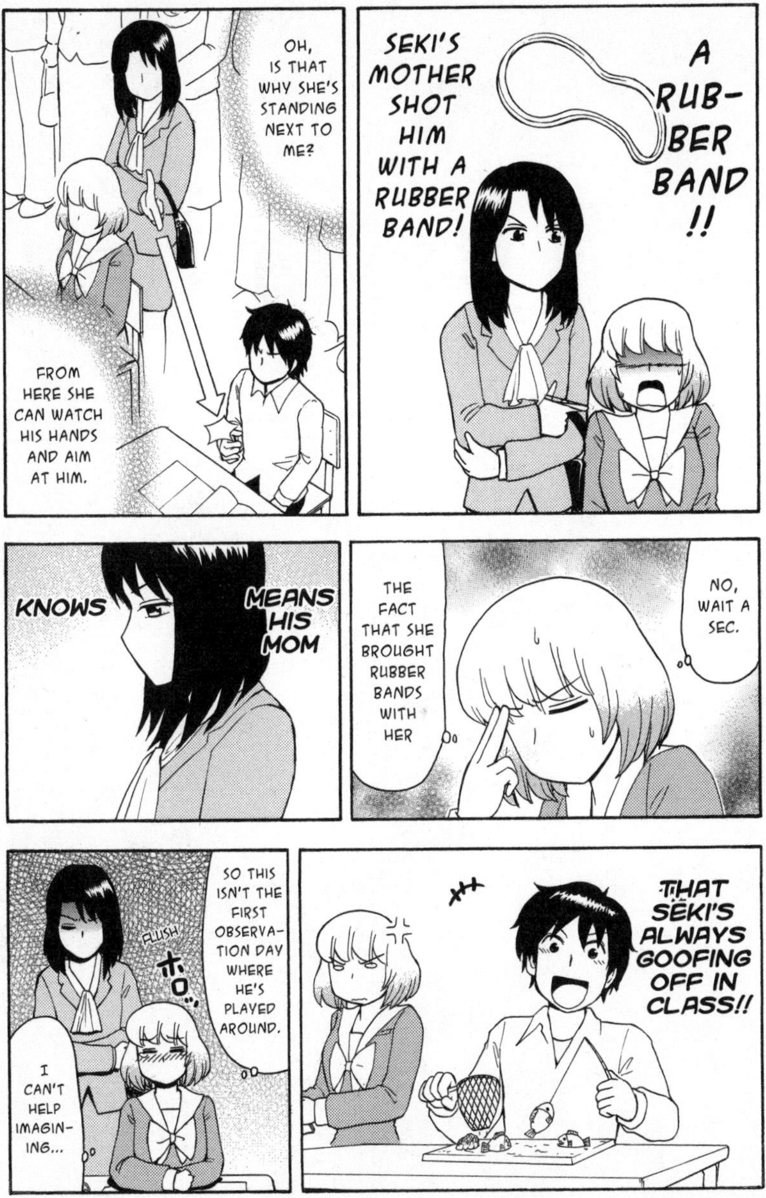
SEKI'S MOTHER SHOT HIM WITH A RUBBER BAND!
A RUB-BER BAND !!
OH, IS THAT WHY SHE'S STANDING NEXT TO ME?
FROM HERE SHE CAN WATCH HIS HANDS AND AIM AT HIM.
NO, WAIT A SEC.
THE FACT THAT SHE BROUGHT RUBBER BANDS WITH HER
MEANS HIS MOM
KNOWS
THAT SEKI'S ALWAYS GOOFING OFF IN CLASS!!
SO THIS ISN'T THE FIRST OBSERVA-TION DAY WHERE HE'S PLAYED AROUND.
FLUSH
ホロッ
I CAN'T HELP IMAGIN-ING...

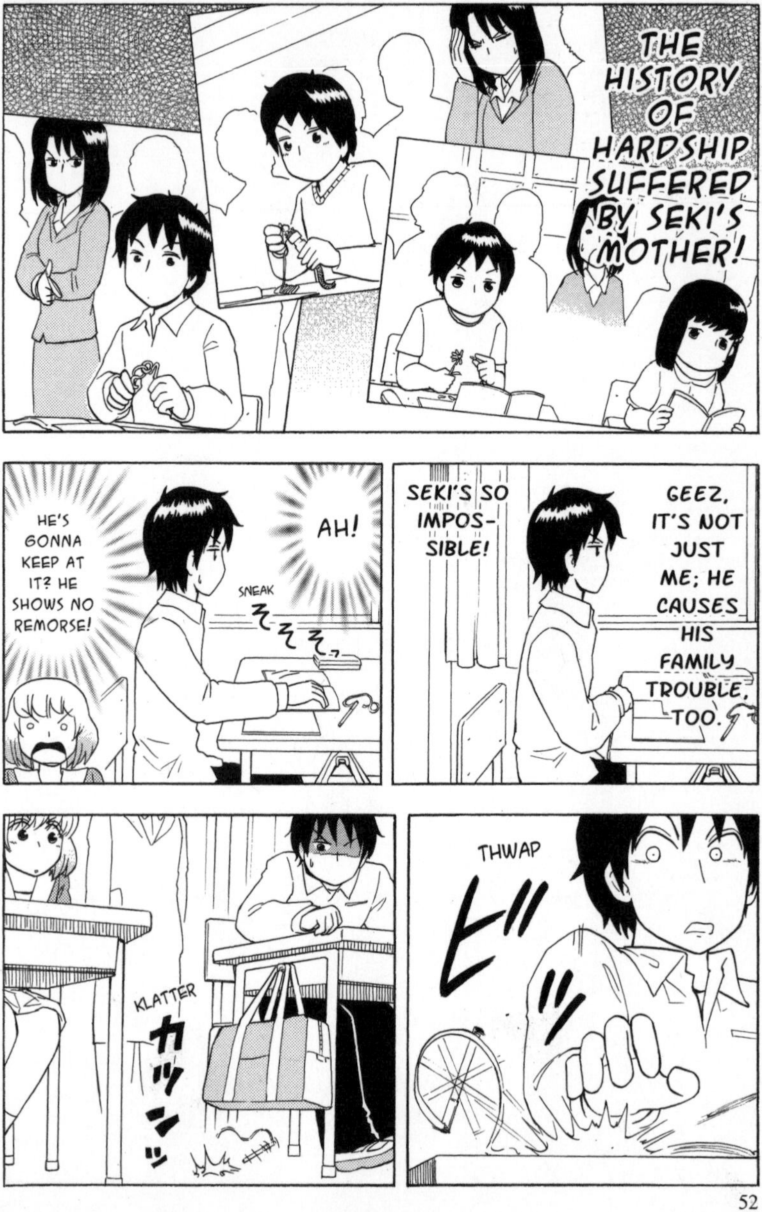
THE HISTORY OF HARDSHIP SUFFERED BY SEKI'S MOTHER!
GEEZ, IT'S NOT JUST ME; HE CAUSES HIS FAMILY TROUBLE, TOO.
SEKI'S SO IMPOS-SIBLE!
AH!
SNEAK
HE'S GONNA KEEP AT IT? HE SHOWS NO REMORSE!
THWAP
KLATTER

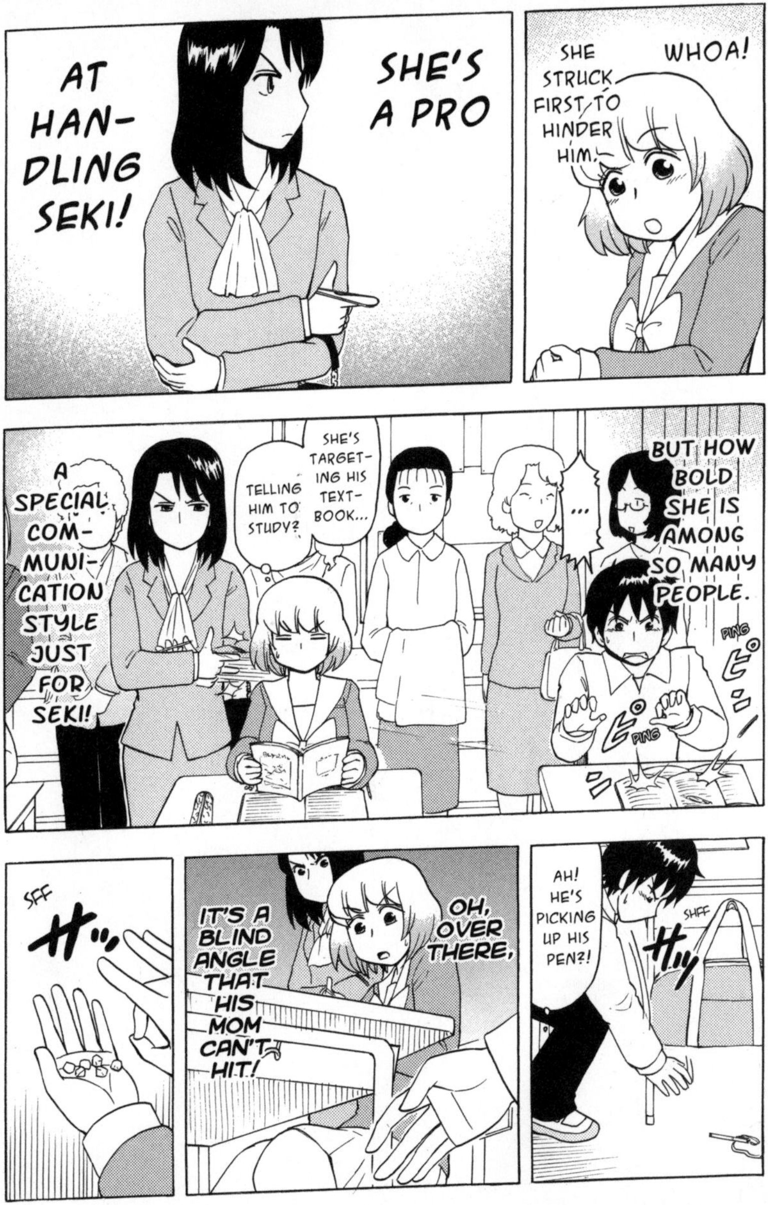
WHOA!
SHE STRUCK FIRST TO HINDER HIM.
SHE'S A PRO
AT HAN-DLING SEKI!
BUT HOW BOLD SHE IS AMONG SO MANY PEOPLE.
...
PING
PING
SHE'S TARGET-ING HIS TEXT-BOOK...
TELLING HIM TO STUDY?
A SPECIAL COM-MUNI-CATION STYLE JUST FOR SEKI!
AH! HE'S PICKING UP HIS PEN?!
SHFF
OH, OVER THERE,
IT'S A BLIND ANGLE THAT HIS MOM CAN'T HIT!
SFF

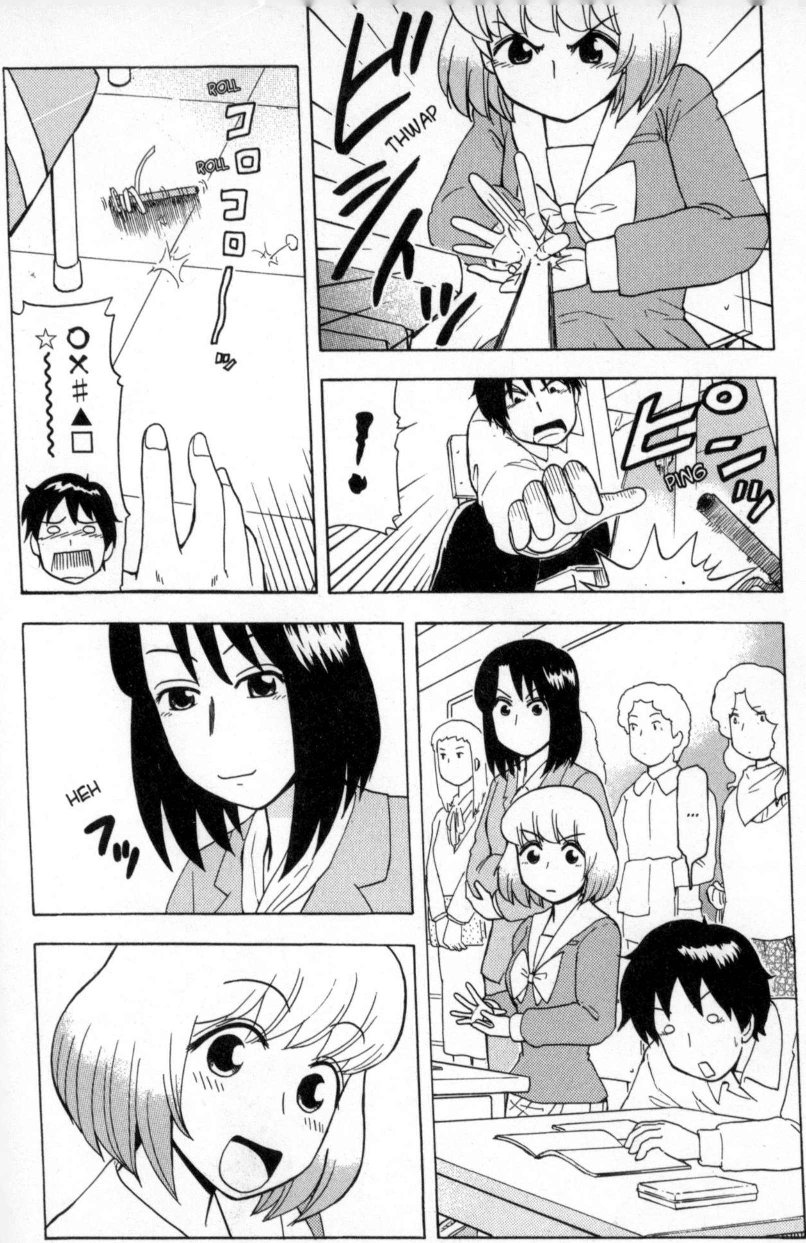

ビシィッ
THWAP
ピーンッ
PING
!
ROLL
ROLL
コロコローーッ
○×#▲□☆~~~
...
HEH
フッ

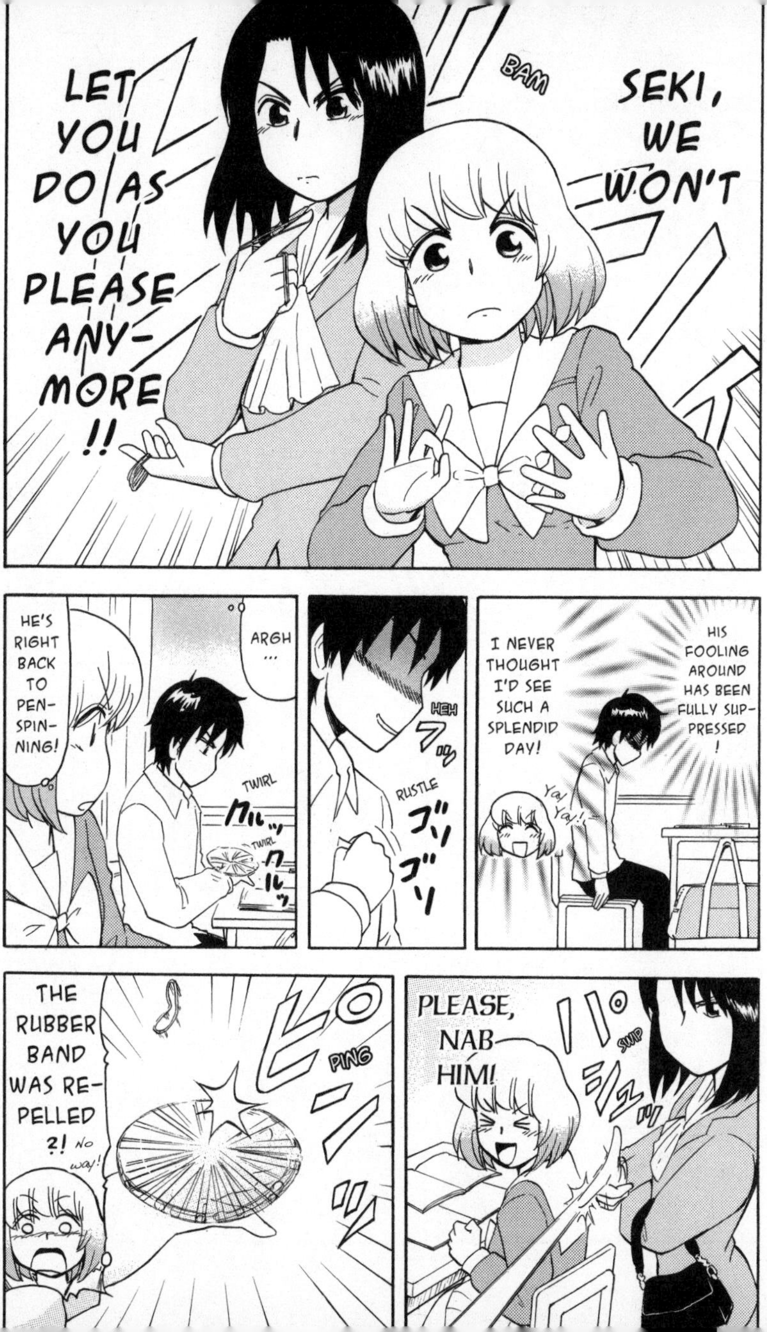
SEKI, WE WON'T
BAM
LET YOU DO AS YOU PLEASE ANYMORE!!
HIS FOOLING AROUND HAS BEEN FULLY SUPPRESSED!
I NEVER THOUGHT I'D SEE SUCH A SPLENDID DAY!
Yay Yay!
HEH
RUSTLE
ARGH ...
HE'S RIGHT BACK TO PEN-SPINNING!
TWIRL
TWIRL
PLEASE, NAB HIM!
SWIP
PING
THE RUBBER BAND WAS REPELLED?!
No way!

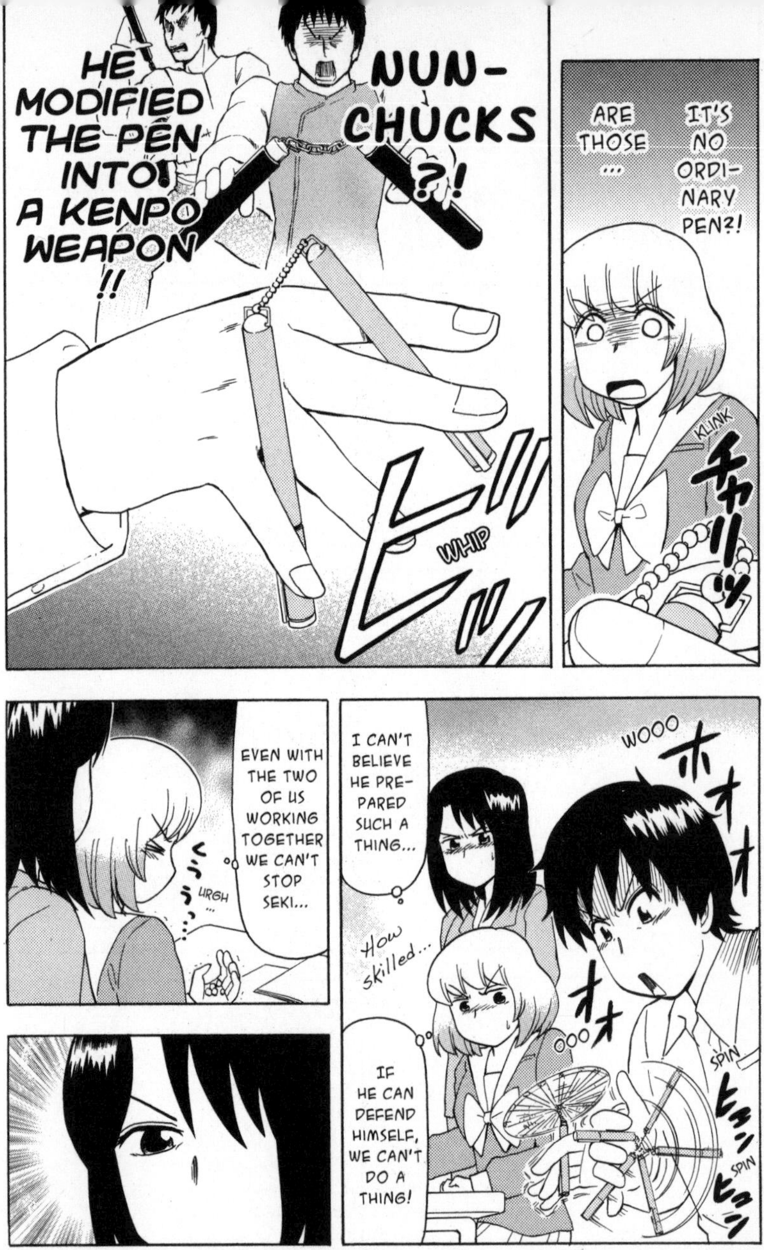

ARE THOSE ...
IT'S NO ORDINARY PEN?!
KLINK
チャリッ
NUN-CHUCKS ?!
HE MODIFIED THE PEN INTO A KENPO WEAPON !!
WHIP
ビッ
I CAN'T BELIEVE HE PREPARED SUCH A THING...
WOOO
ホオオ
How skilled...
オオ
IF HE CAN DEFEND HIMSELF, WE CAN'T DO A THING!
SPIN
ヒュン
SPIN
ヒュン
EVEN WITH THE TWO OF US WORKING TOGETHER WE CAN'T STOP SEKI...
URGH ...
くぅぅ...

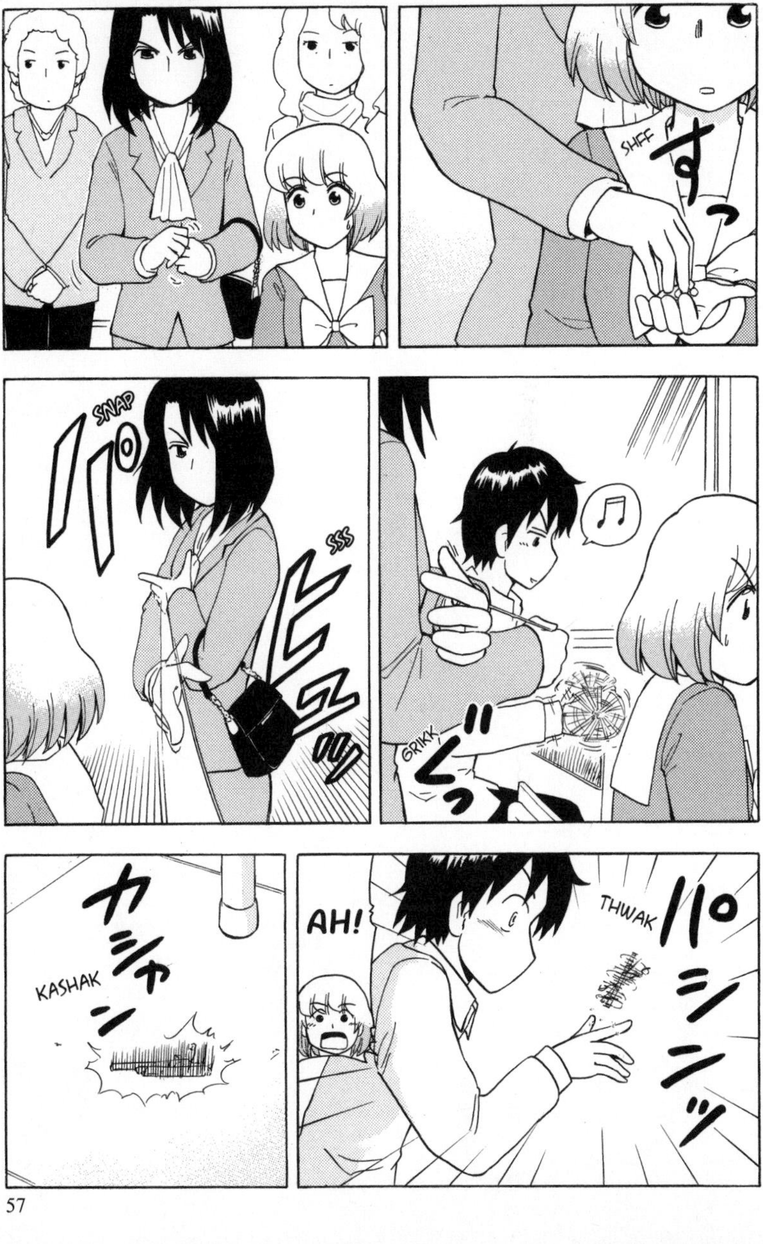
SHFF
すっ
♪
GRIKK
ぐっ
SNAP
パ
SSS
AH!
THWAK
パシンッ
KASHAK
カシャン

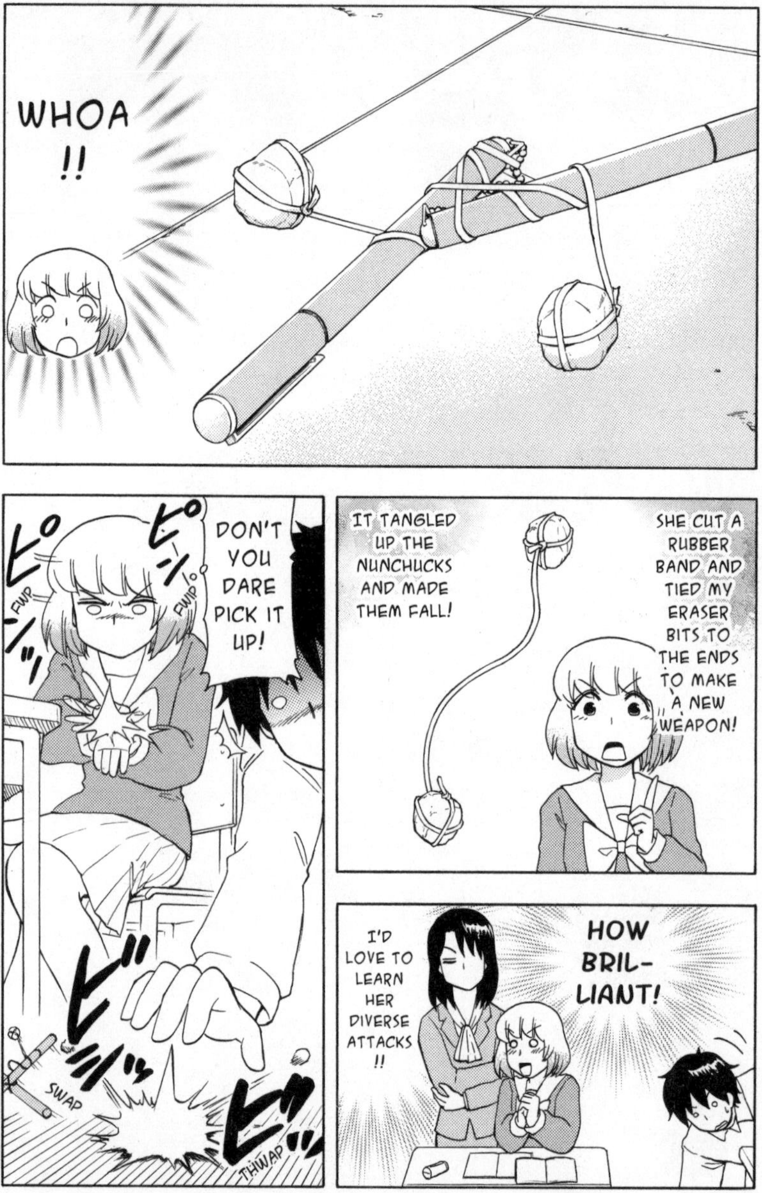
WHOA !!
SHE CUT A RUBBER BAND AND TIED MY ERASER BITS TO THE ENDS TO MAKE A NEW WEAPON!
IT TANGLED UP THE NUNCHUCKS AND MADE THEM FALL!
HOW BRIL- LIANT!
I'D LOVE TO LEARN HER DIVERSE ATTACKS !!
DON'T YOU DARE PICK IT UP!
FWIP
FWIP
SWAP
THWAP

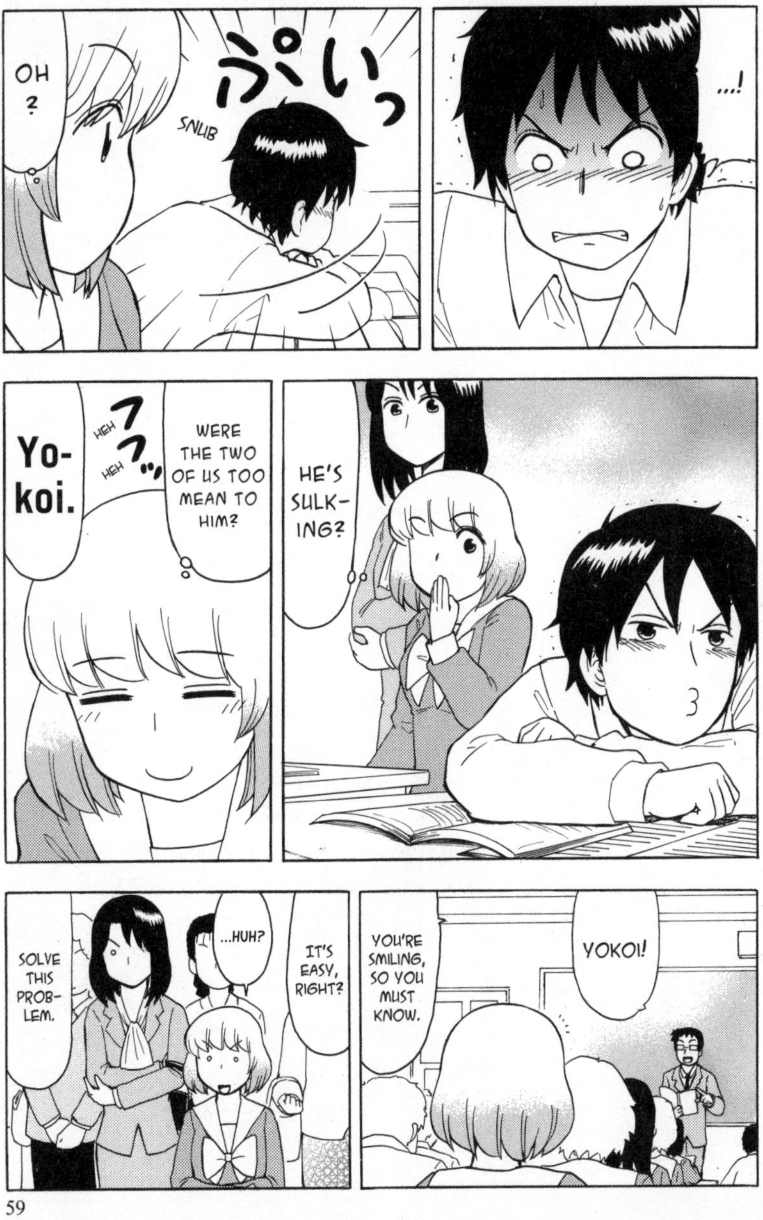

...!
ぷいっ
SNUB
OH?
HE'S SULKING?
WERE THE TWO OF US TOO MEAN TO HIM?
HEH HEH
Yo-koi.
YOKOI!
YOU'RE SMILING, SO YOU MUST KNOW.
IT'S EASY, RIGHT?
...HUH?
SOLVE THIS PROBLEM.

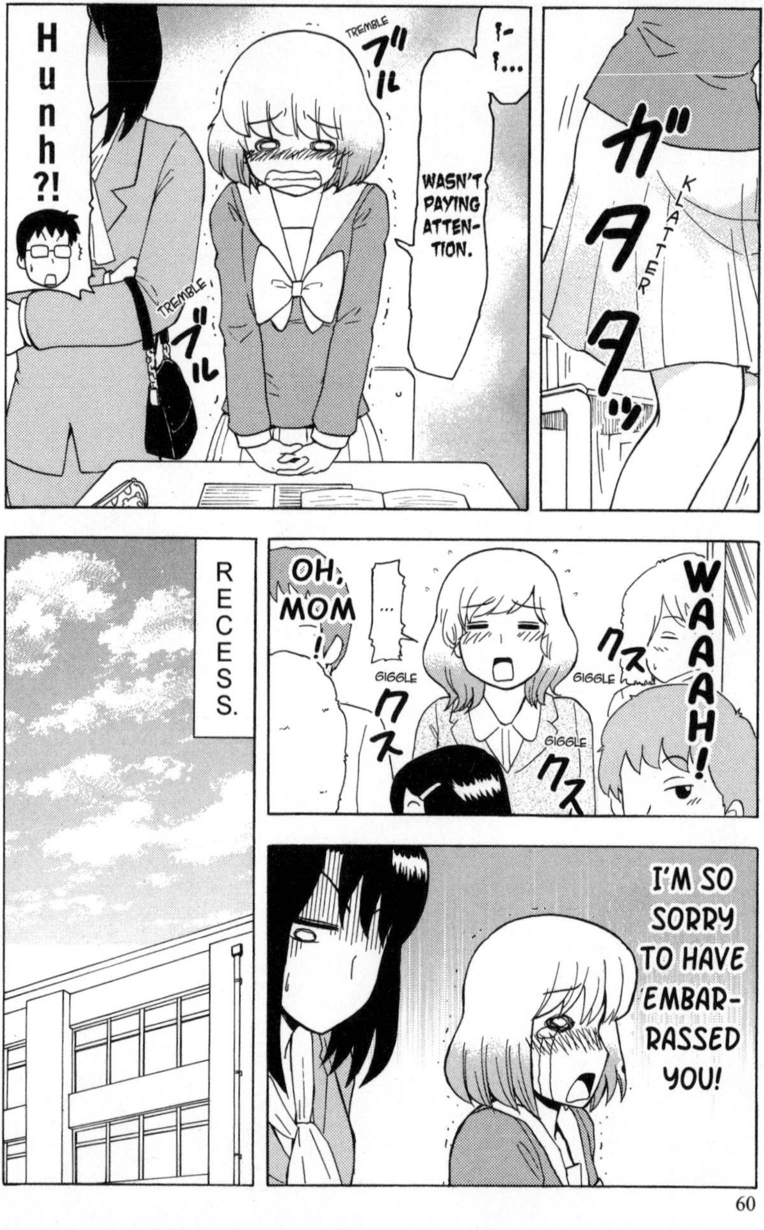

ガタタッ
KLATTER
I- I...
WASN'T PAYING ATTEN-TION.
TREMBLE
ブル
Hunh?!
TREMBLE
ブル
WAAAAH!
GIGGLE
クス
...
OH, MOM!
GIGGLE
クス
GIGGLE
クス
I'M SO SORRY TO HAVE EMBAR-RASSED YOU!
RECESS.

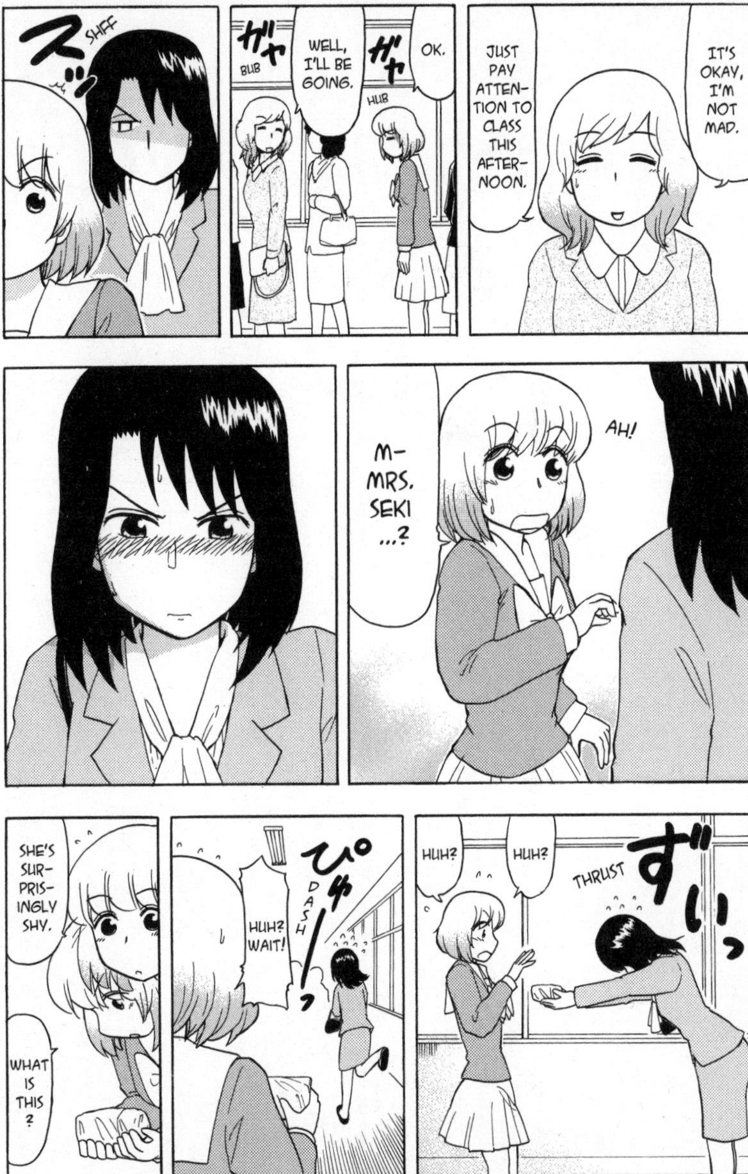
IT'S OKAY, I'M NOT MAD.
JUST PAY ATTENTION TO CLASS THIS AFTERNOON.
OK.
ガヤ
HUB
WELL, I'LL BE GOING.
ガヤ
BUB
ズッ
SHFF
AH!
M-MRS. SEKI ...?
ずいっ
THRUST
HUH?
HUH?
ぴゅーっ
DASH
HUH? WAIT!
SHE'S SURPRISINGLY SHY.
WHAT IS THIS?

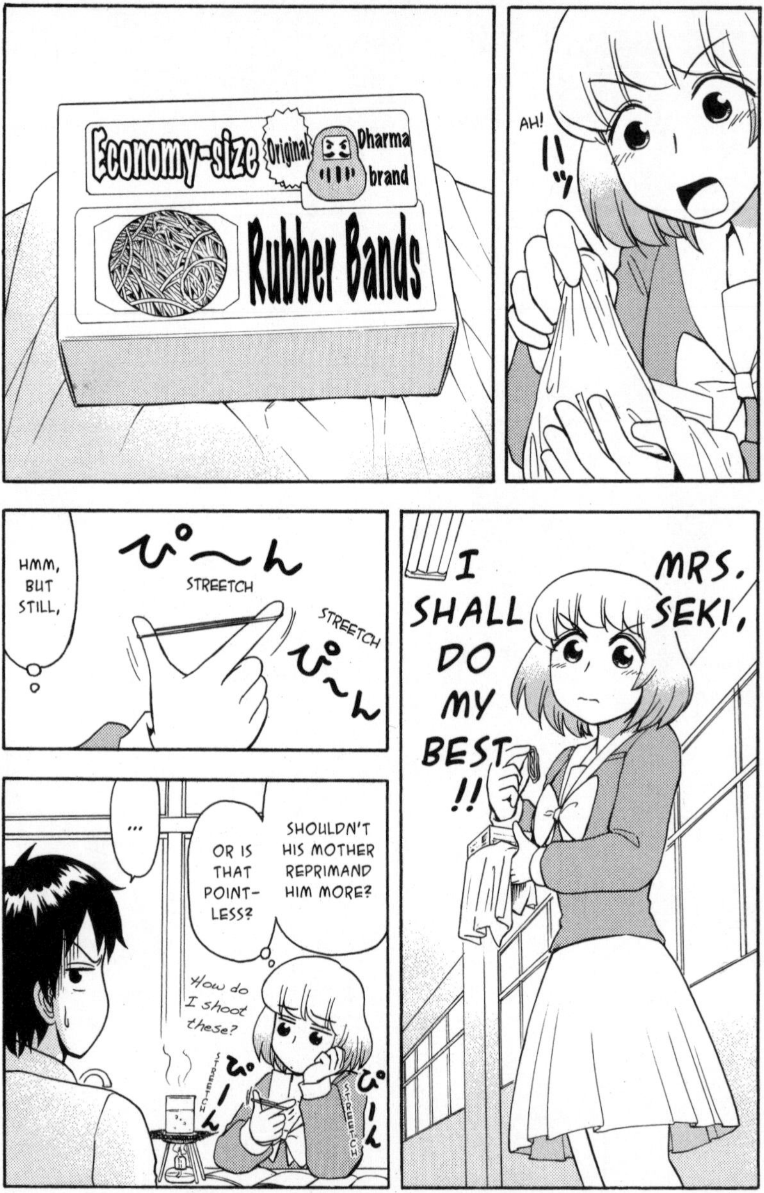
AH!
ハッ
Economy-size
Original
Dharma brand
Rubber Bands
MRS. SEKI,
I SHALL DO MY BEST!!
HMM, BUT STILL,
ぴ〜ん
STREETCH
STREETCH
ぴ〜ん
SHOULDN'T HIS MOTHER REPRIMAND HIM MORE?
OR IS THAT POINT-LESS?
...
How do I shoot these?
ぴーん
STREETCH
ぴーん
STREETCH

My Neighbor Seki

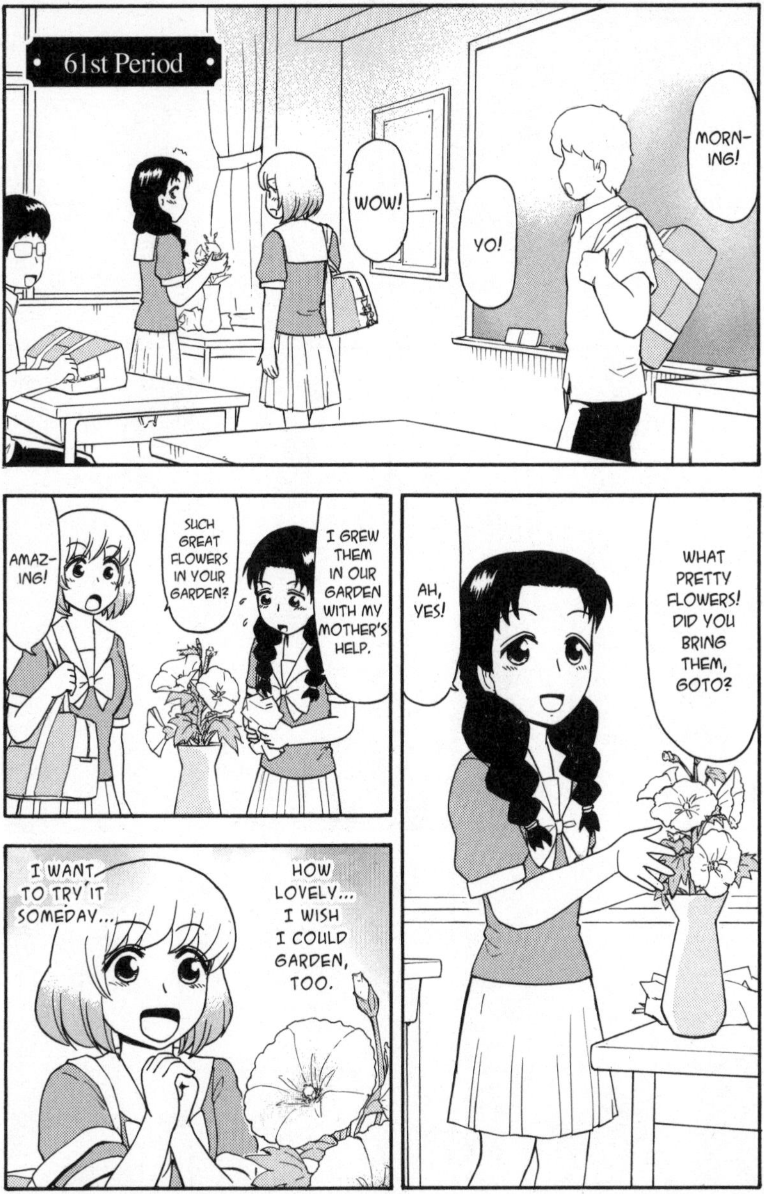
61st Period
MORN-ING!
YO!
WOW!
WHAT PRETTY FLOWERS! DID YOU BRING THEM, GOTO?
AH, YES!
I GREW THEM IN OUR GARDEN WITH MY MOTHER'S HELP.
SUCH GREAT FLOWERS IN YOUR GARDEN?
AMAZ-ING!
HOW LOVELY... I WISH I COULD GARDEN, TOO.
I WANT TO TRY IT SOMEDAY...

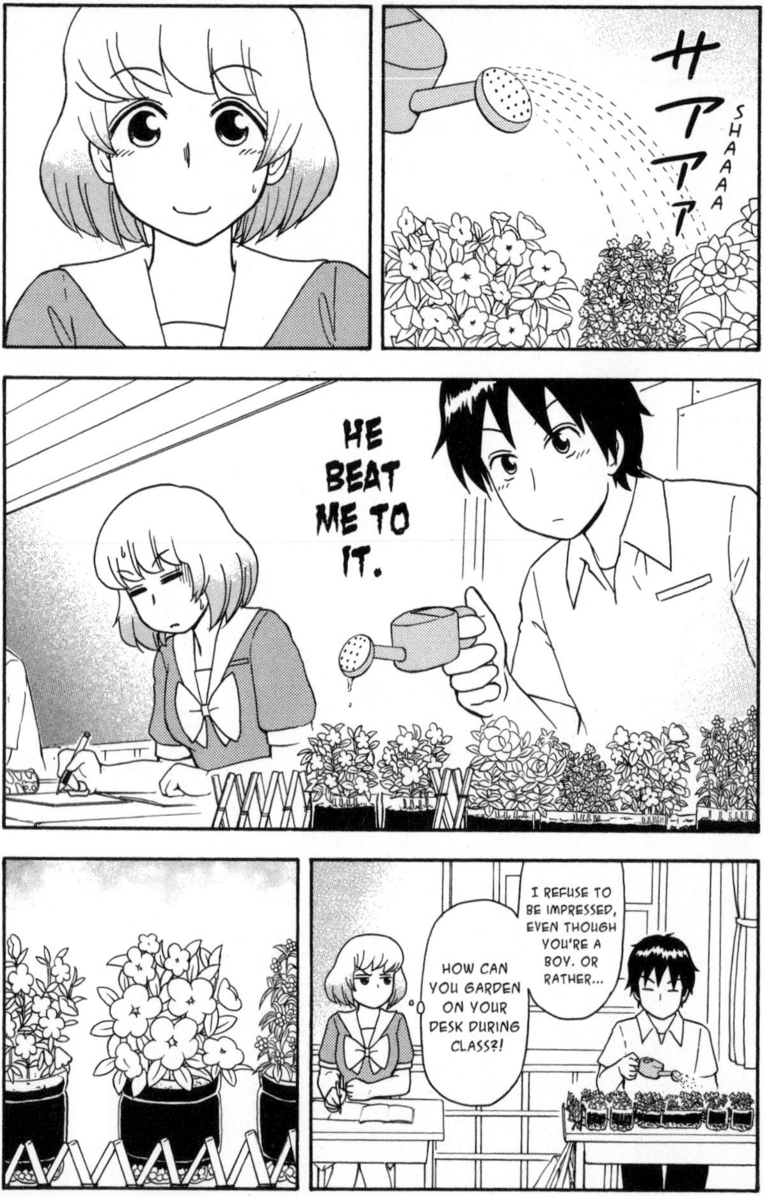
サアア
SHAAAA
HE BEAT ME TO IT.
I REFUSE TO BE IMPRESSED, EVEN THOUGH YOU'RE A BOY. OR RATHER...
HOW CAN YOU GARDEN ON YOUR DESK DURING CLASS?!

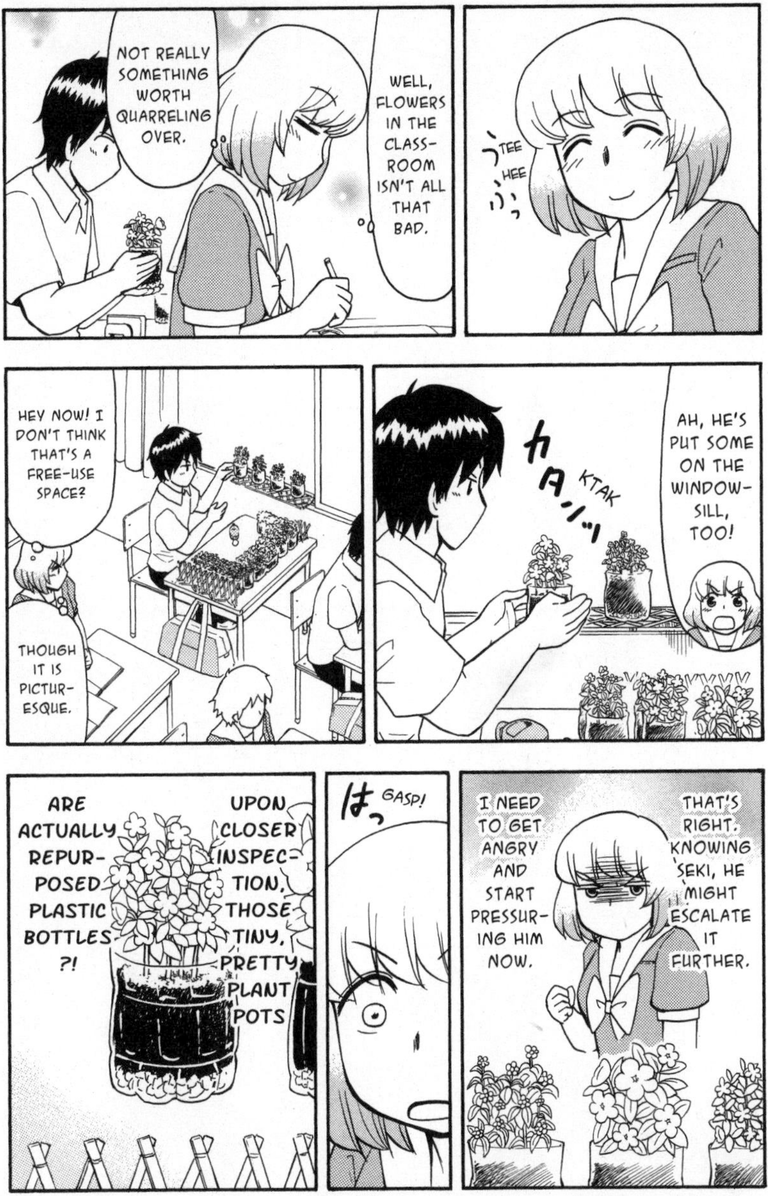
TEE HEE
WELL, FLOWERS IN THE CLASS-ROOM ISN'T ALL THAT BAD.
NOT REALLY SOMETHING WORTH QUARRELING OVER.
AH, HE'S PUT SOME ON THE WINDOW-SILL, TOO!
カタンッ
KTAK
HEY NOW! I DON'T THINK THAT'S A FREE-USE SPACE?
THOUGH IT IS PICTUR-ESQUE.
THAT'S RIGHT. KNOWING SEKI, HE MIGHT ESCALATE IT FURTHER.
I NEED TO GET ANGRY AND START PRESSUR-ING HIM NOW.
はっ
GASP!
UPON CLOSER INSPEC-TION, THOSE TINY, PRETTY PLANT POTS
ARE ACTUALLY REPUR-POSED PLASTIC BOTTLES?!

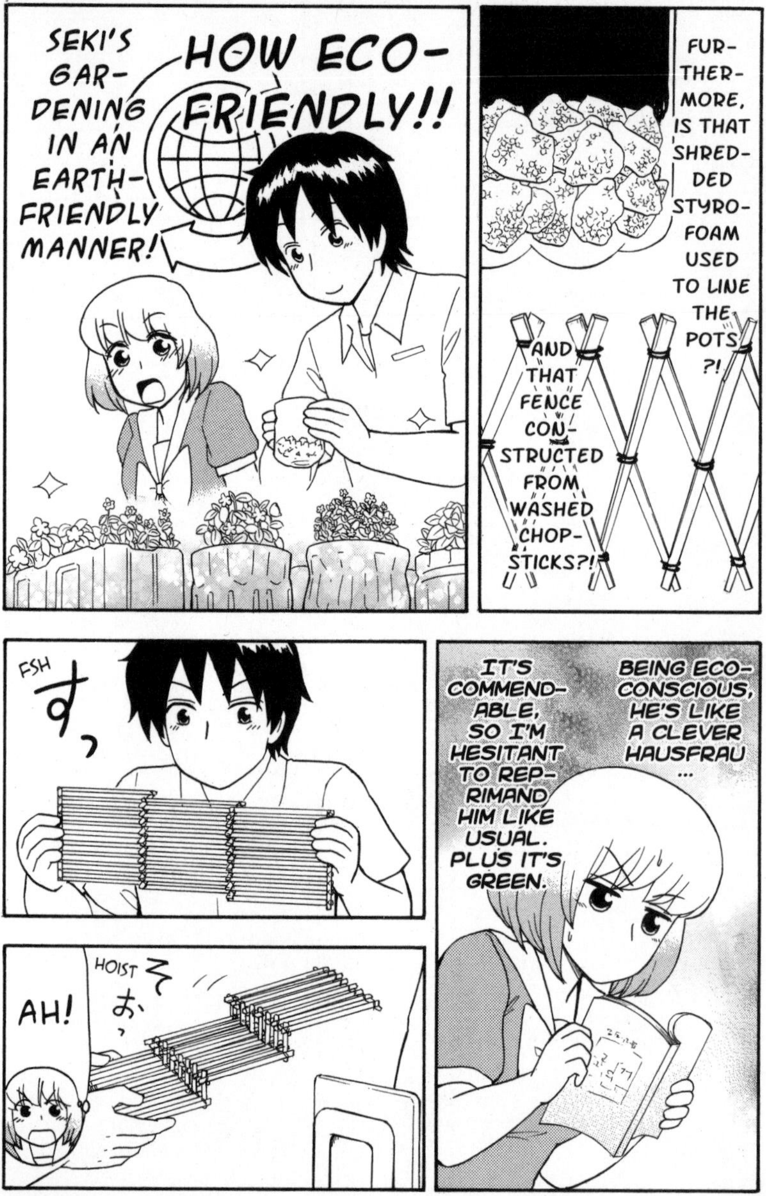
FURTHERMORE, IS THAT SHREDDED STYROFOAM USED TO LINE THE POTS?!
AND THAT FENCE CONSTRUCTED FROM WASHED CHOPSTICKS?!
HOW ECO-FRIENDLY!!
SEKI'S GARDENING IN AN EARTH-FRIENDLY MANNER!
BEING ECO-CONSCIOUS, HE'S LIKE A CLEVER HAUSFRAU...
IT'S COMMENDABLE, SO I'M HESITANT TO REPRIMAND HIM LIKE USUAL. PLUS IT'S GREEN.
FSH
すっ
HOIST
そお
AH!

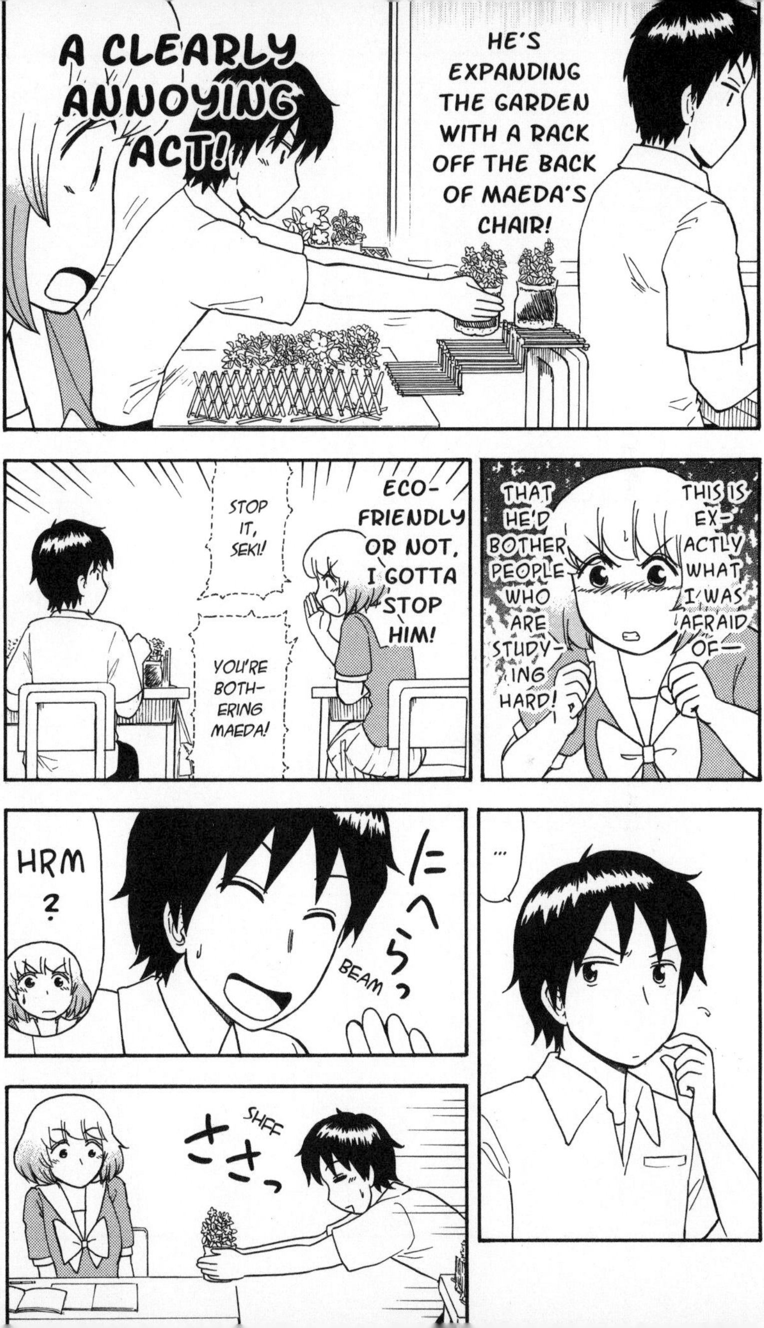
HE'S EXPANDING THE GARDEN WITH A RACK OFF THE BACK OF MAEDA'S CHAIR!
A CLEARLY ANNOYING ACT!
THIS IS EX-ACTLY WHAT I WAS AFRAID OF—
THAT HE'D BOTHER PEOPLE WHO ARE STUDY-ING HARD!
ECO-FRIENDLY OR NOT, I GOTTA STOP HIM!
STOP IT, SEKI!
YOU'RE BOTH-ERING MAEDA!
...
にへらっ
BEAM
HRM?
SHFF
ささっ

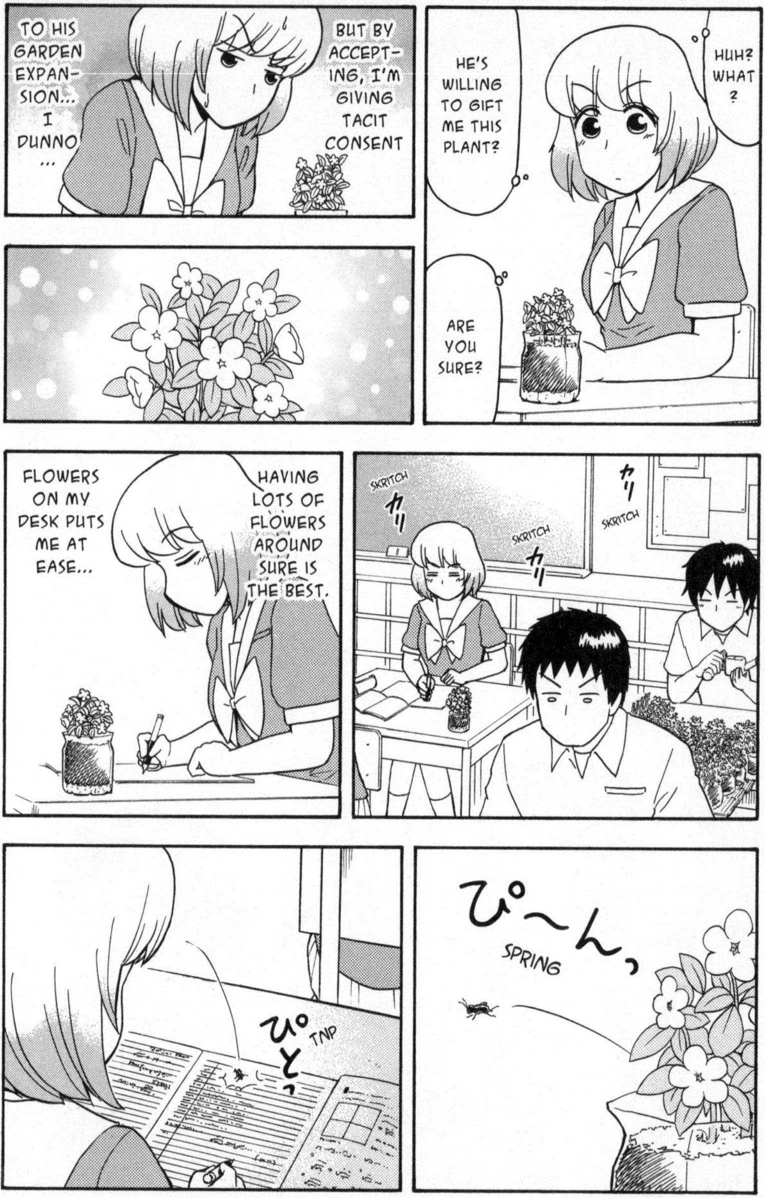
HUH? WHAT?
HE'S WILLING TO GIFT ME THIS PLANT?
ARE YOU SURE?
BUT BY ACCEPTING, I'M GIVING TACIT CONSENT
TO HIS GARDEN EXPANSION... I DUNNO...
カリ
SKRITCH
カリ
SKRITCH
カリ
SKRITCH
HAVING LOTS OF FLOWERS AROUND SURE IS THE BEST.
FLOWERS ON MY DESK PUTS ME AT EASE...
ぴ〜ん
SPRING
ぴと
TNP

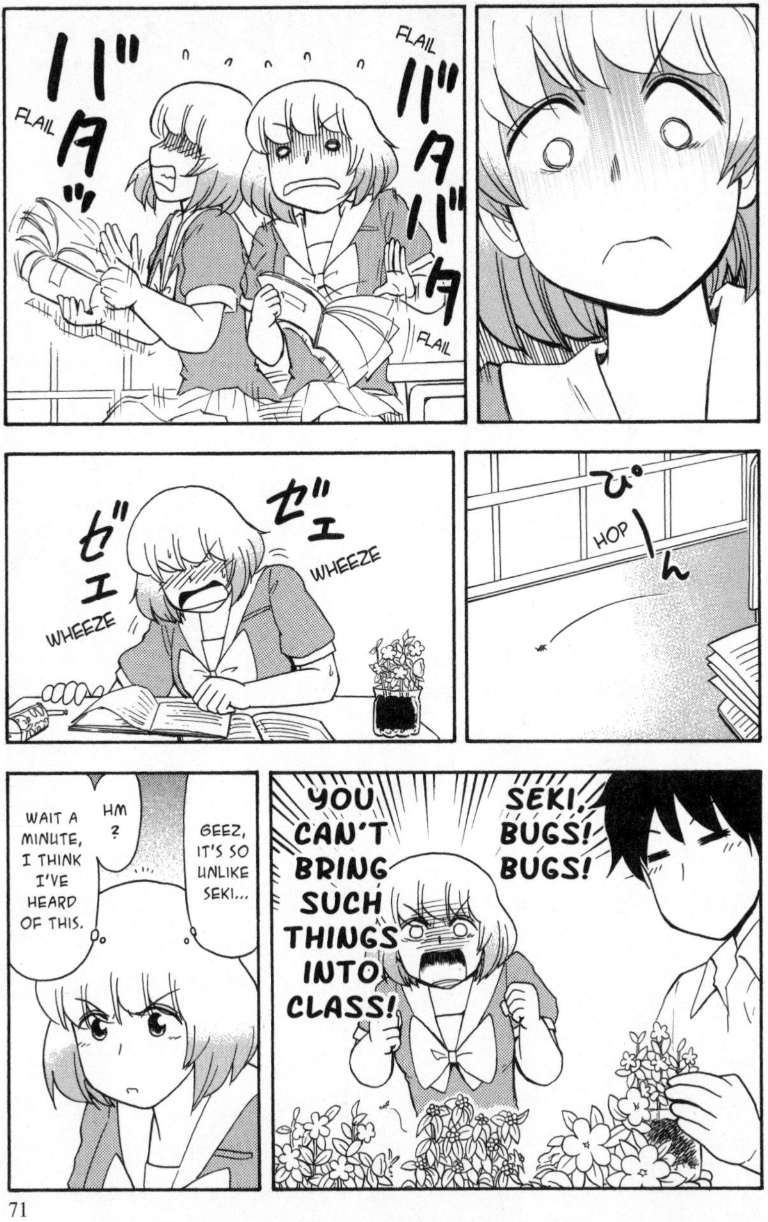
FLAIL
バタバタ
バタッ
FLAIL
FLAIL
ぴーん
HOP
ゼェ
WHEEZE
ゼェ
WHEEZE
SEKI, BUGS! BUGS!
YOU CAN'T BRING SUCH THINGS INTO CLASS!
GEEZ, IT'S SO UNLIKE SEKI...
HM ?
WAIT A MINUTE, I THINK I'VE HEARD OF THIS.

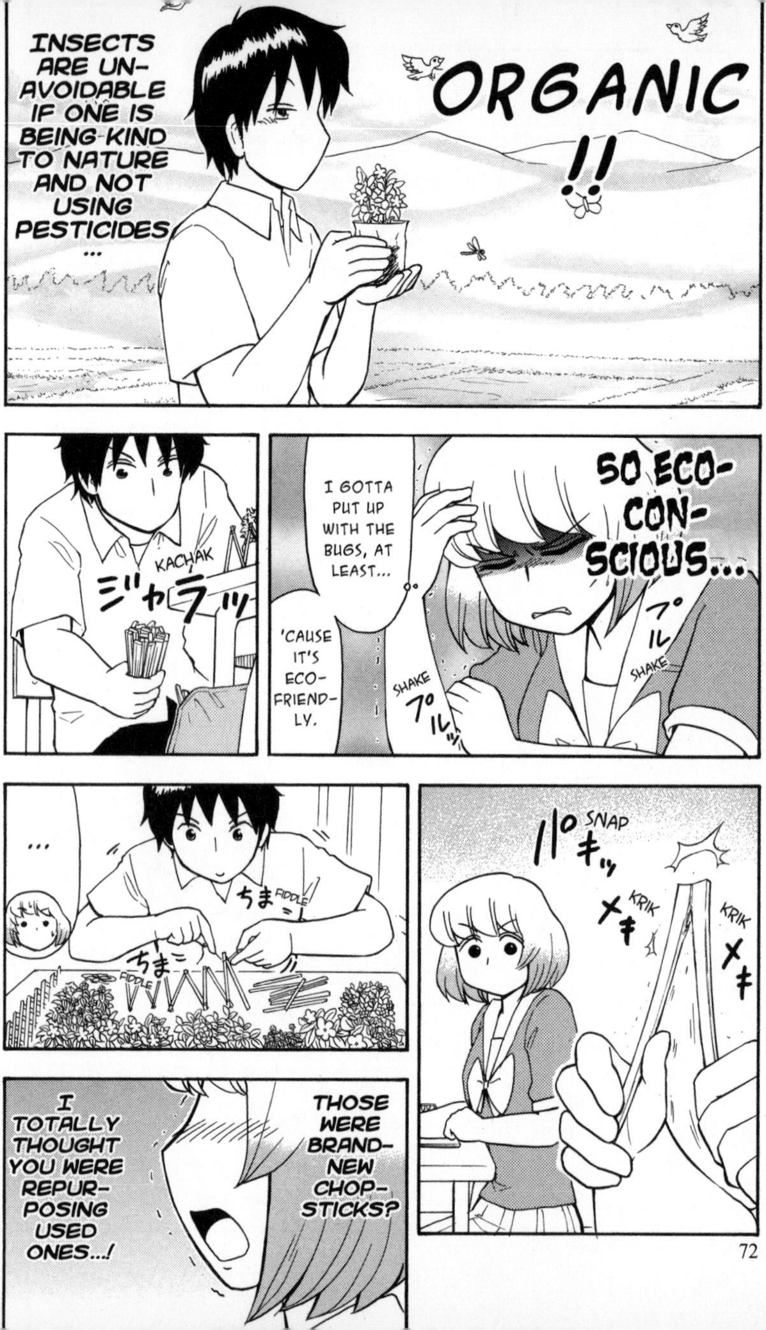
ORGANIC!!
INSECTS ARE UNAVOIDABLE IF ONE IS BEING KIND TO NATURE AND NOT USING PESTICIDES...
SO ECO-CONSCIOUS...
プル SHAKE
I GOTTA PUT UP WITH THE BUGS, AT LEAST...
'CAUSE IT'S ECO-FRIENDLY.
SHAKE プルッ
KACHAK ジャラッ
SNAP パキッ
KRIK メキ
KRIK メキ
...
ちま FIDDLE
ちま FIDDLE
THOSE WERE BRAND-NEW CHOPSTICKS?
I TOTALLY THOUGHT YOU WERE REPURPOSING USED ONES...!

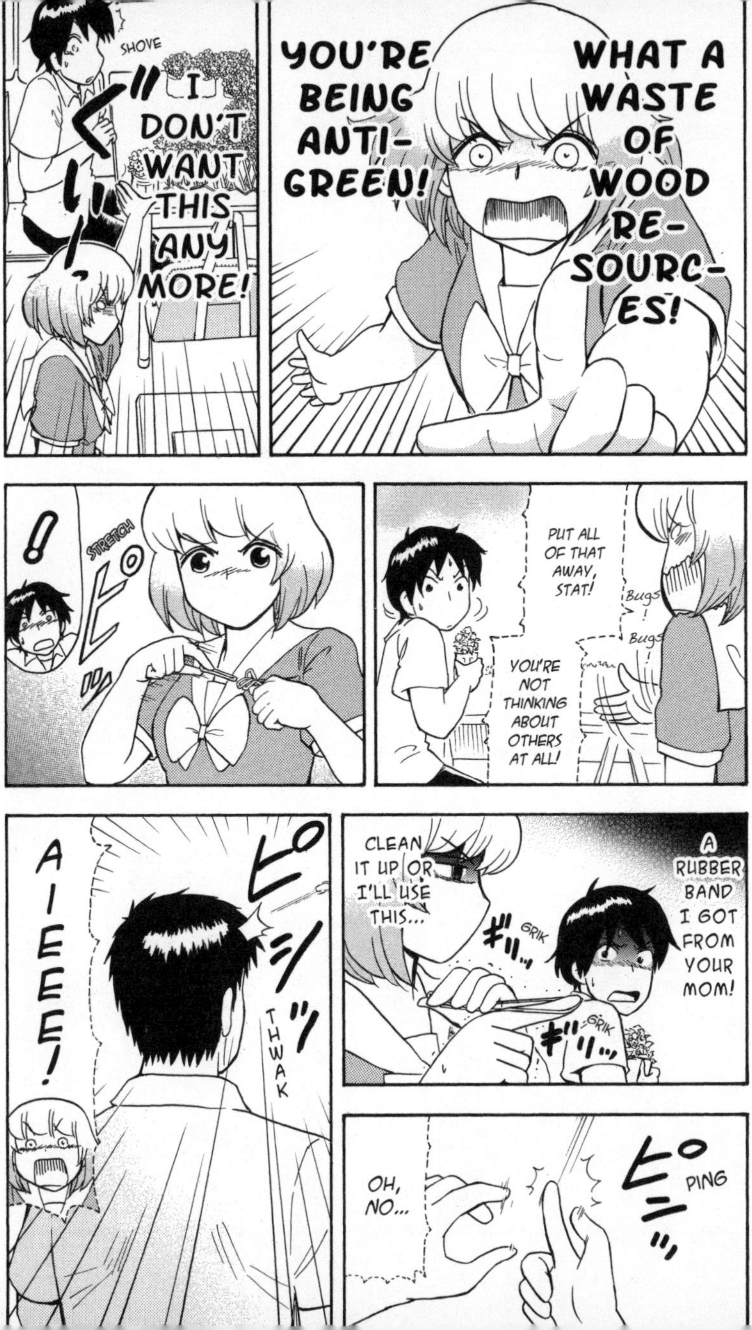
WHAT A WASTE OF WOOD RE-SOURC-ES!
YOU'RE BEING ANTI-GREEN!
SHOVE
I DON'T WANT THIS ANY MORE!
Bugs! Bugs
PUT ALL OF THAT AWAY, STAT!
YOU'RE NOT THINKING ABOUT OTHERS AT ALL!
STRETCH
A RUBBER BAND I GOT FROM YOUR MOM!
CLEAN IT UP OR I'LL USE THIS...
GRIK
GRIK
PING
OH, NO...
THWAK
AIEEEE!

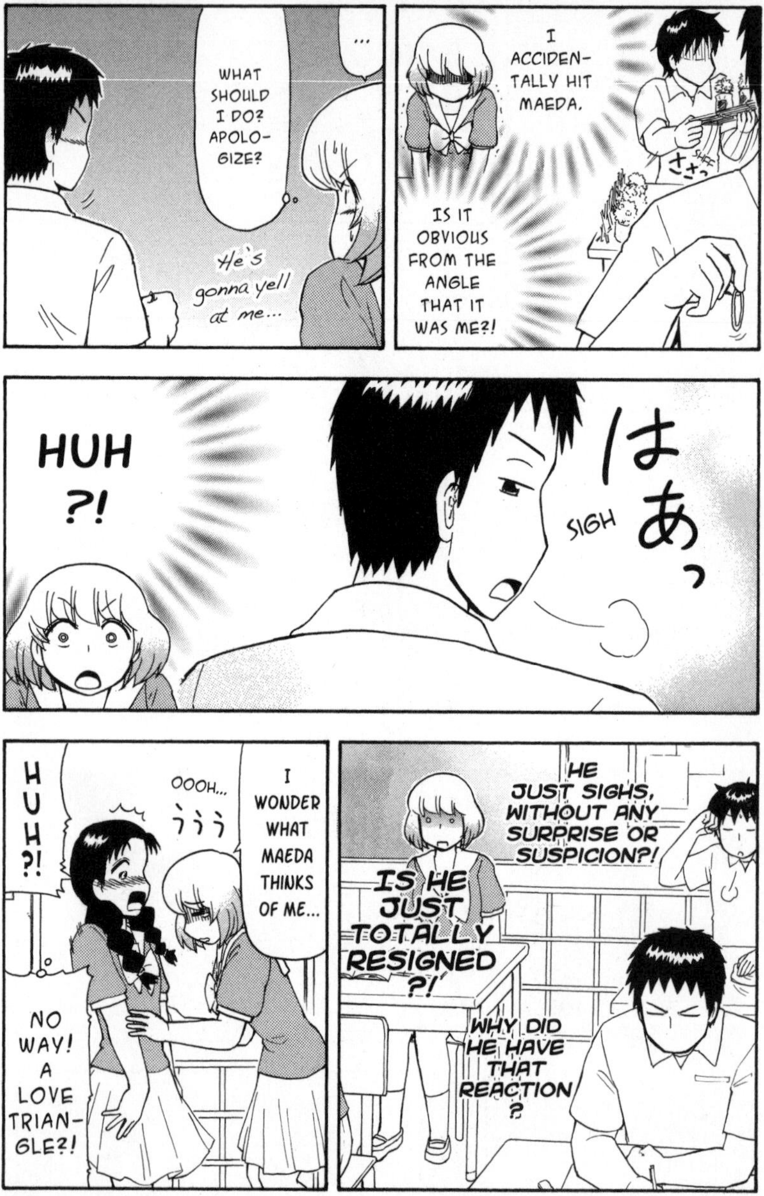

I ACCIDENTALLY HIT MAEDA.
SHFF
IS IT OBVIOUS FROM THE ANGLE THAT IT WAS ME?!
...
WHAT SHOULD I DO? APOLOGIZE?
He's gonna yell at me...
はあっ
SIGH
HUH?!
HE JUST SIGHS, WITHOUT ANY SURPRISE OR SUSPICION?!
IS HE JUST TOTALLY RESIGNED?!
WHY DID HE HAVE THAT REACTION?
I WONDER WHAT MAEDA THINKS OF ME...
OOOH...
ううう
HUH?!
NO WAY! A LOVE TRIANGLE?!

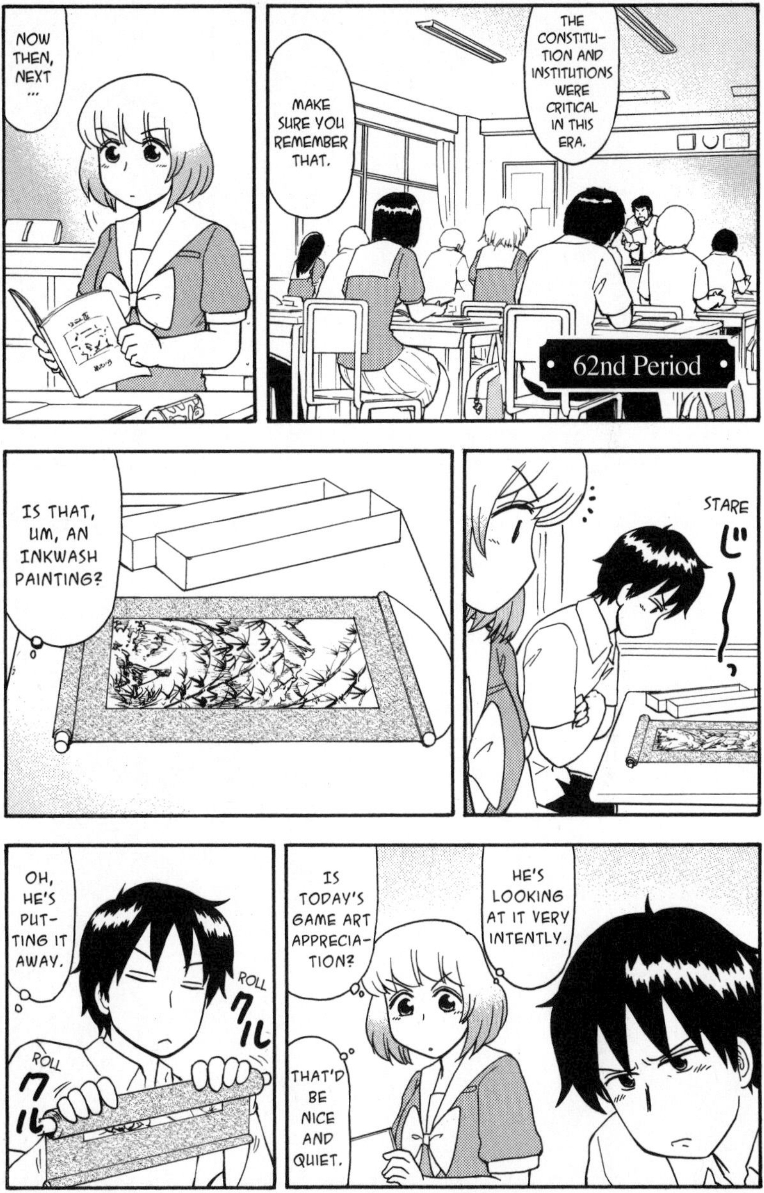
THE CONSTITUTION AND INSTITUTIONS WERE CRITICAL IN THIS ERA.
MAKE SURE YOU REMEMBER THAT.
• 62nd Period •
NOW THEN, NEXT ...
STARE
じー
IS THAT, UM, AN INKWASH PAINTING?
HE'S LOOKING AT IT VERY INTENTLY.
IS TODAY'S GAME ART APPRECIATION?
THAT'D BE NICE AND QUIET.
OH, HE'S PUTTING IT AWAY.
ROLL
クル
ROLL
クル

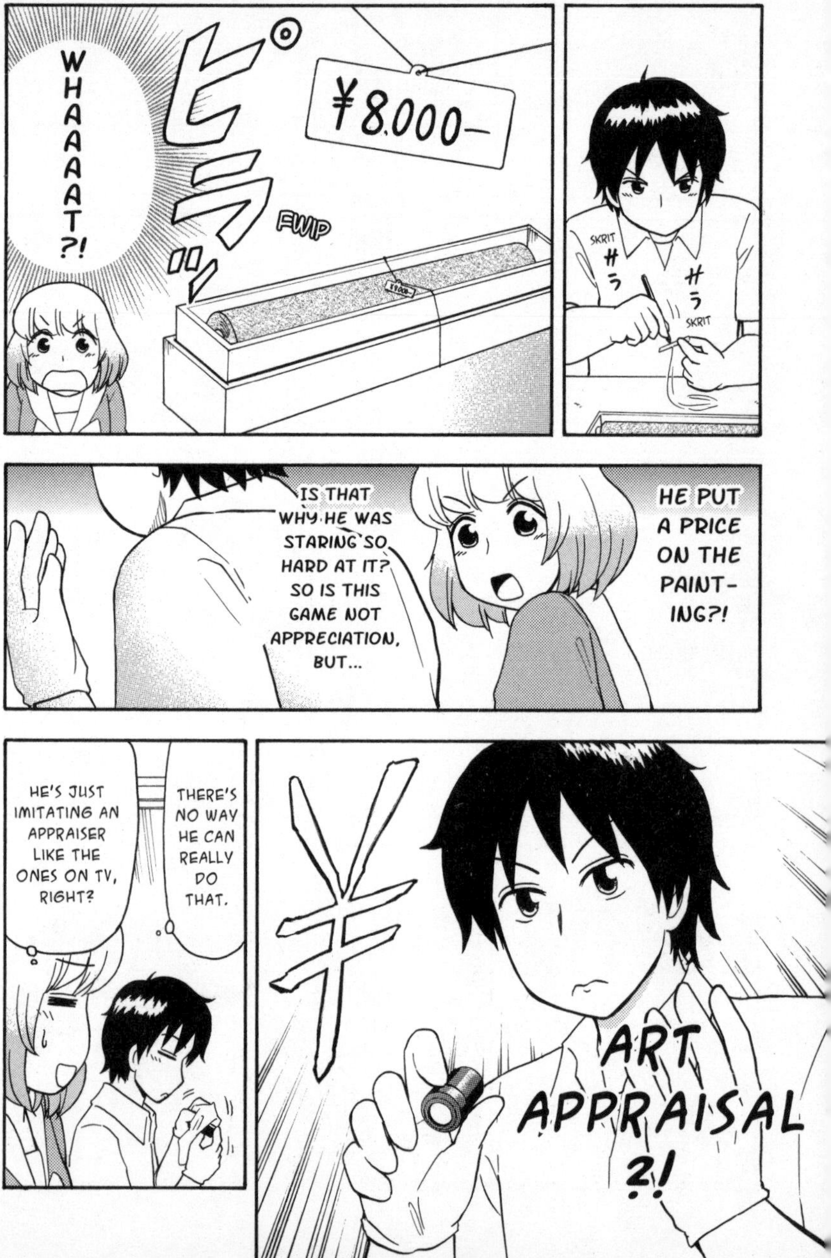
SKRIT
SKRIT
¥8,000—
ピラ
FWIP
WHAAAAAT?!
HE PUT A PRICE ON THE PAINT-ING?!
IS THAT WHY HE WAS STARING SO HARD AT IT? SO IS THIS GAME NOT APPRECIATION, BUT...
ART APPRAISAL?!
THERE'S NO WAY HE CAN REALLY DO THAT.
HE'S JUST IMITATING AN APPRAISER LIKE THE ONES ON TV, RIGHT?

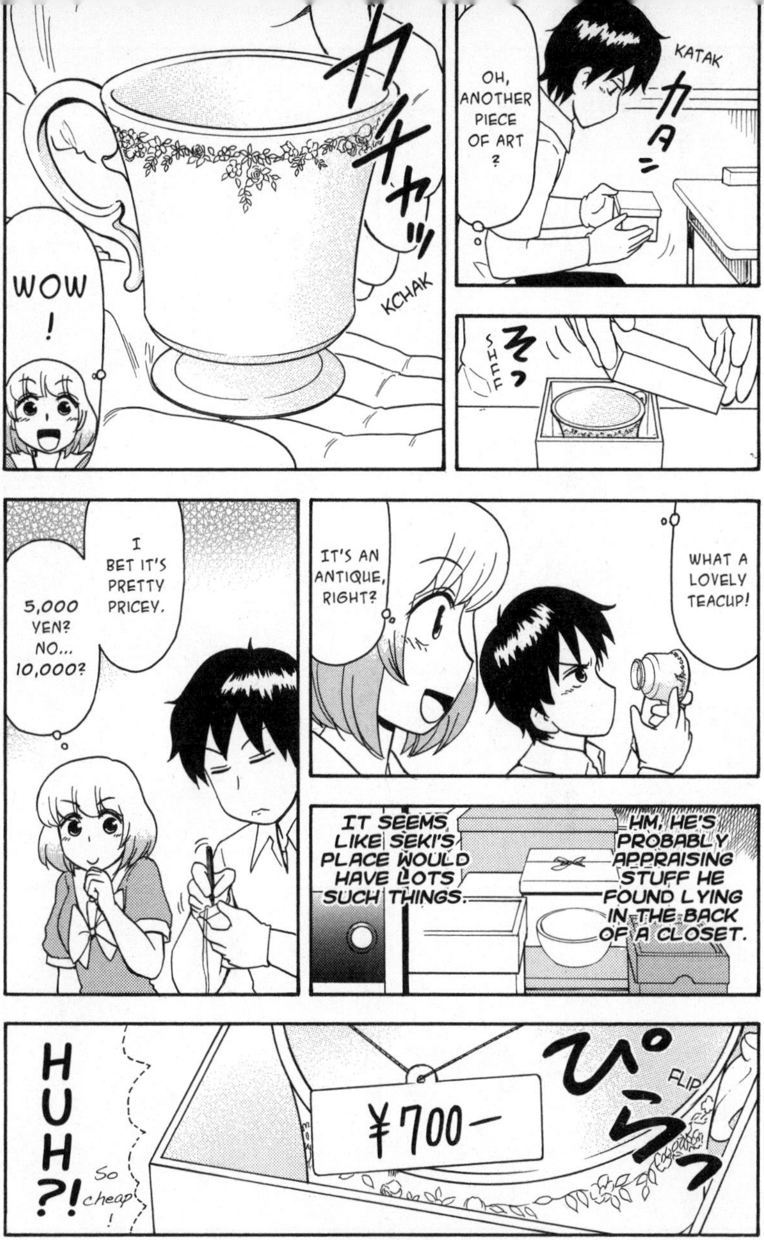
OH, ANOTHER PIECE OF ART?
KATAK
SHFF
KCHAK
WOW!
WHAT A LOVELY TEACUP!
IT'S AN ANTIQUE, RIGHT?
HM, HE'S PROBABLY APPRAISING STUFF HE FOUND LYING IN THE BACK OF A CLOSET.
IT SEEMS LIKE SEKI'S PLACE WOULD HAVE LOTS SUCH THINGS.
I BET IT'S PRETTY PRICEY.
5,000 YEN? NO... 10,000?
FLIP
¥700—
HUH?!
So cheap!

*Note: 1 yen is about 1 U.S. cent.

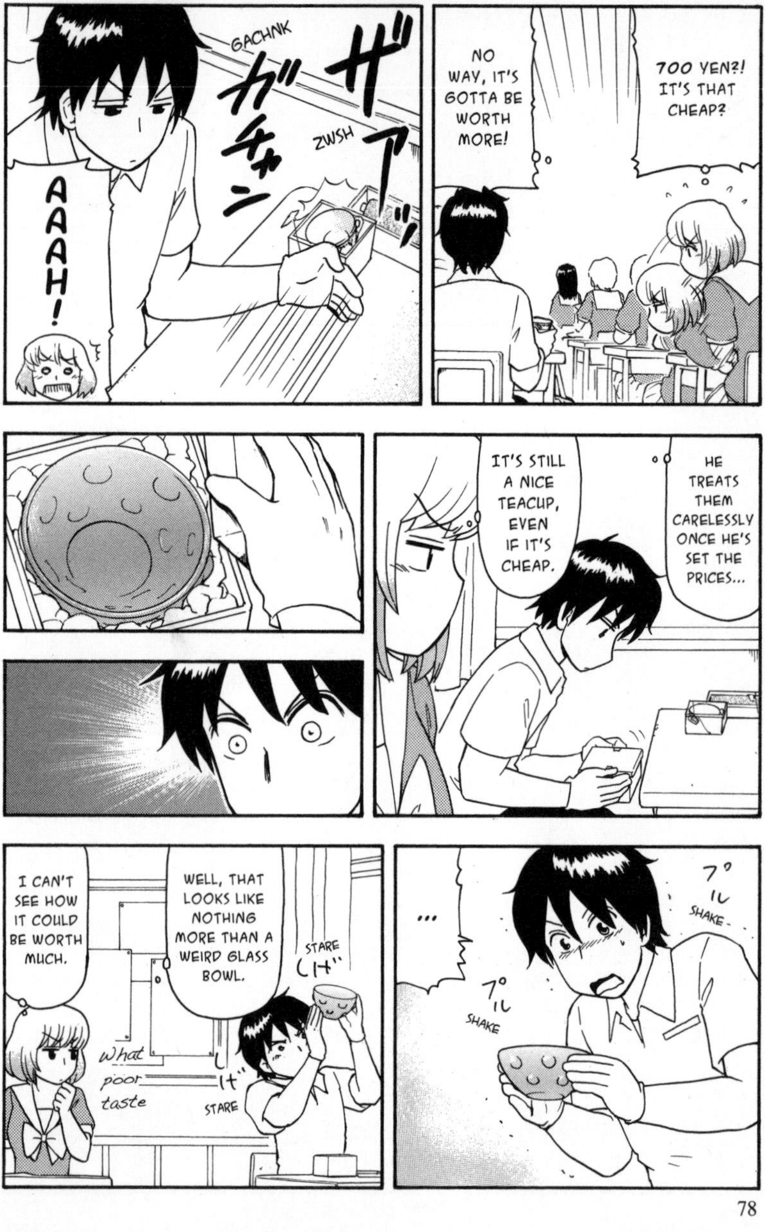
700 YEN?! IT'S THAT CHEAP?
NO WAY, IT'S GOTTA BE WORTH MORE!
ザァッ
ZWSH
ガチャン
GACHNK
AAAAH!
HE TREATS THEM CARELESSLY ONCE HE'S SET THE PRICES...
IT'S STILL A NICE TEACUP, EVEN IF IT'S CHEAP.
プル
SHAKE
...
プル
SHAKE
STARE
WELL, THAT LOOKS LIKE NOTHING MORE THAN A WEIRD GLASS BOWL.
I CAN'T SEE HOW IT COULD BE WORTH MUCH.
STARE
What poor taste

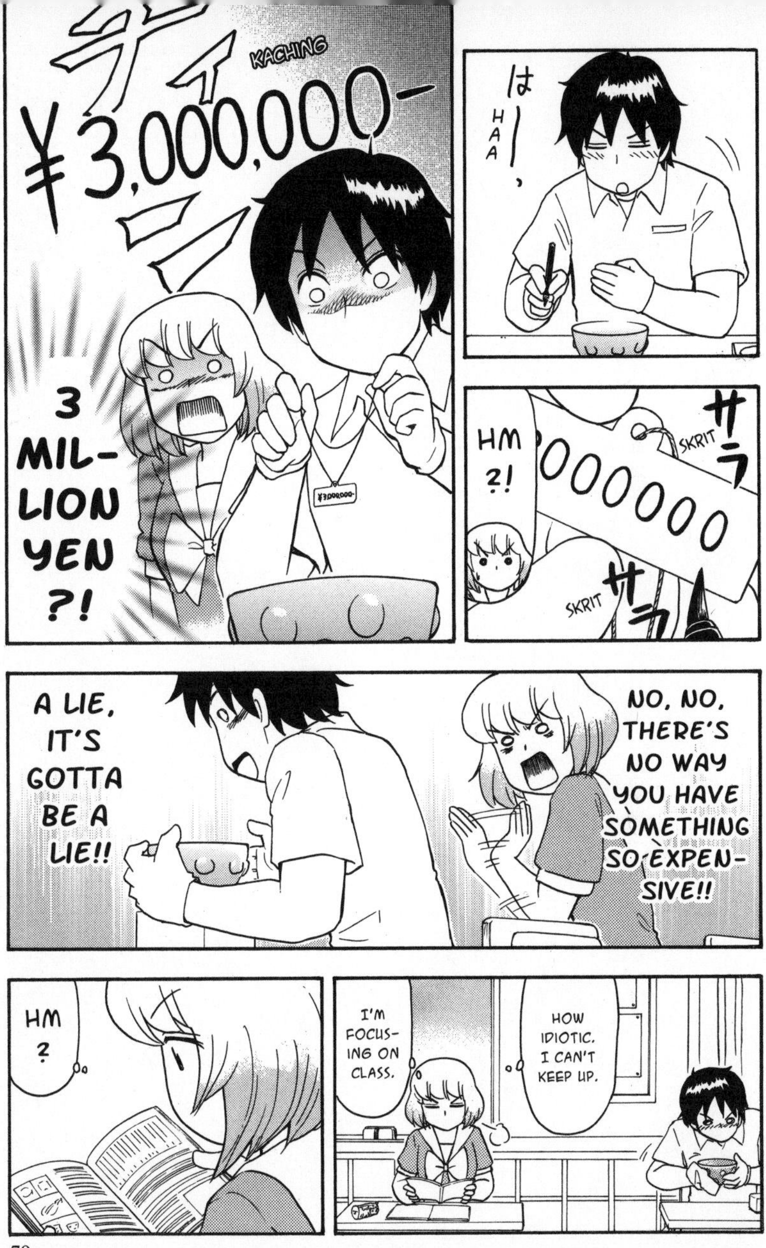

は
HAA
—,
HM ?!
000000
サラ
SKRIT
サラ
SKRIT
チィ
KACHING
¥3,000,000—
3 MIL-LION YEN ?!
NO, NO, THERE'S NO WAY YOU HAVE SOMETHING SO EXPEN-SIVE!!
A LIE, IT'S GOTTA BE A LIE!!
HOW IDIOTIC. I CAN'T KEEP UP.
I'M FOCUS-ING ON CLASS.
HM ?

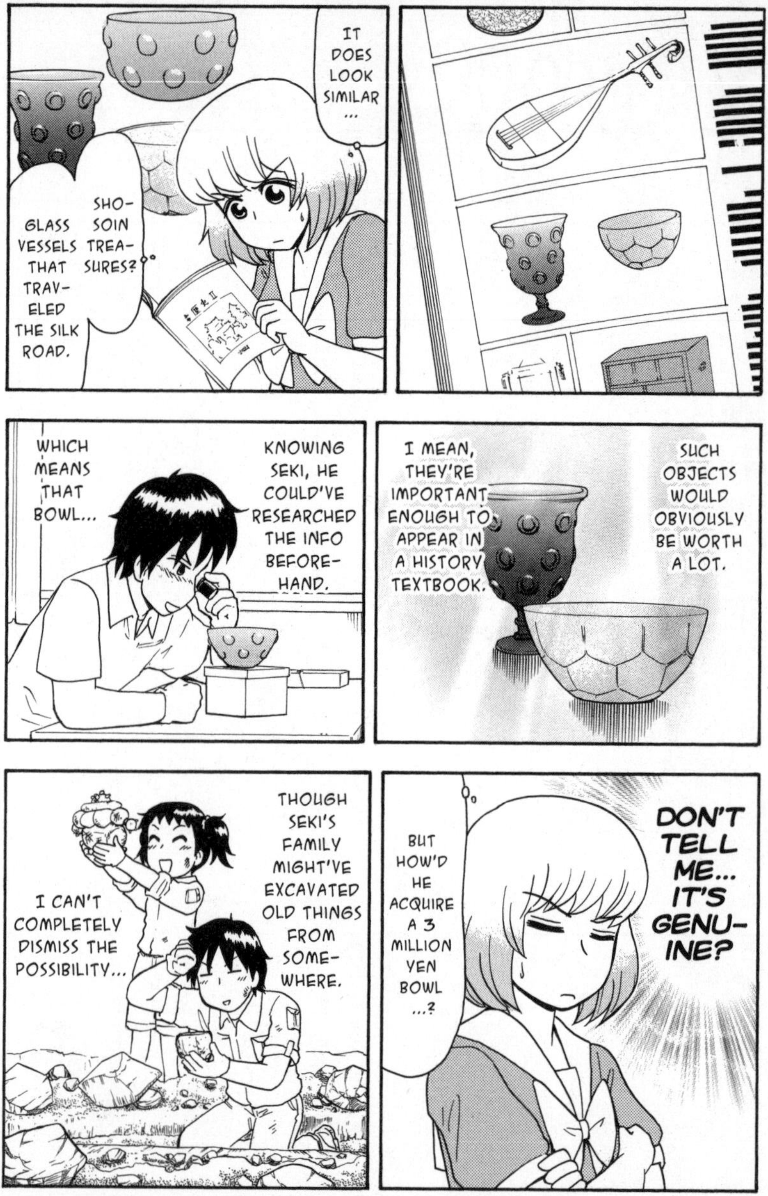

IT DOES LOOK SIMILAR...
SHOSOIN TREASURES?
GLASS VESSELS THAT TRAVELED THE SILK ROAD.
SUCH OBJECTS WOULD OBVIOUSLY BE WORTH A LOT.
I MEAN, THEY'RE IMPORTANT ENOUGH TO APPEAR IN A HISTORY TEXTBOOK.
KNOWING SEKI, HE COULD'VE RESEARCHED THE INFO BEFOREHAND.
WHICH MEANS THAT BOWL...
DON'T TELL ME... IT'S GENUINE?
BUT HOW'D HE ACQUIRE A 3 MILLION YEN BOWL...?
THOUGH SEKI'S FAMILY MIGHT'VE EXCAVATED OLD THINGS FROM SOMEWHERE.
I CAN'T COMPLETELY DISMISS THE POSSIBILITY...

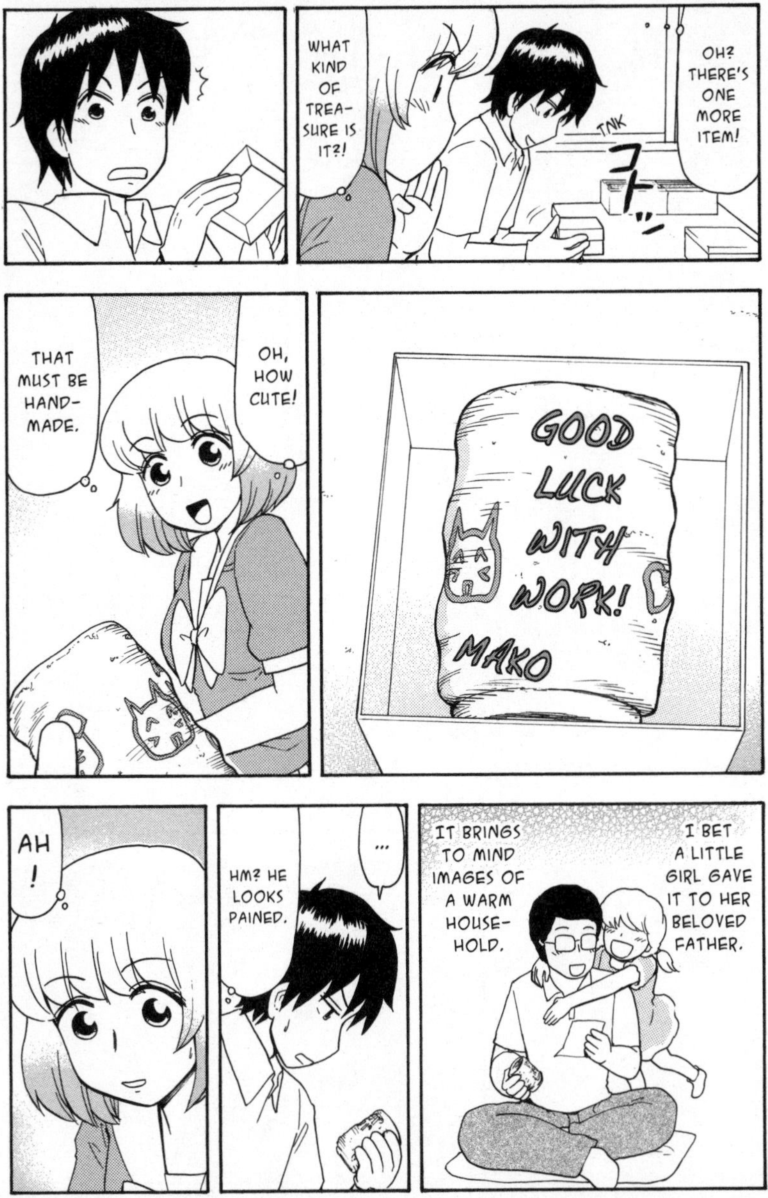
OH? THERE'S ONE MORE ITEM!
TNK
WHAT KIND OF TREASURE IS IT?!
GOOD LUCK WITH WORK!
MAKO
OH, HOW CUTE!
THAT MUST BE HANDMADE.
I BET A LITTLE GIRL GAVE IT TO HER BELOVED FATHER.
IT BRINGS TO MIND IMAGES OF A WARM HOUSEHOLD.
...
HM? HE LOOKS PAINED.
AH!

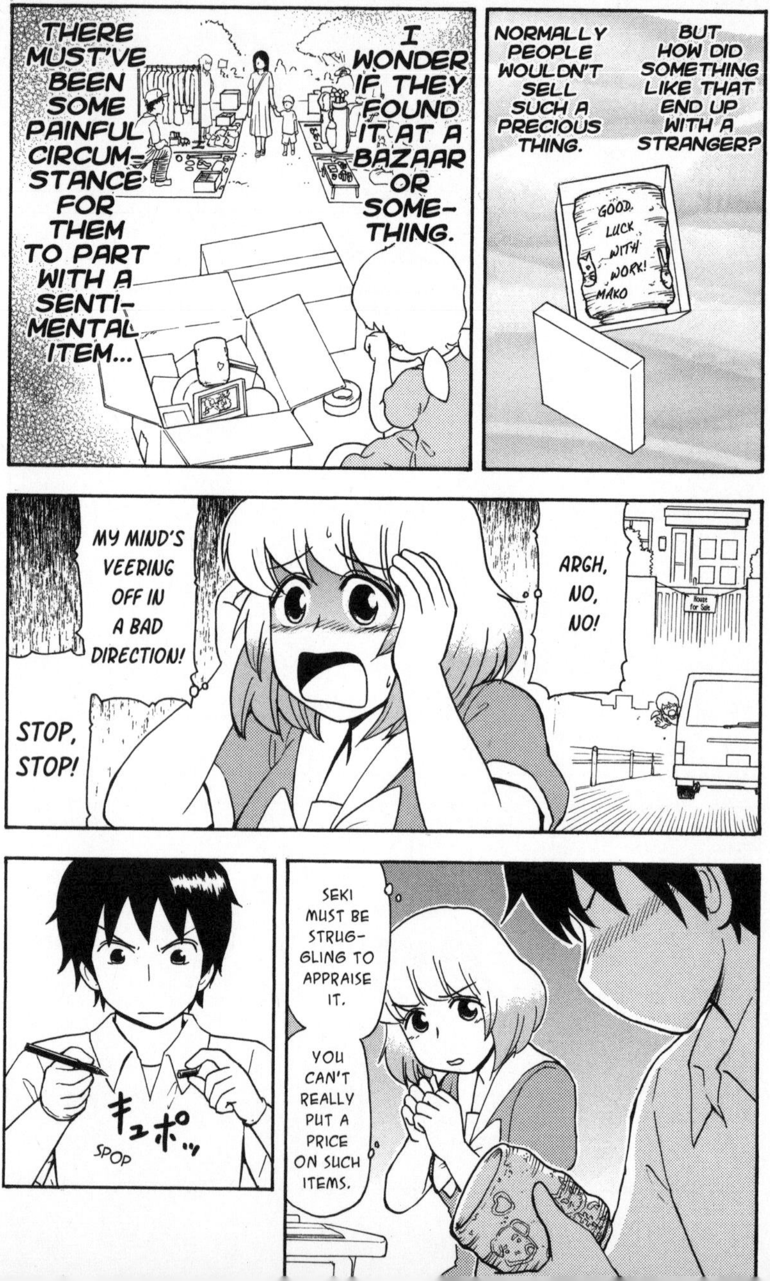
BUT HOW DID SOMETHING LIKE THAT END UP WITH A STRANGER?
NORMALLY PEOPLE WOULDN'T SELL SUCH A PRECIOUS THING.
GOOD LUCK WITH WORK! MAKO
I WONDER IF THEY FOUND IT AT A BAZAAR OR SOME-THING.
THERE MUST'VE BEEN SOME PAINFUL CIRCUM-STANCE FOR THEM TO PART WITH A SENTI-MENTAL ITEM...
ARGH, NO, NO!
House for Sale
MY MIND'S VEERING OFF IN A BAD DIRECTION!
STOP, STOP!
SEKI MUST BE STRUG-GLING TO APPRAISE IT.
YOU CAN'T REALLY PUT A PRICE ON SUCH ITEMS.
キュポッ
SPOP

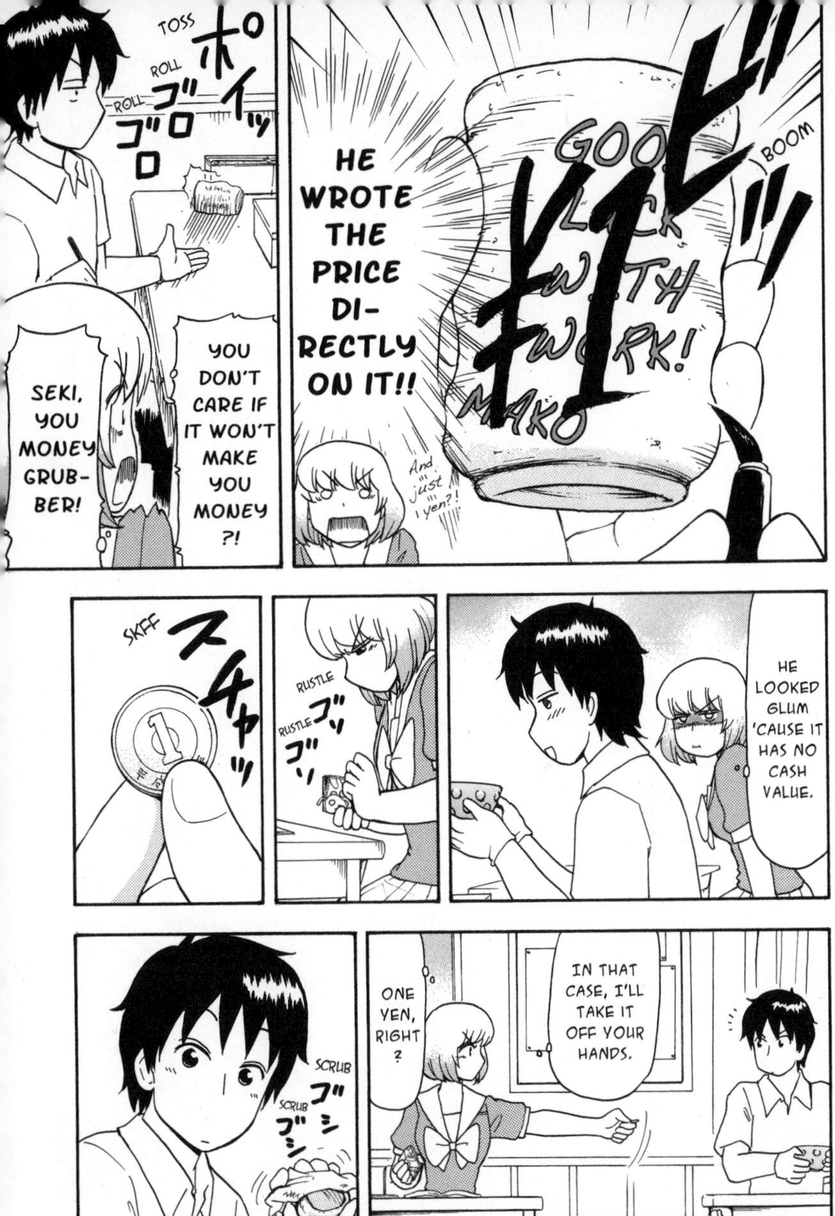
HE WROTE THE PRICE DI- RECTLY ON IT!!
BOOM
¥1
And just 1 yen?!
TOSS
ポイッ
ROLL ROLL
ゴロゴロ
YOU DON'T CARE IF IT WON'T MAKE YOU MONEY ?!
SEKI, YOU MONEY GRUB- BER!
HE LOOKED GLUM 'CAUSE IT HAS NO CASH VALUE.
RUSTLE RUSTLE
ゴソゴソ
SKFF
IN THAT CASE, I'LL TAKE IT OFF YOUR HANDS.
ONE YEN, RIGHT ?
SCRUB SCRUB
ゴシゴシ

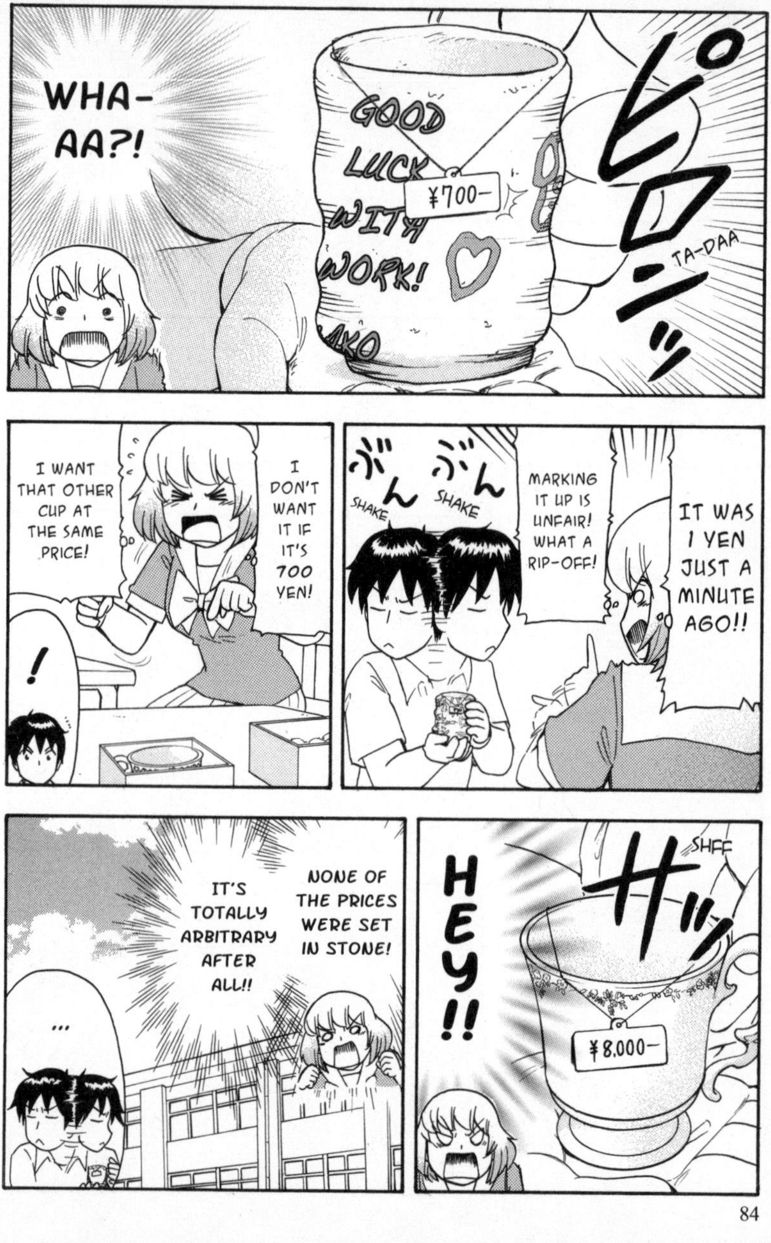
GOOD LUCK WITH WORK!
¥700-
TA-DAA
WHA-AA?!
IT WAS 1 YEN JUST A MINUTE AGO!!
MARKING IT UP IS UNFAIR! WHAT A RIP-OFF!
ぶん ぶん
SHAKE SHAKE
I DON'T WANT IT IF IT'S 700 YEN!
I WANT THAT OTHER CUP AT THE SAME PRICE!
!
サッ
SHFF
HEY!!
¥8,000-
NONE OF THE PRICES WERE SET IN STONE!
IT'S TOTALLY ARBITRARY AFTER ALL!!
...

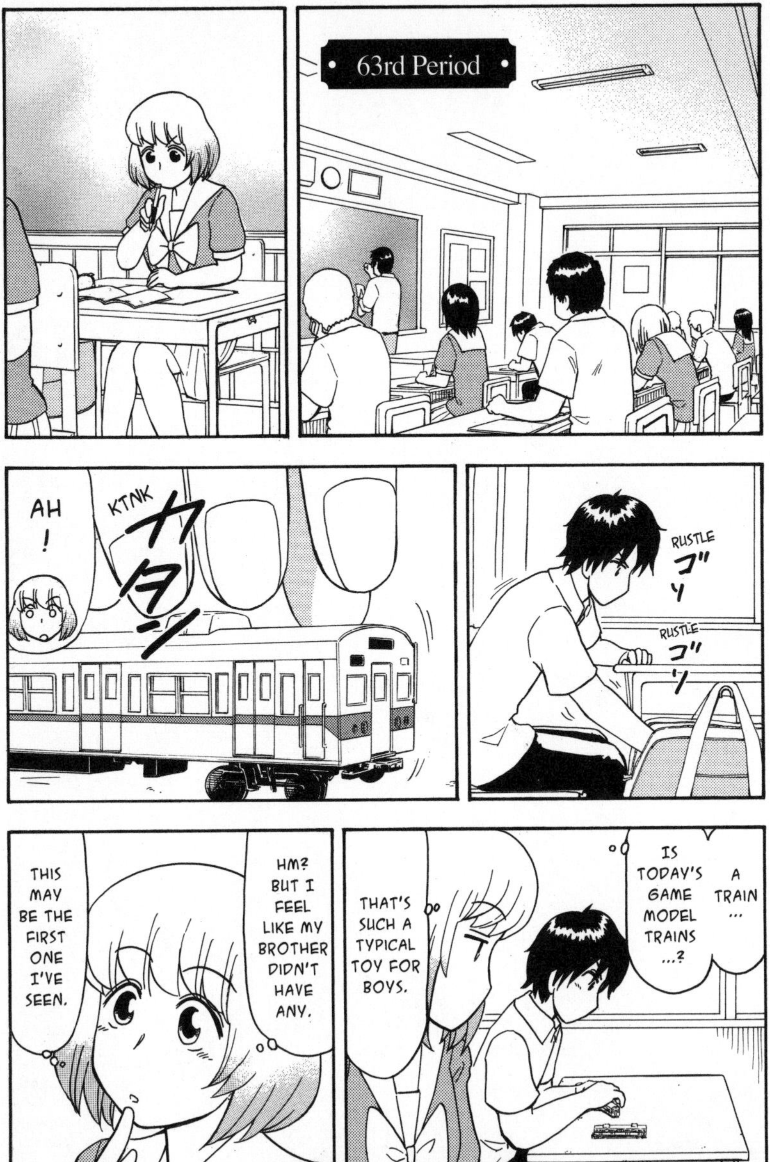
63rd Period
RUSTLE
ゴソ
RUSTLE
ゴソ
AH!
KTNK
カタン
A TRAIN...
IS TODAY'S GAME MODEL TRAINS...?
THAT'S SUCH A TYPICAL TOY FOR BOYS.
HM? BUT I FEEL LIKE MY BROTHER DIDN'T HAVE ANY.
THIS MAY BE THE FIRST ONE I'VE SEEN.

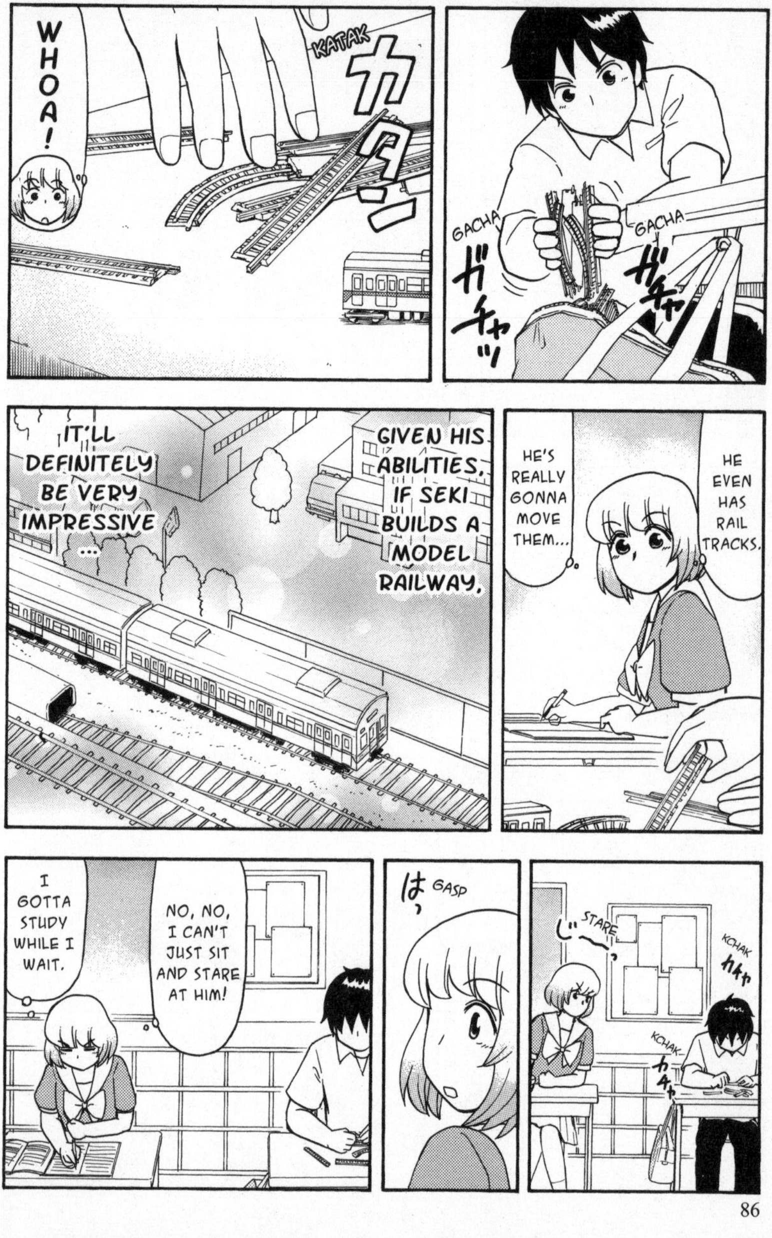
GACHA
GACHA
WHOA!
KATAK
HE EVEN HAS RAIL TRACKS.
HE'S REALLY GONNA MOVE THEM...
GIVEN HIS ABILITIES, IF SEKI BUILDS A MODEL RAILWAY,
IT'LL DEFINITELY BE VERY IMPRESSIVE...
KCHAK
KCHAK
STARE
GASP
NO, NO, I CAN'T JUST SIT AND STARE AT HIM!
I GOTTA STUDY WHILE I WAIT.

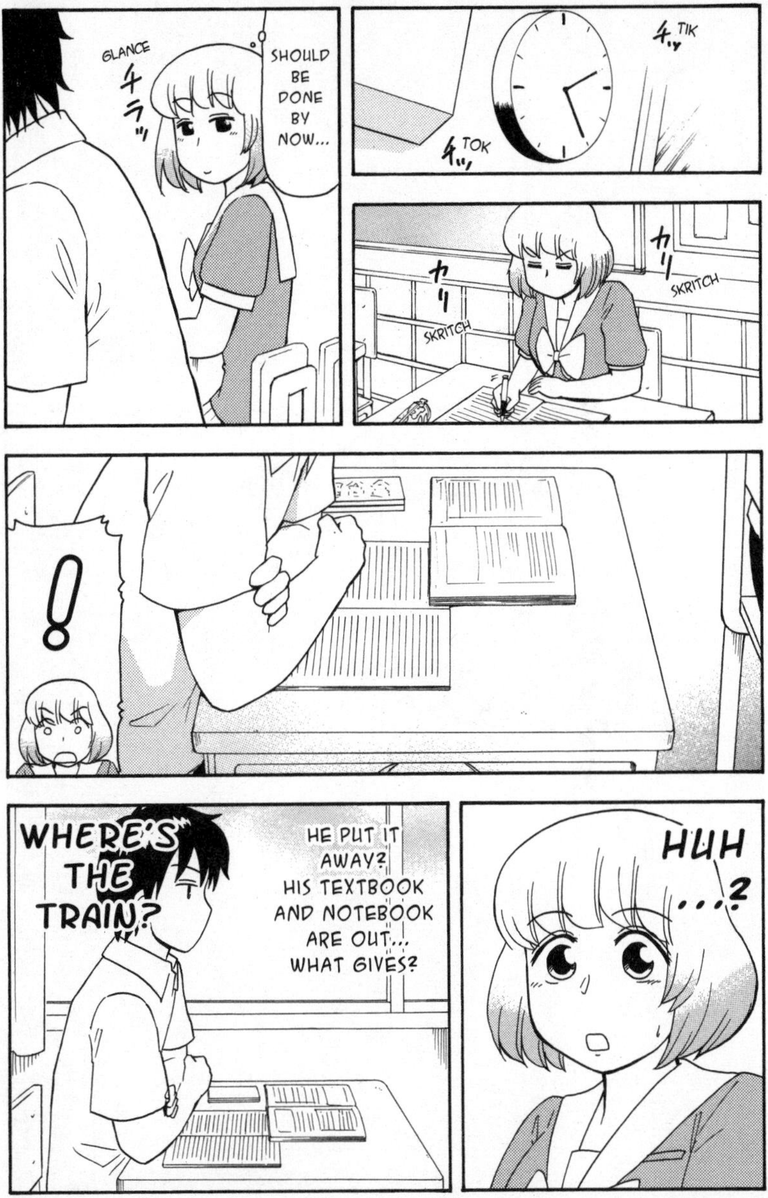

チッ TIK
チッ TOK
カリ SKRITCH
カリ SKRITCH
SHOULD BE DONE BY NOW...
GLANCE チラッ
!
HUH...?
HE PUT IT AWAY? HIS TEXTBOOK AND NOTEBOOK ARE OUT... WHAT GIVES?
WHERE'S THE TRAIN?

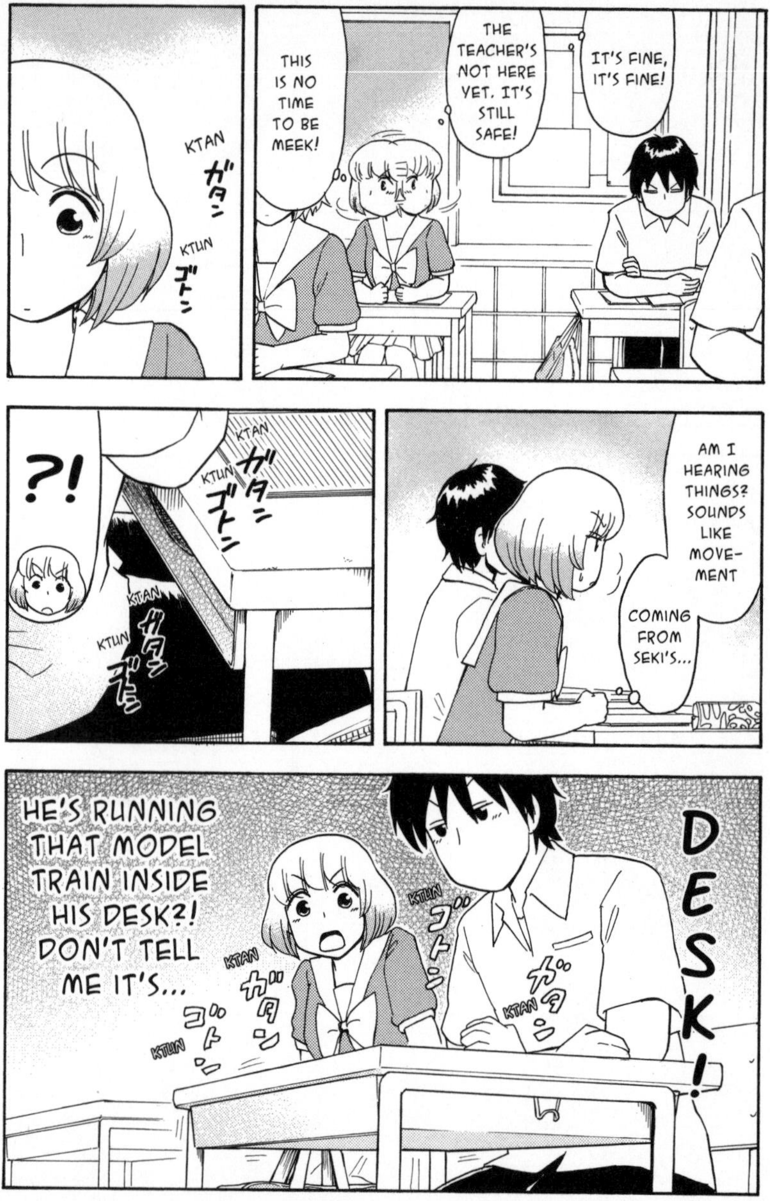
IT'S FINE, IT'S FINE!
THE TEACHER'S NOT HERE YET. IT'S STILL SAFE!
THIS IS NO TIME TO BE MEEK!
KTAN
ガタン
KTUN
ゴトン
AM I HEARING THINGS? SOUNDS LIKE MOVEMENT
COMING FROM SEKI'S...
KTAN
ガタン
KTUN
ゴトン
?!
KTAN
ガタン
KTUN
ゴトン
DESK!
KTAN
ガタン
KTUN
ゴトン
KTAN
ガタン
KTUN
ゴトン
HE'S RUNNING THAT MODEL TRAIN INSIDE HIS DESK?! DON'T TELL ME IT'S...

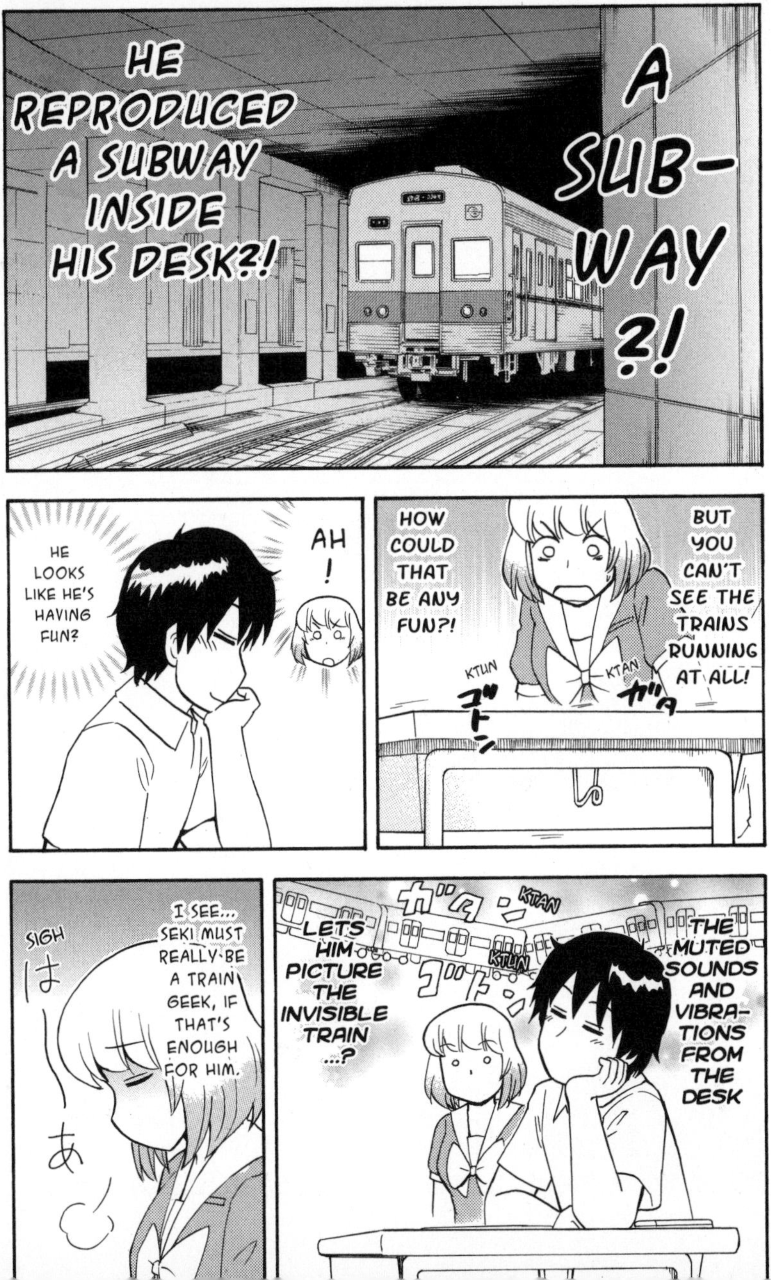
A SUB-WAY?!
HE REPRODUCED A SUBWAY INSIDE HIS DESK?!
BUT YOU CAN'T SEE THE TRAINS RUNNING AT ALL!
KTAN
HOW COULD THAT BE ANY FUN?!
KTUN
AH!
HE LOOKS LIKE HE'S HAVING FUN?
THE MUTED SOUNDS AND VIBRATIONS FROM THE DESK
KTAN
KTUN
LETS HIM PICTURE THE INVISIBLE TRAIN ...?
I SEE... SEKI MUST REALLY BE A TRAIN GEEK, IF THAT'S ENOUGH FOR HIM.
SIGH

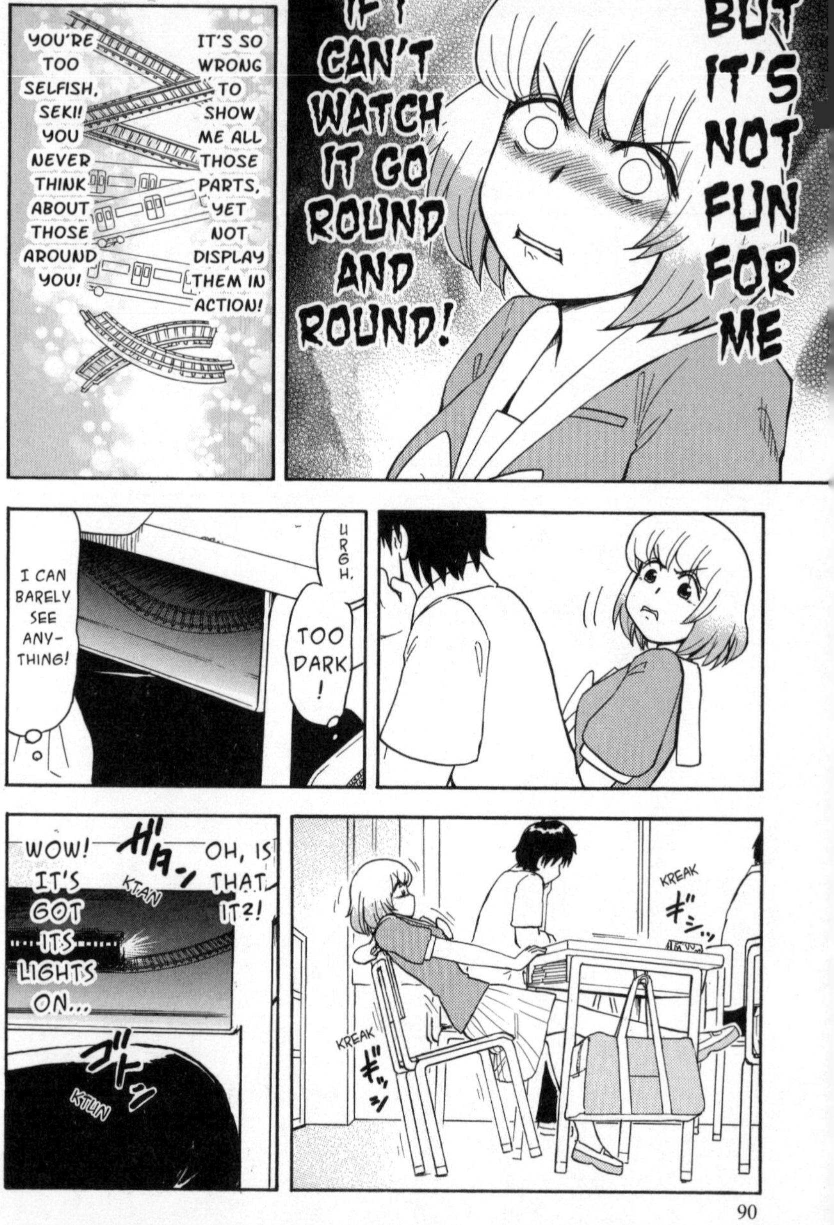
BUT IT'S NOT FUN FOR ME
IF I CAN'T WATCH IT GO ROUND AND ROUND!
IT'S SO WRONG TO SHOW ME ALL THOSE PARTS, YET NOT DISPLAY THEM IN ACTION!
YOU'RE TOO SELFISH, SEKI! YOU NEVER THINK ABOUT THOSE AROUND YOU!
URGH.
TOO DARK!
I CAN BARELY SEE ANY-THING!
KREAK
KREAK
OH, IS THAT IT?!
KTAN
WOW! IT'S GOT ITS LIGHTS ON...
KTUN

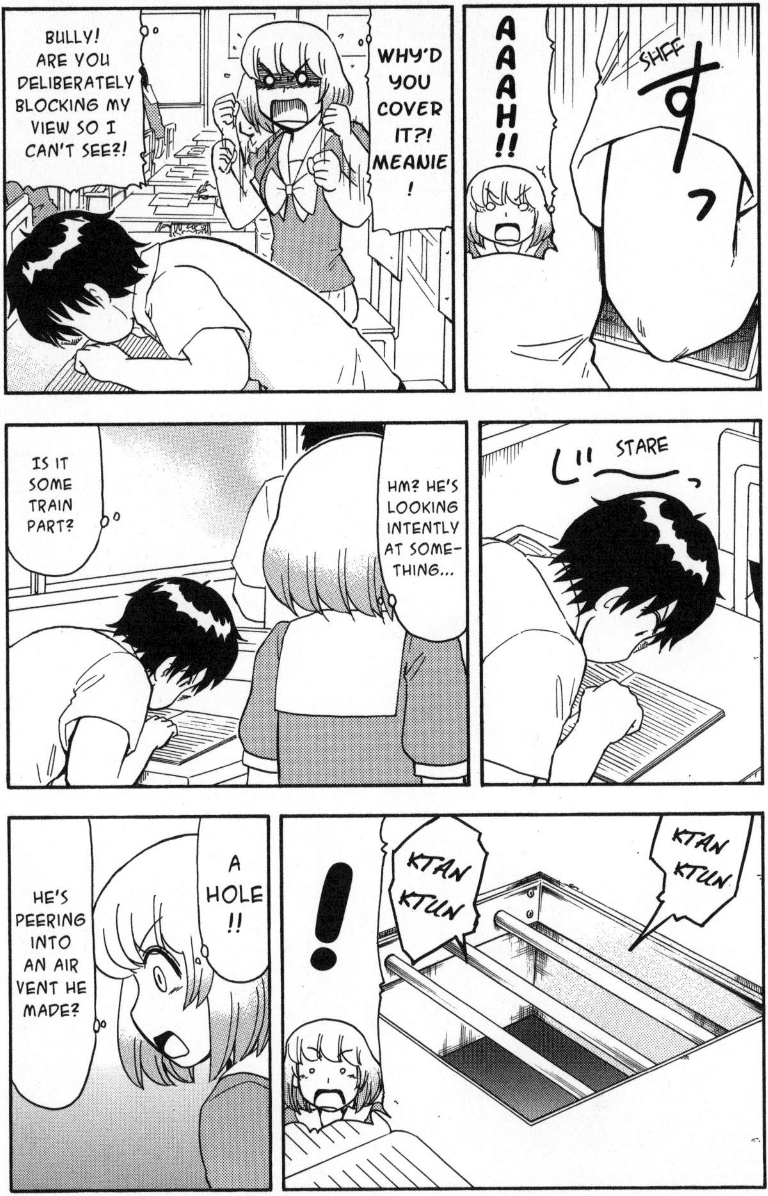
AAAAH!!
SHFF
WHY'D YOU COVER IT?! MEANIE!
BULLY! ARE YOU DELIBERATELY BLOCKING MY VIEW SO I CAN'T SEE?!
STARE
HM? HE'S LOOKING INTENTLY AT SOME-THING...
IS IT SOME TRAIN PART?
KTAN KTUN
KTAN KTUN
!
A HOLE!!
HE'S PEERING INTO AN AIR VENT HE MADE?

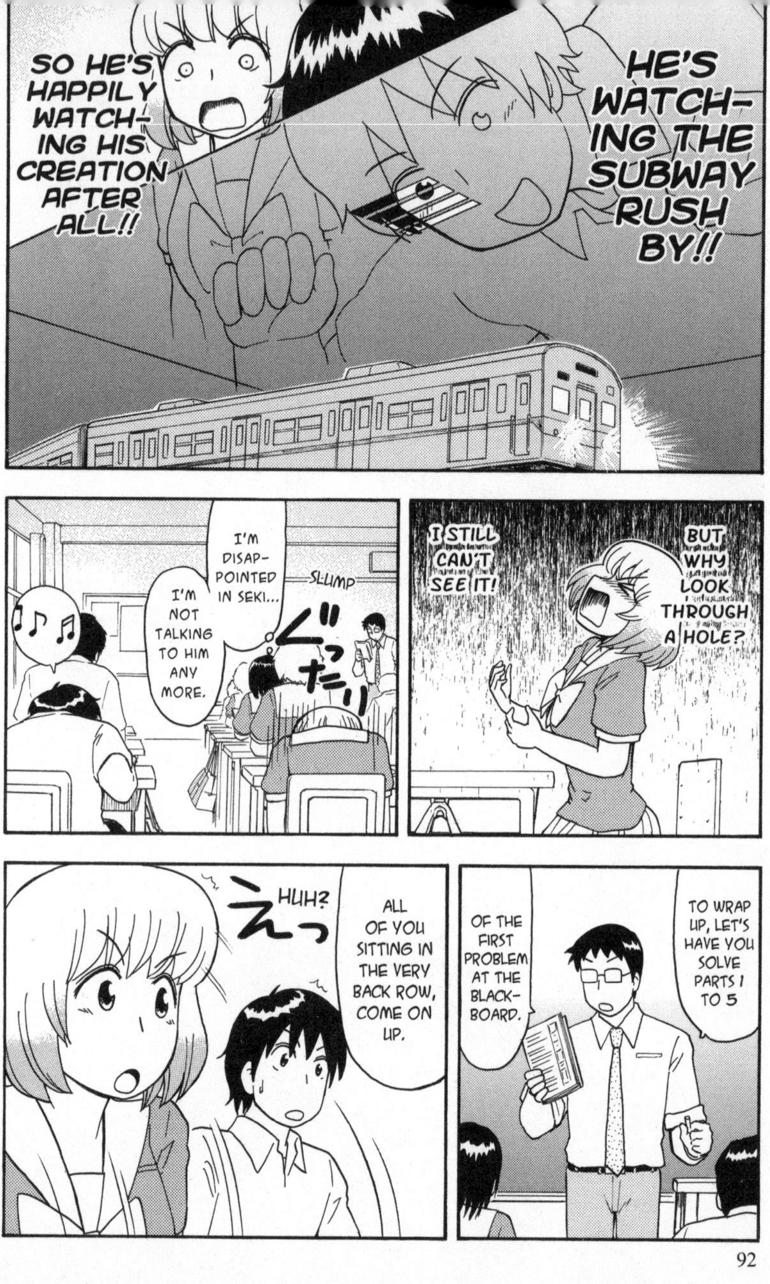
HE'S WATCH-ING THE SUBWAY RUSH BY!!
SO HE'S HAPPILY WATCH-ING HIS CREATION AFTER ALL!!
BUT WHY LOOK THROUGH A HOLE?
I STILL CAN'T SEE IT!
I'M DISAP-POINTED IN SEKI...
SLUMP
ぐったり
I'M NOT TALKING TO HIM ANY MORE.
TO WRAP UP, LET'S HAVE YOU SOLVE PARTS 1 TO 5
OF THE FIRST PROBLEM AT THE BLACK-BOARD.
ALL OF YOU SITTING IN THE VERY BACK ROW, COME ON UP.
HUH?
えっ

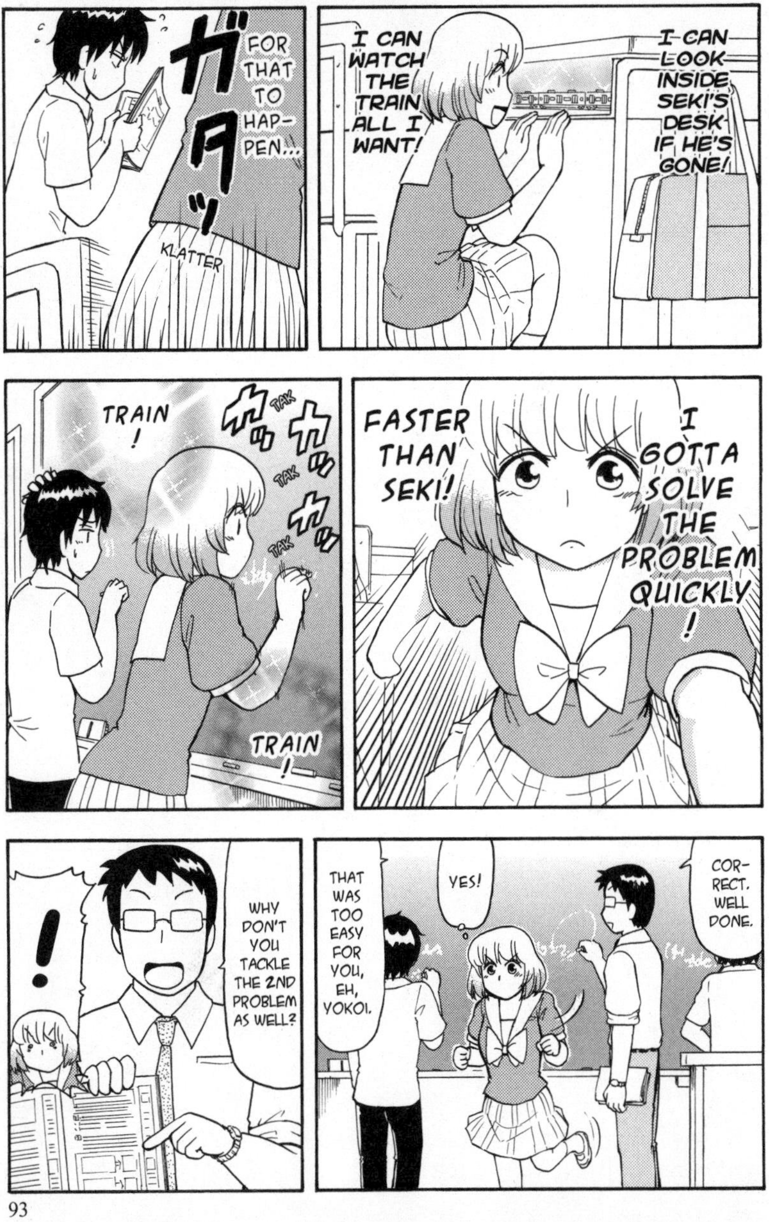

I CAN LOOK INSIDE SEKI'S DESK IF HE'S GONE!
I CAN WATCH THE TRAIN ALL I WANT!
FOR THAT TO HAP-PEN...
ガタッ
KLATTER
I GOTTA SOLVE THE PROBLEM QUICKLY!
FASTER THAN SEKI!
カッ
TAK
カッ
TAK
カッ
TAK
TRAIN!
TRAIN!
CORRECT. WELL DONE.
YES!
THAT WAS TOO EASY FOR YOU, EH, YOKOI.
WHY DON'T YOU TACKLE THE 2ND PROBLEM AS WELL?
!

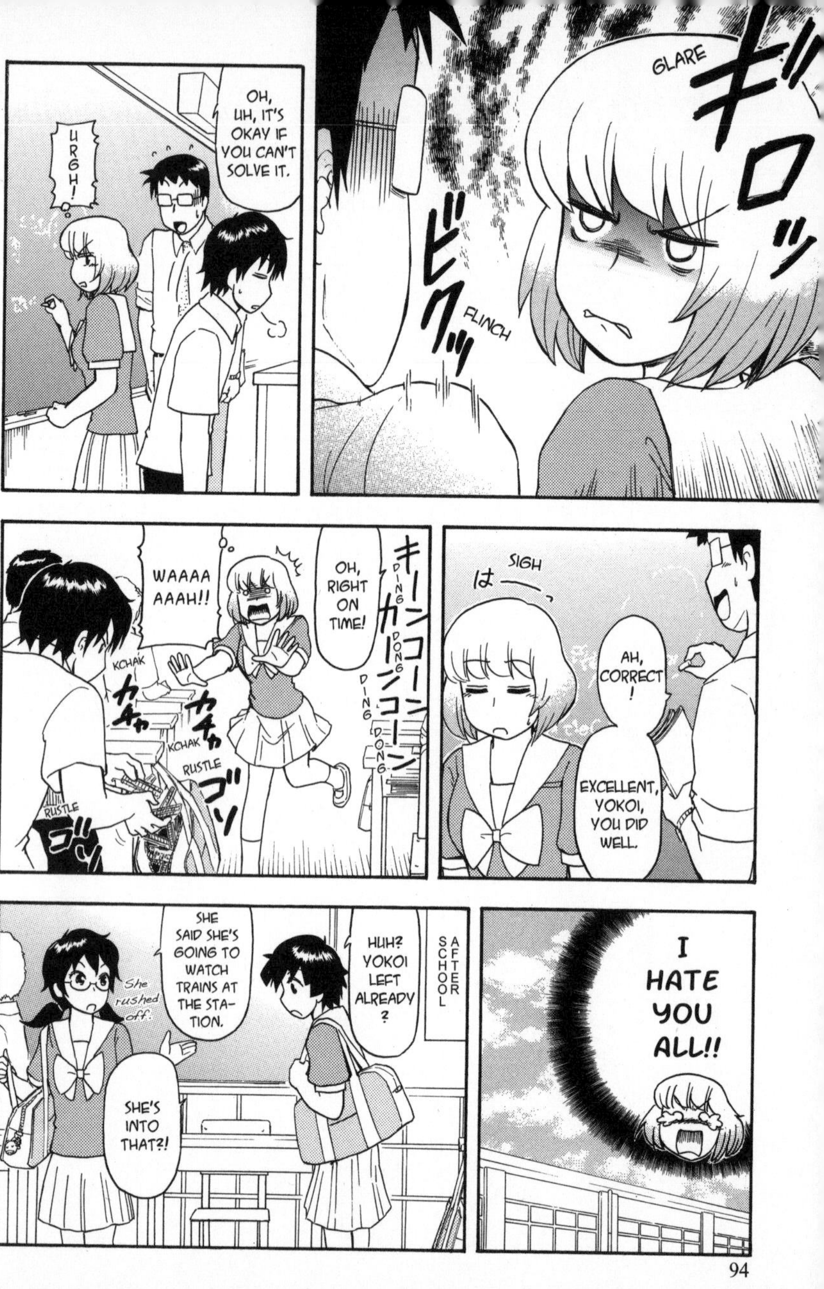
ギロッ
GLARE
ビクッ
FLINCH
OH, UH, IT'S OKAY IF YOU CAN'T SOLVE IT.
URGH!
は
SIGH
AH, CORRECT!
EXCELLENT, YOKOI, YOU DID WELL.
キーンコーン カーンコーン
DING DONG DING DONG
OH, RIGHT ON TIME!
WAAAAAAAH!!
KCHAK
KCHAK
RUSTLE
RUSTLE
I HATE YOU ALL!!
AFTER SCHOOL
HUH? YOKOI LEFT ALREADY?
SHE SAID SHE'S GOING TO WATCH TRAINS AT THE STATION.
She rushed off.
SHE'S INTO THAT?!

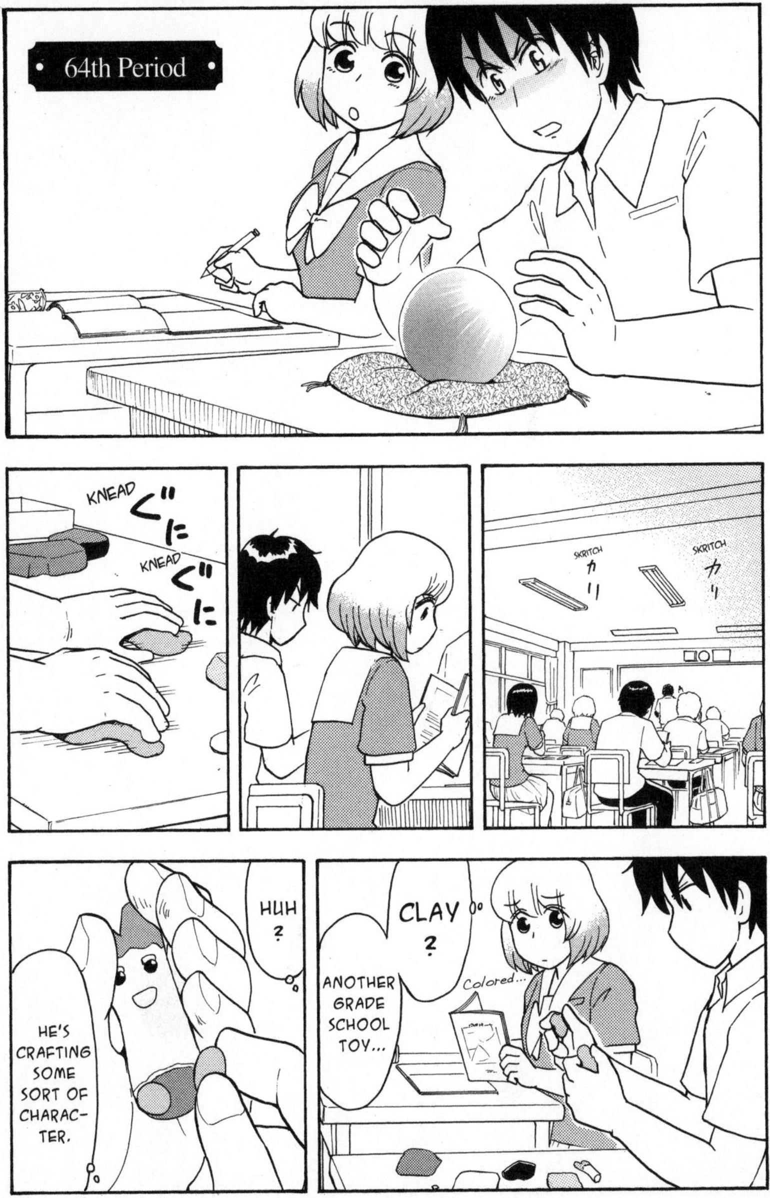
64th Period
SKRITCH カリ
SKRITCH カリ
KNEAD ぐに
KNEAD ぐに
CLAY?
Colored...
ANOTHER GRADE SCHOOL TOY...
HUH?
HE'S CRAFTING SOME SORT OF CHARACTER.

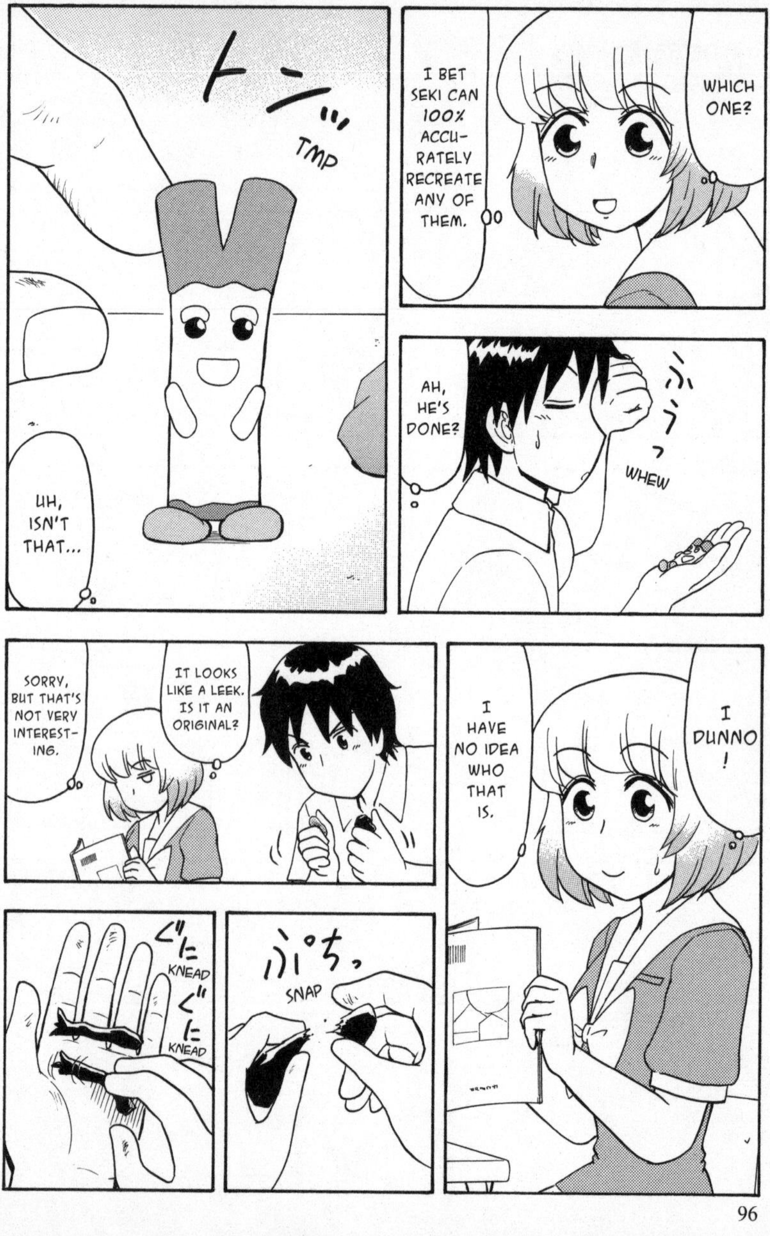
WHICH ONE?
I BET SEKI CAN 100% ACCU-RATELY RECREATE ANY OF THEM.
ふぅっ
WHEW
AH, HE'S DONE?
トンッ
TMP
UH, ISN'T THAT...
I DUNNO!
I HAVE NO IDEA WHO THAT IS.
IT LOOKS LIKE A LEEK. IS IT AN ORIGINAL?
SORRY, BUT THAT'S NOT VERY INTEREST-ING.
ぷちっ
SNAP
ぐに
KNEAD
ぐに
KNEAD

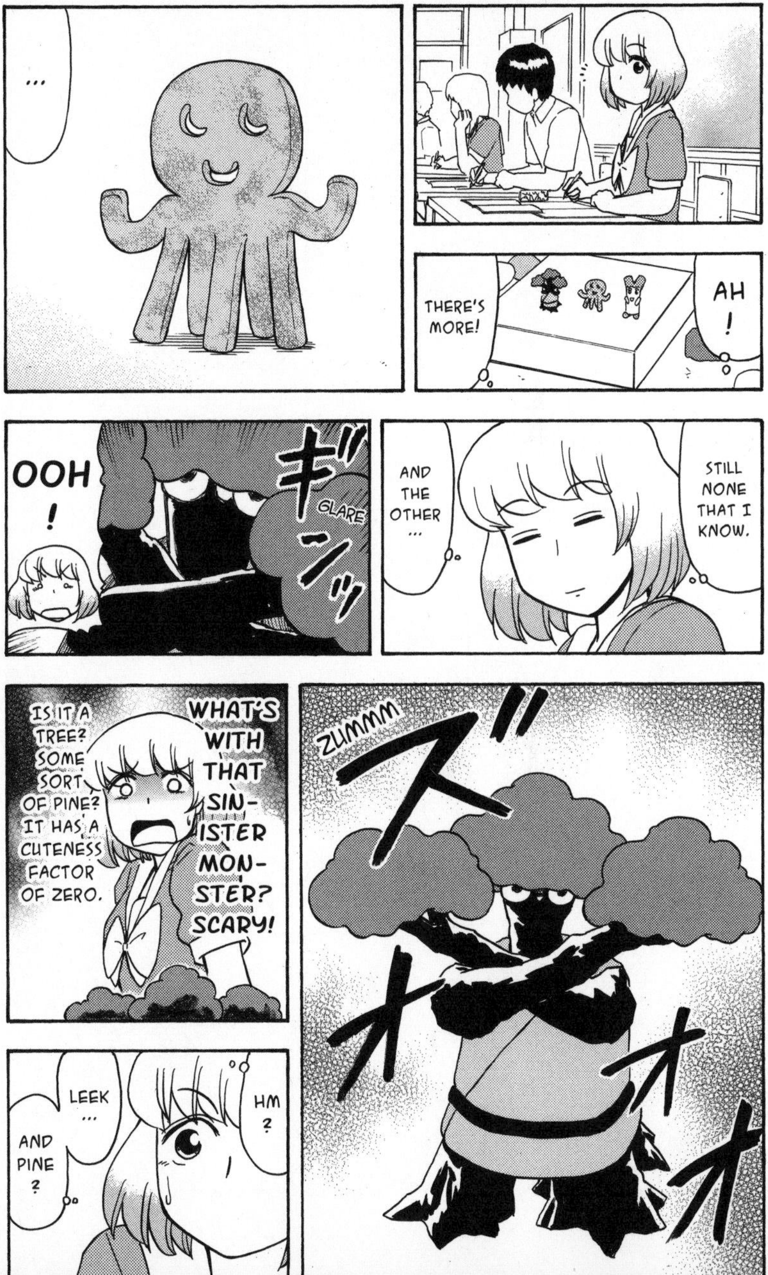
AH !
THERE'S MORE!
...
STILL NONE THAT I KNOW.
AND THE OTHER ...
ギーッ
GLARE
OOH !
ズオオオ
ZUMMM
WHAT'S WITH THAT SIN-ISTER MON-STER? SCARY!
IS IT A TREE? SOME SORT OF PINE? IT HAS A CUTENESS FACTOR OF ZERO.
HM ?
LEEK ... AND PINE ?

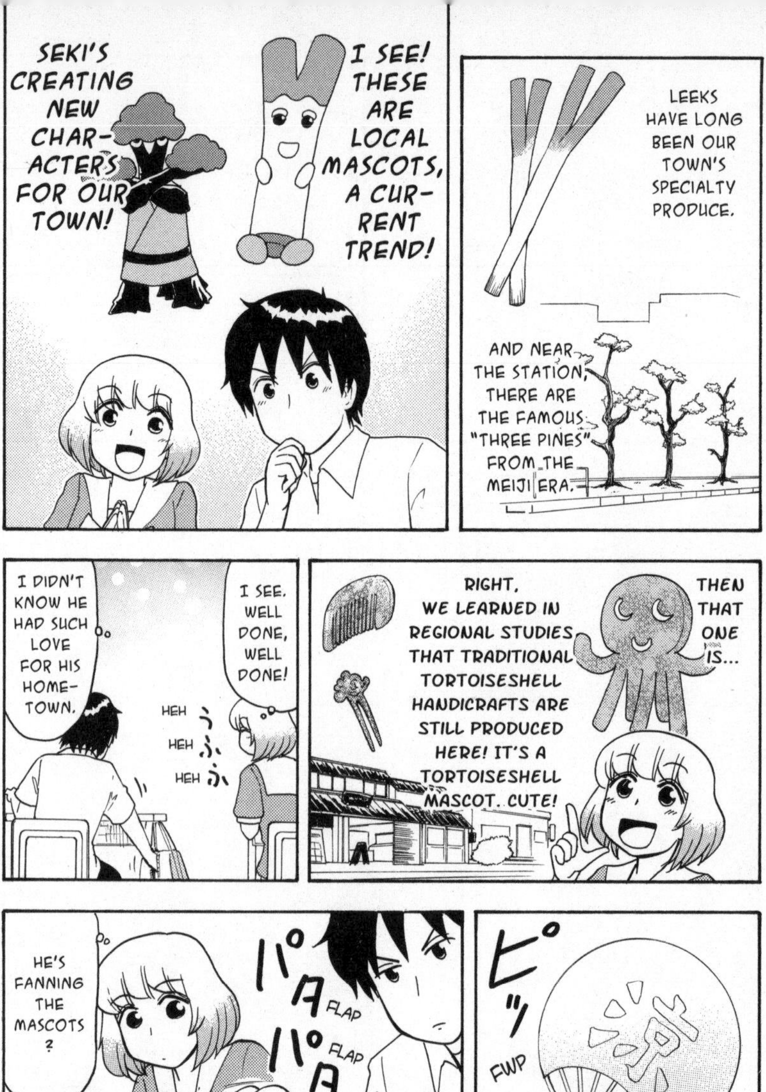
LEEKS HAVE LONG BEEN OUR TOWN'S SPECIALTY PRODUCE.
AND NEAR THE STATION, THERE ARE THE FAMOUS "THREE PINES" FROM THE MEIJI ERA.
I SEE! THESE ARE LOCAL MASCOTS, A CUR-RENT TREND!
SEKI'S CREATING NEW CHAR-ACTERS FOR OUR TOWN!
THEN THAT ONE IS...
RIGHT, WE LEARNED IN REGIONAL STUDIES THAT TRADITIONAL TORTOISESHELL HANDICRAFTS ARE STILL PRODUCED HERE! IT'S A TORTOISESHELL MASCOT. CUTE!
I SEE. WELL DONE, WELL DONE!
うふふ
HEH HEH HEH
I DIDN'T KNOW HE HAD SUCH LOVE FOR HIS HOME-TOWN.
ピッ
FWP
Cool
パタパタ
FLAP FLAP
HE'S FANNING THE MASCOTS?

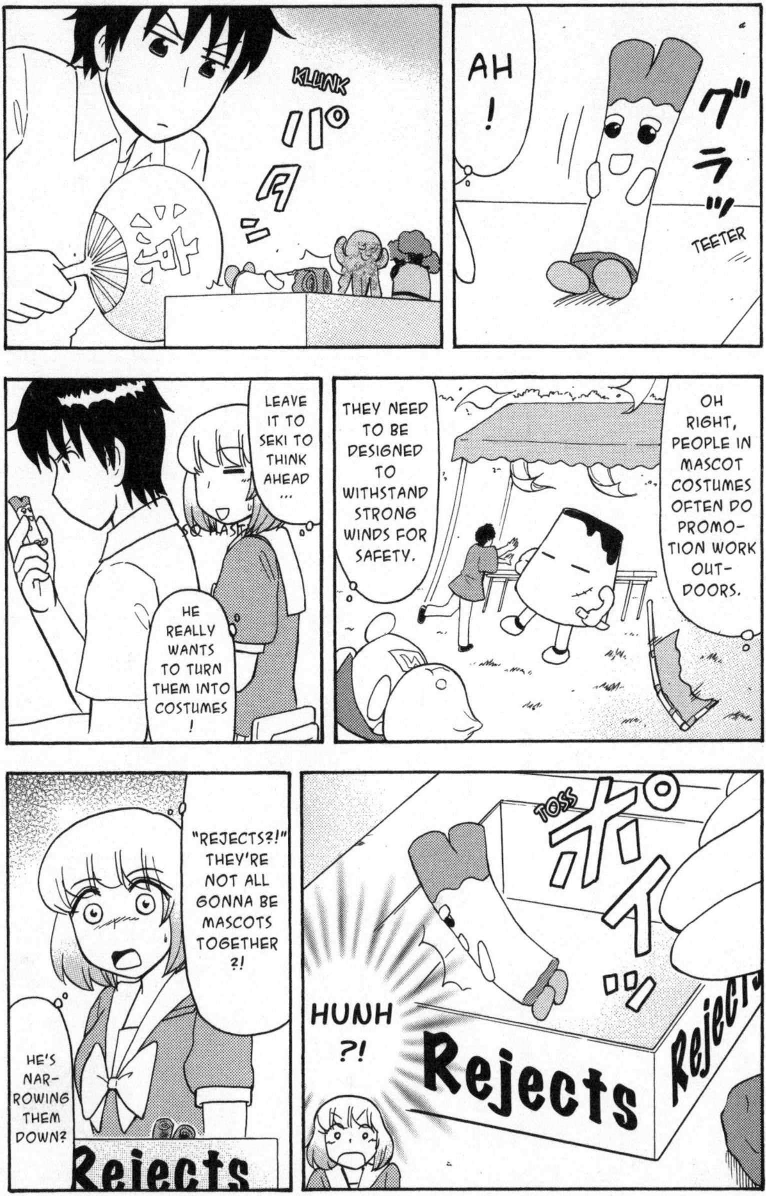
AH !
グラッ
TEETER
KLUNK
パタッ
OH RIGHT, PEOPLE IN MASCOT COSTUMES OFTEN DO PROMO-TION WORK OUT-DOORS.
THEY NEED TO BE DESIGNED TO WITHSTAND STRONG WINDS FOR SAFETY.
LEAVE IT TO SEKI TO THINK AHEAD ...
HE REALLY WANTS TO TURN THEM INTO COSTUMES !
TOSS
ポイッ
HUNH ?!
Rejects
Rejects
"REJECTS?!" THEY'RE NOT ALL GONNA BE MASCOTS TOGETHER ?!
HE'S NAR-ROWING THEM DOWN?
Rejects

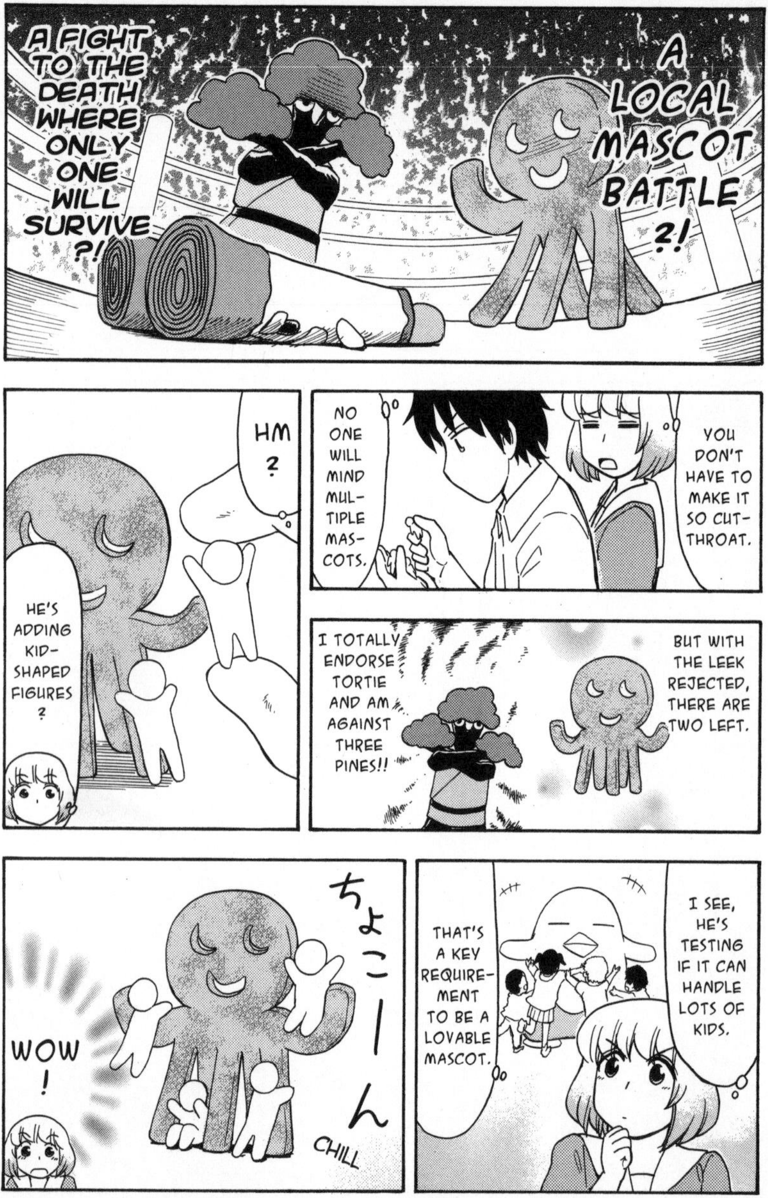
A LOCAL MASCOT BATTLE ?!
A FIGHT TO THE DEATH WHERE ONLY ONE WILL SURVIVE ?!
YOU DON'T HAVE TO MAKE IT SO CUT-THROAT.
NO ONE WILL MIND MUL-TIPLE MAS-COTS.
BUT WITH THE LEEK REJECTED, THERE ARE TWO LEFT.
I TOTALLY ENDORSE TORTIE AND AM AGAINST THREE PINES!!
HM ?
HE'S ADDING KID-SHAPED FIGURES ?
I SEE, HE'S TESTING IF IT CAN HANDLE LOTS OF KIDS.
THAT'S A KEY REQUIRE-MENT TO BE A LOVABLE MASCOT.
ちょこーん
CHILL
WOW !

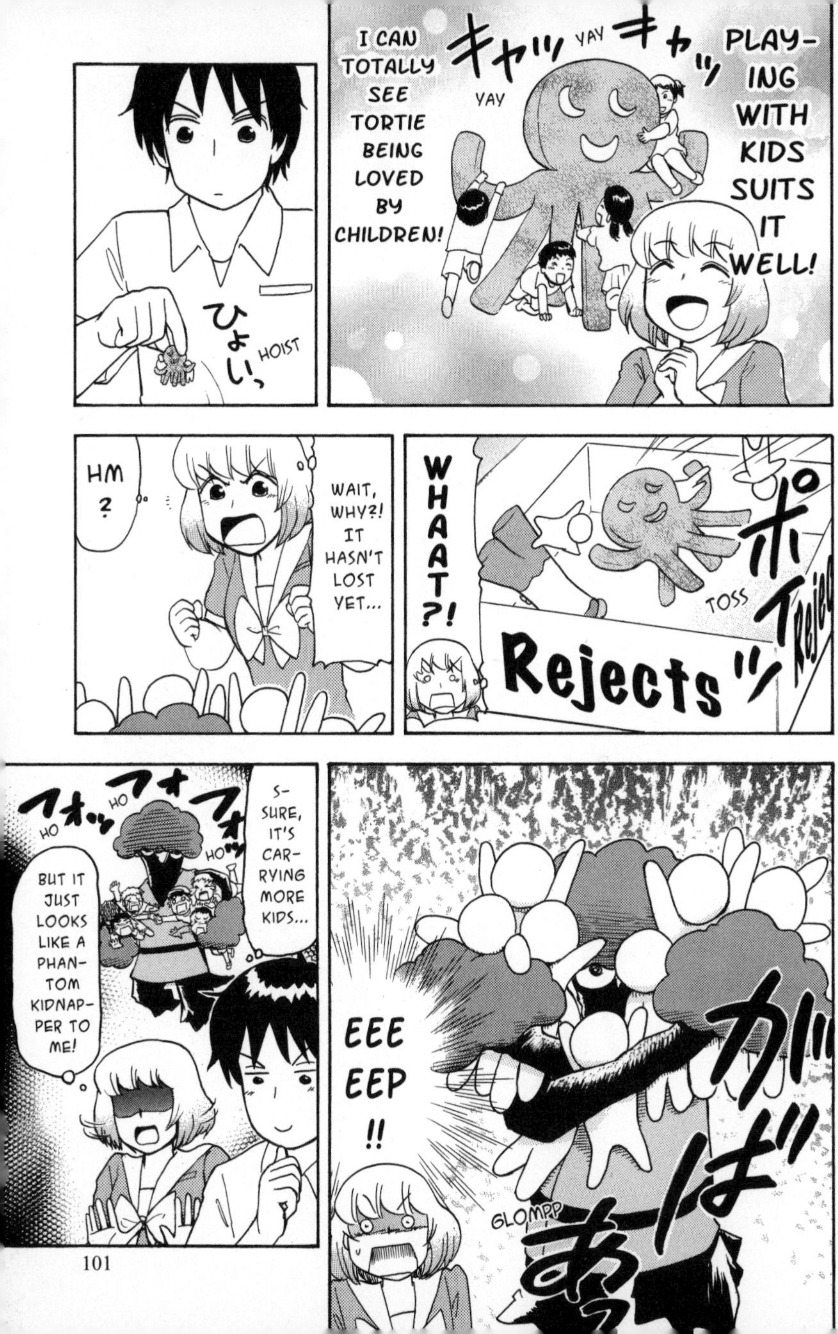
キャッ
YAY
キャッ
PLAYING WITH KIDS SUITS IT WELL!
YAY
I CAN TOTALLY SEE TORTIE BEING LOVED BY CHILDREN!
ひょいっ
HOIST
ポイッ
TOSS
WHAAAT?!
Rejects
WAIT, WHY?! IT HASN'T LOST YET...
HM?
がばぁっ
GLOMPP
EEEEEP!!
S-SURE, IT'S CARRYING MORE KIDS...
フォッフォフォッ
HO HO HO
BUT IT JUST LOOKS LIKE A PHANTOM KIDNAPPER TO ME!

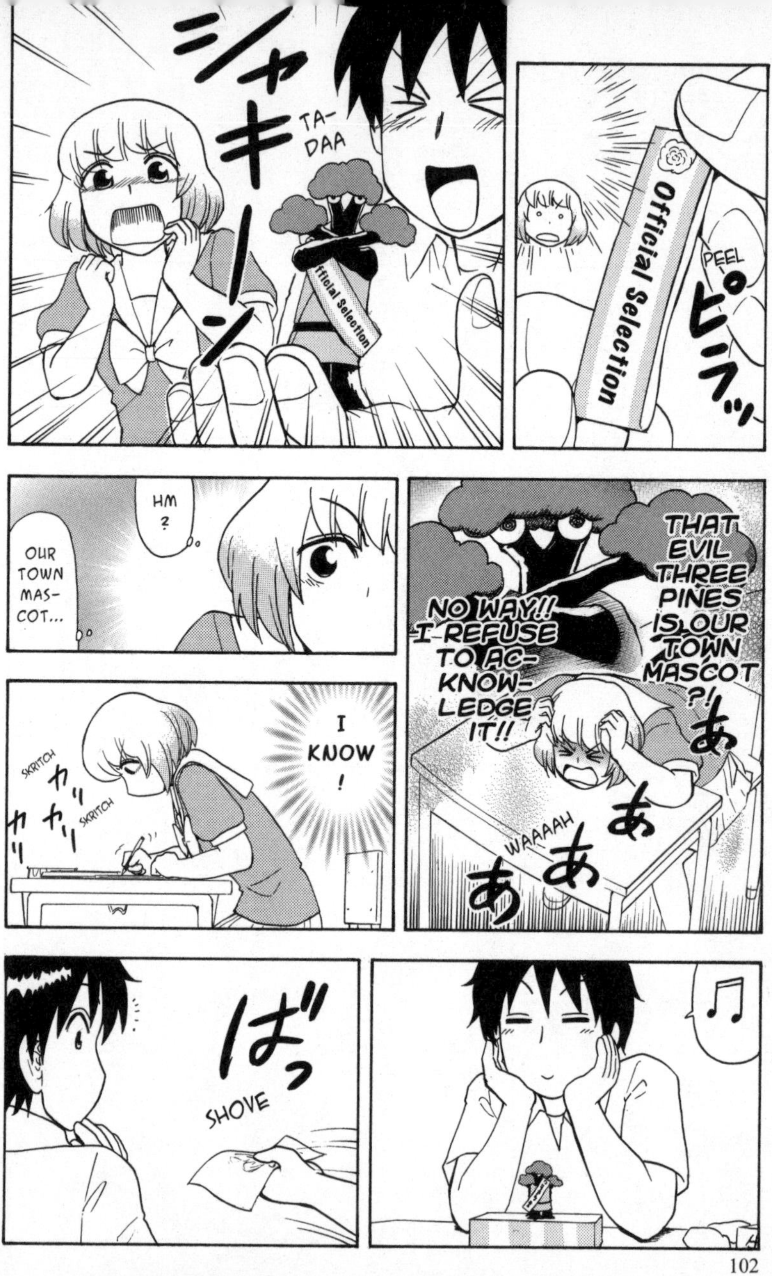
Official Selection
PEEL
シャキーン
TA-DAA
Official Selection
THAT EVIL THREE PINES IS OUR TOWN MASCOT?!
NO WAY!! I REFUSE TO ACKNOWLEDGE IT!!
あああ
あ
WAAAAH
HM?
OUR TOWN MASCOT...
I KNOW!
SKRITCH
カリカリ
SKRITCH
カリ
♫
ばっ
SHOVE

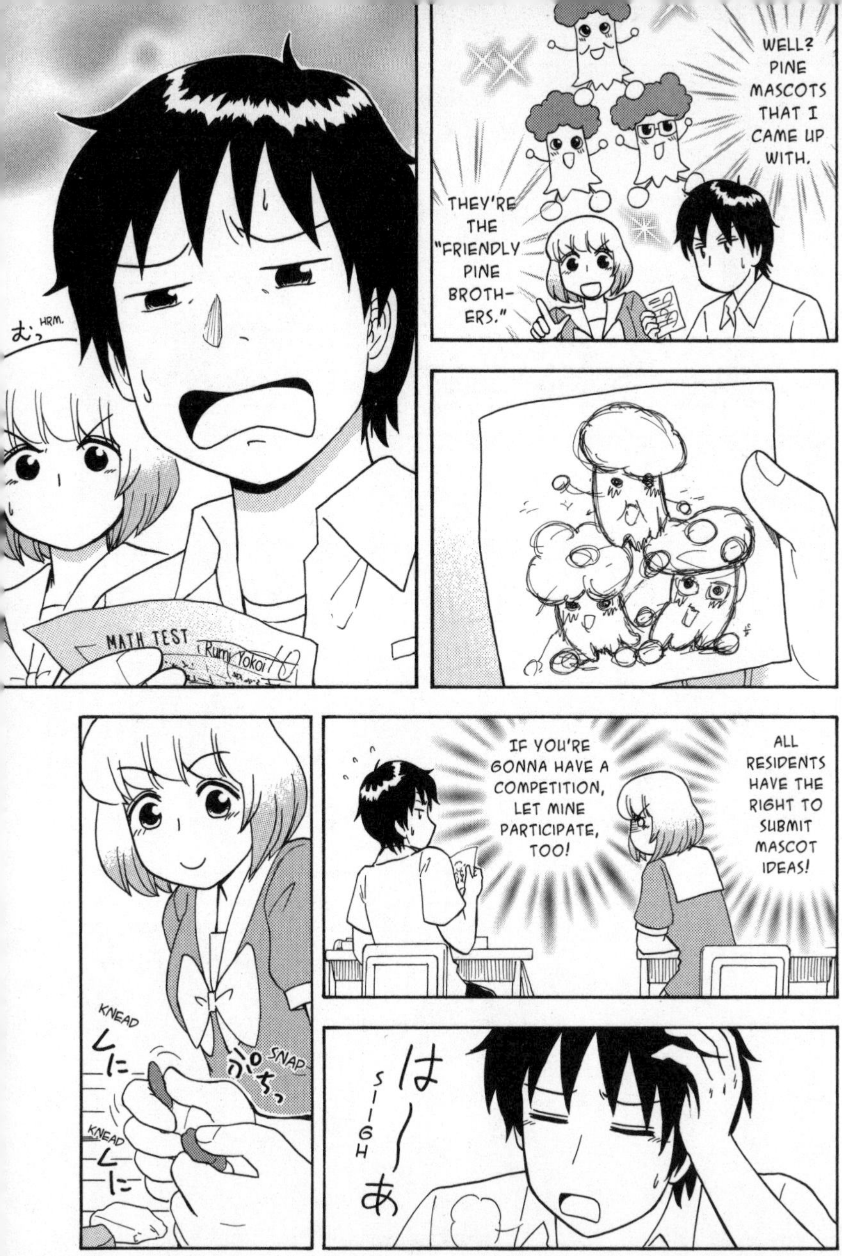
WELL? PINE MASCOTS THAT I CAME UP WITH.
THEY'RE THE "FRIENDLY PINE BROTHERS."
むっ HRM.
MATH TEST
Rumi Yokoi
ALL RESIDENTS HAVE THE RIGHT TO SUBMIT MASCOT IDEAS!
IF YOU'RE GONNA HAVE A COMPETITION, LET MINE PARTICIPATE, TOO!
はーあ SIIGH
ぷちっ SNAP
ムに KNEAD
ムに KNEAD

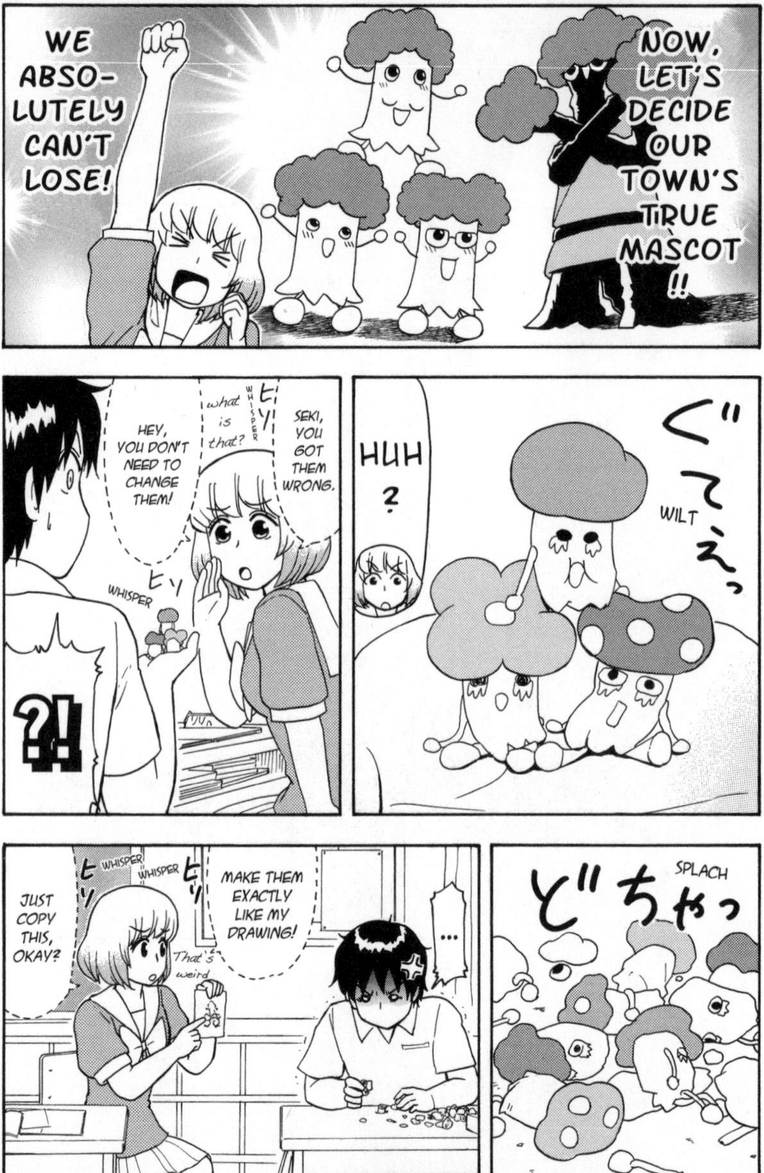
NOW, LET'S DECIDE OUR TOWN'S TRUE MASCOT !!
WE ABSO-LUTELY CAN'T LOSE!
ぐてぇっ
WILT
HUH ?
SEKI, YOU GOT THEM WRONG.
ヒソ
WHISPER
what is that?
HEY, YOU DON'T NEED TO CHANGE THEM!
ヒソ
WHISPER
?!
どちゃっ
SPLACH
...
MAKE THEM EXACTLY LIKE MY DRAWING!
ヒソ
WHISPER
ヒソ
WHISPER
That's weird
JUST COPY THIS, OKAY?

My Neighbor Seki

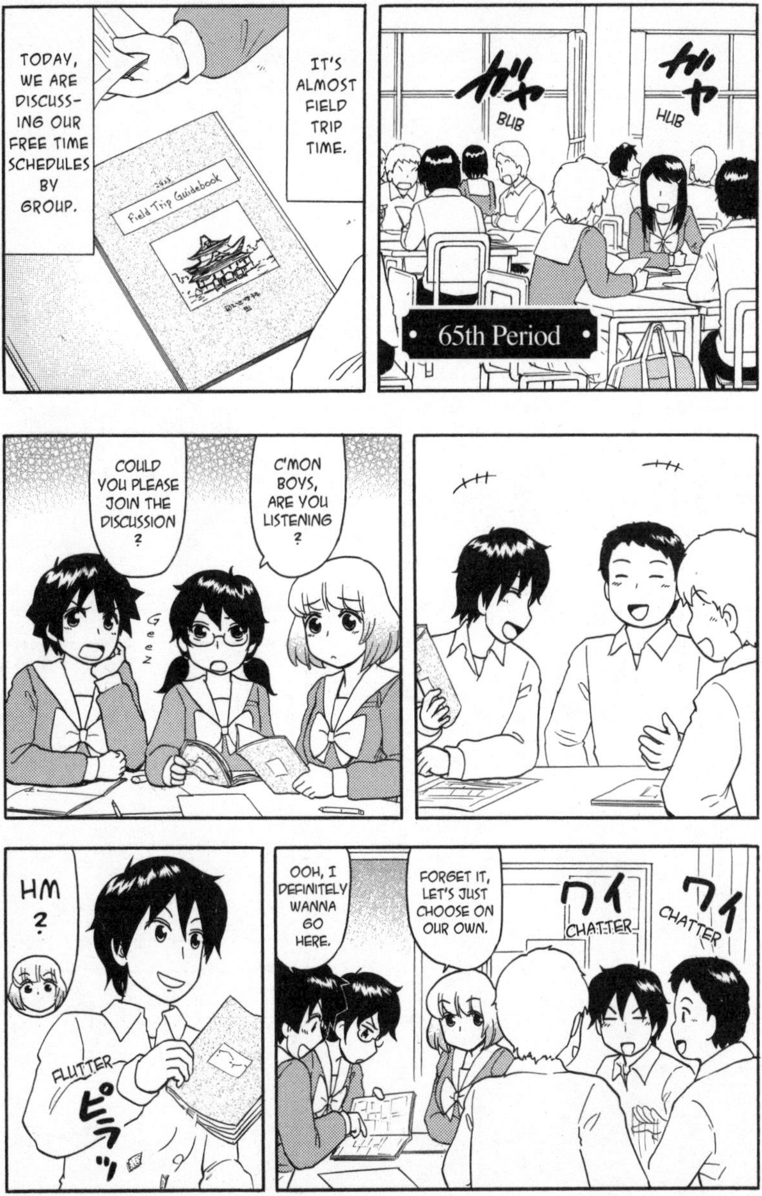
ガヤ
HUB
ガヤ
BUB
65th Period
IT'S ALMOST FIELD TRIP TIME.
TODAY, WE ARE DISCUSSING OUR FREE TIME SCHEDULES BY GROUP.
Field Trip Guidebook
C'MON BOYS, ARE YOU LISTENING?
COULD YOU PLEASE JOIN THE DISCUSSION?
Geez
ワイ
CHATTER
ワイ
CHATTER
FORGET IT, LET'S JUST CHOOSE ON OUR OWN.
OOH, I DEFINITELY WANNA GO HERE.
HM?
FLUTTER
ピラッ

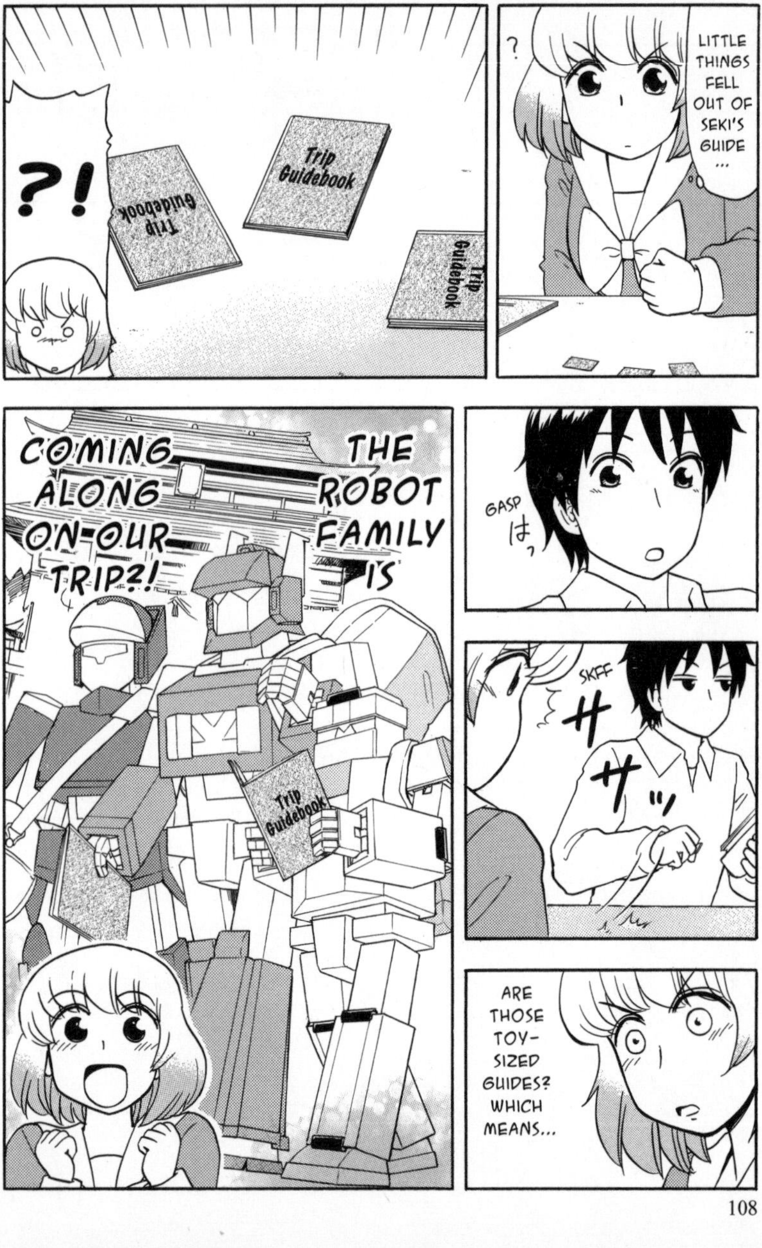
?
LITTLE THINGS FELL OUT OF SEKI'S GUIDE ...
?!
Trip Guidebook
Trip Guidebook
Trip Guidebook
GASP は
SKFF サ サッ
ARE THOSE TOY-SIZED GUIDES? WHICH MEANS...
THE ROBOT FAMILY IS
COMING ALONG ON OUR TRIP?!
Trip Guidebook

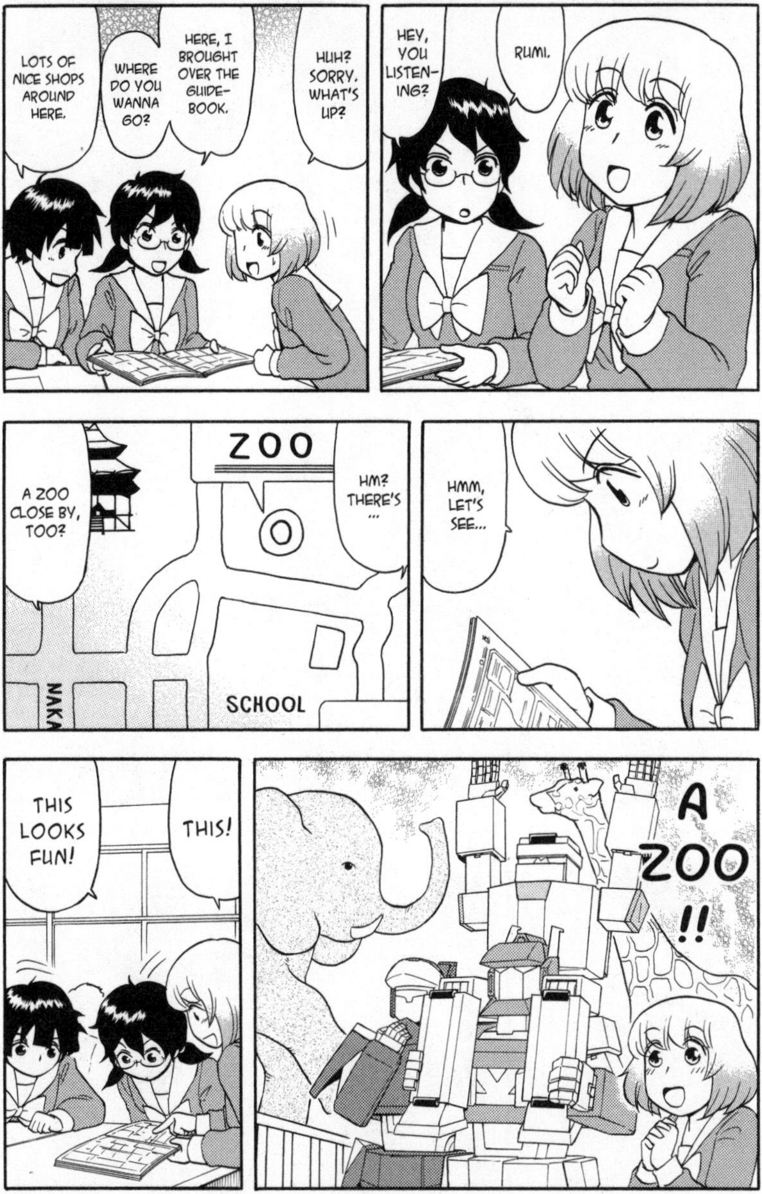
RUMI.
HEY, YOU LISTEN-ING?
HUH? SORRY. WHAT'S UP?
HERE, I BROUGHT OVER THE GUIDE-BOOK.
WHERE DO YOU WANNA GO?
LOTS OF NICE SHOPS AROUND HERE.
HMM, LET'S SEE...
HM? THERE'S ...
ZOO
A ZOO CLOSE BY, TOO?
NAKA
SCHOOL
A ZOO !!
THIS!
THIS LOOKS FUN!

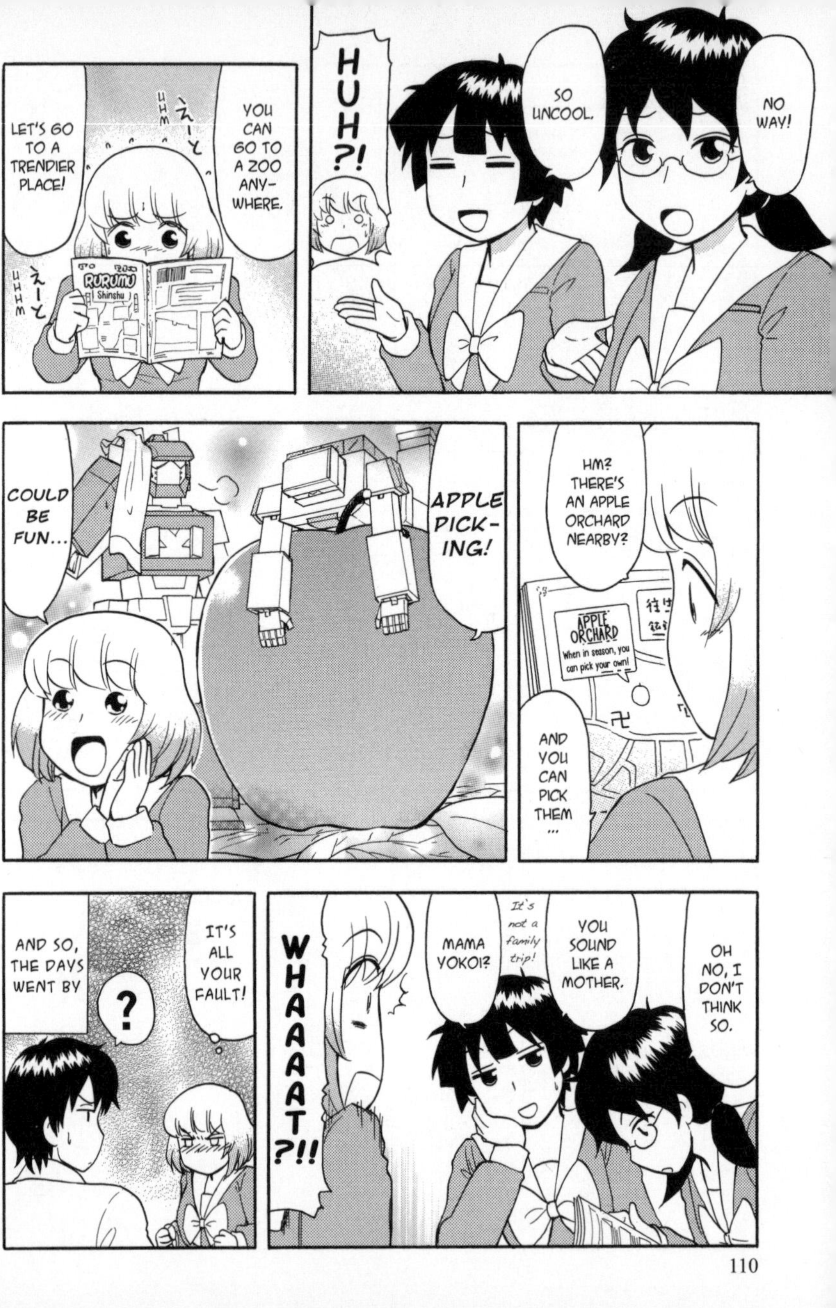
NO WAY!
SO UNCOOL.
HUH?!
YOU CAN GO TO A ZOO ANYWHERE.
えーと UHHM
LET'S GO TO A TRENDIER PLACE!
RURUMU Shinshu
えーと UHHM
HM? THERE'S AN APPLE ORCHARD NEARBY?
APPLE ORCHARD
When in season, you can pick your own!
AND YOU CAN PICK THEM ...
APPLE PICKING!
COULD BE FUN...
OH NO, I DON'T THINK SO.
YOU SOUND LIKE A MOTHER.
It's not a family trip!
MAMA YOKOI?
WHAAAAAT?!!
IT'S ALL YOUR FAULT!
?
AND SO, THE DAYS WENT BY

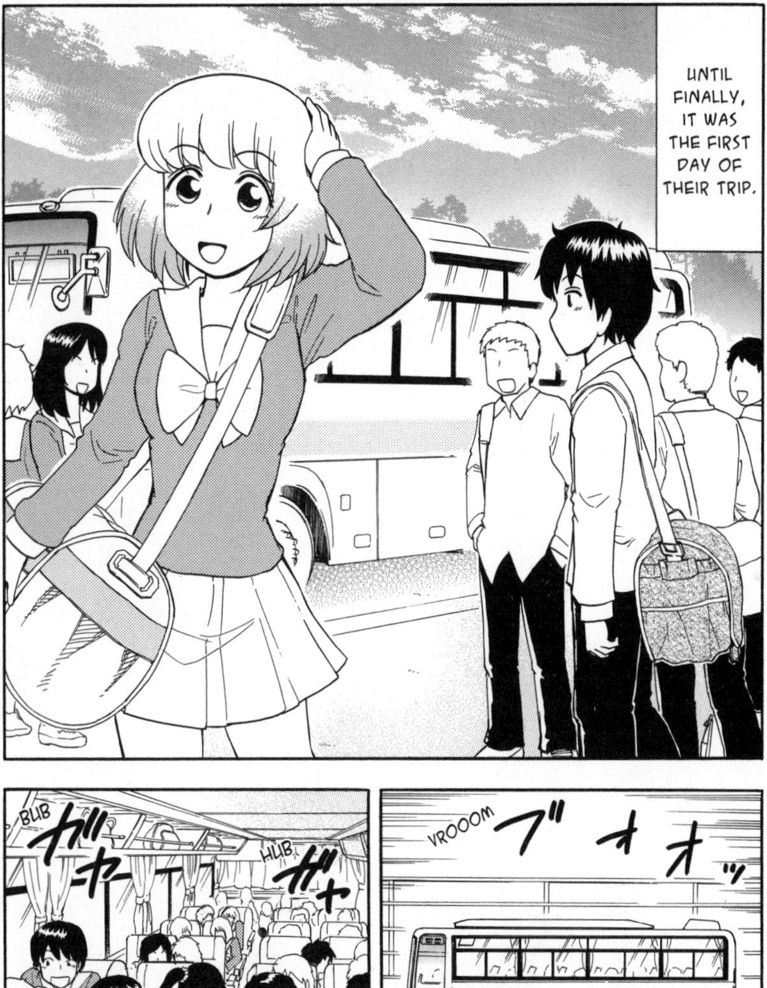
UNTIL FINALLY, IT WAS THE FIRST DAY OF THEIR TRIP.
VROOOM
ブオオッ
BUB
ガヤー
HUB
ガヤ

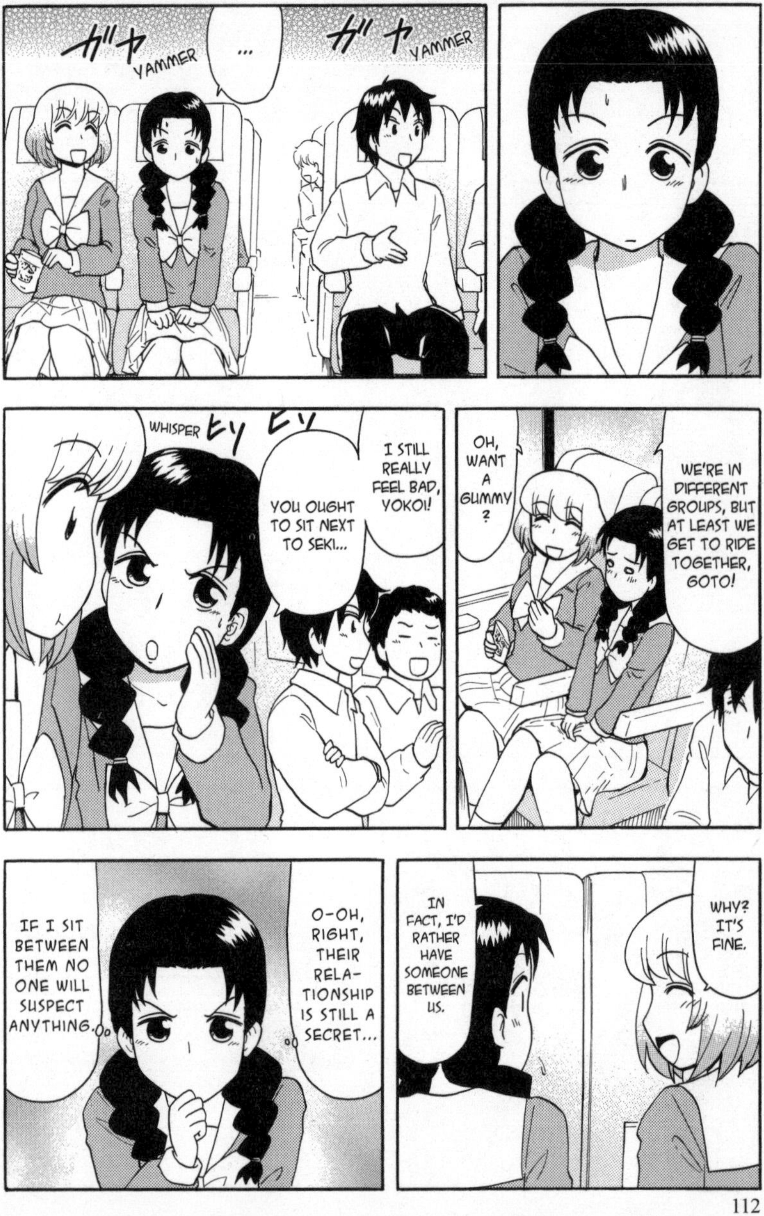
ガヤ
YAMMER
...
ガヤ
YAMMER
WE'RE IN DIFFERENT GROUPS, BUT AT LEAST WE GET TO RIDE TOGETHER, GOTO!
OH, WANT A GUMMY?
I STILL REALLY FEEL BAD, YOKOI!
YOU OUGHT TO SIT NEXT TO SEKI...
ヒソ ヒソ
WHISPER
WHY? IT'S FINE.
IN FACT, I'D RATHER HAVE SOMEONE BETWEEN US.
O-OH, RIGHT, THEIR RELATIONSHIP IS STILL A SECRET...
IF I SIT BETWEEN THEM NO ONE WILL SUSPECT ANYTHING.

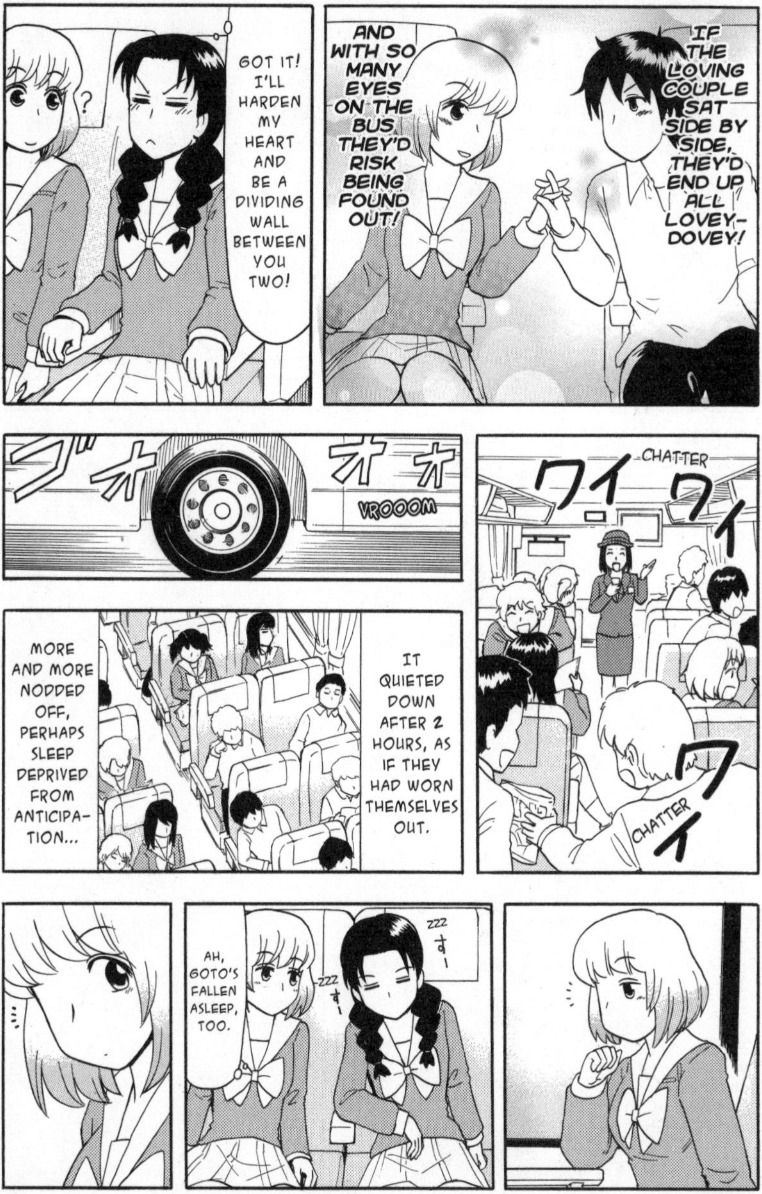
IF THE LOVING COUPLE SAT SIDE BY SIDE, THEY'D END UP ALL LOVEY-DOVEY!
AND WITH SO MANY EYES ON THE BUS THEY'D RISK BEING FOUND OUT!
?
GOT IT! I'LL HARDEN MY HEART AND BE A DIVIDING WALL BETWEEN YOU TWO!
ワイ ワイ
CHATTER
ワイ ワイ
CHATTER
ブォオオ
VROOOM
IT QUIETED DOWN AFTER 2 HOURS, AS IF THEY HAD WORN THEMSELVES OUT.
MORE AND MORE NODDED OFF, PERHAPS SLEEP DEPRIVED FROM ANTICIPA-TION...
...
ZZZ
すー
AH, GOTO'S FALLEN ASLEEP, TOO.
ZZZ
すー
...

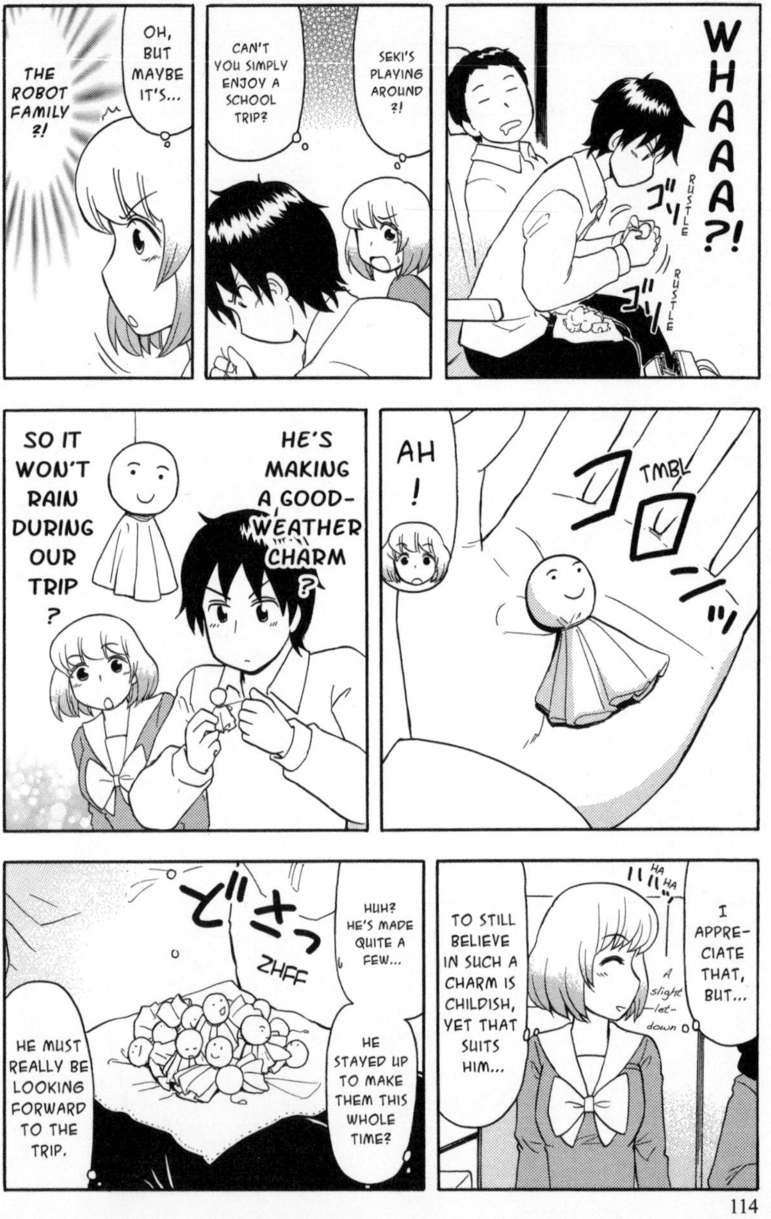
WHAAAA?!
RUSTLE
RUSTLE
SEKI'S PLAYING AROUND?!
CAN'T YOU SIMPLY ENJOY A SCHOOL TRIP?
OH, BUT MAYBE IT'S...
THE ROBOT FAMILY?!
AH!
TMBL
HE'S MAKING A GOOD-WEATHER CHARM?
SO IT WON'T RAIN DURING OUR TRIP?
I APPRECIATE THAT, BUT...
HA HA
A slight let-down
TO STILL BELIEVE IN SUCH A CHARM IS CHILDISH, YET THAT SUITS HIM...
HUH? HE'S MADE QUITE A FEW...
ZHFF
HE STAYED UP TO MAKE THEM THIS WHOLE TIME?
HE MUST REALLY BE LOOKING FORWARD TO THE TRIP.

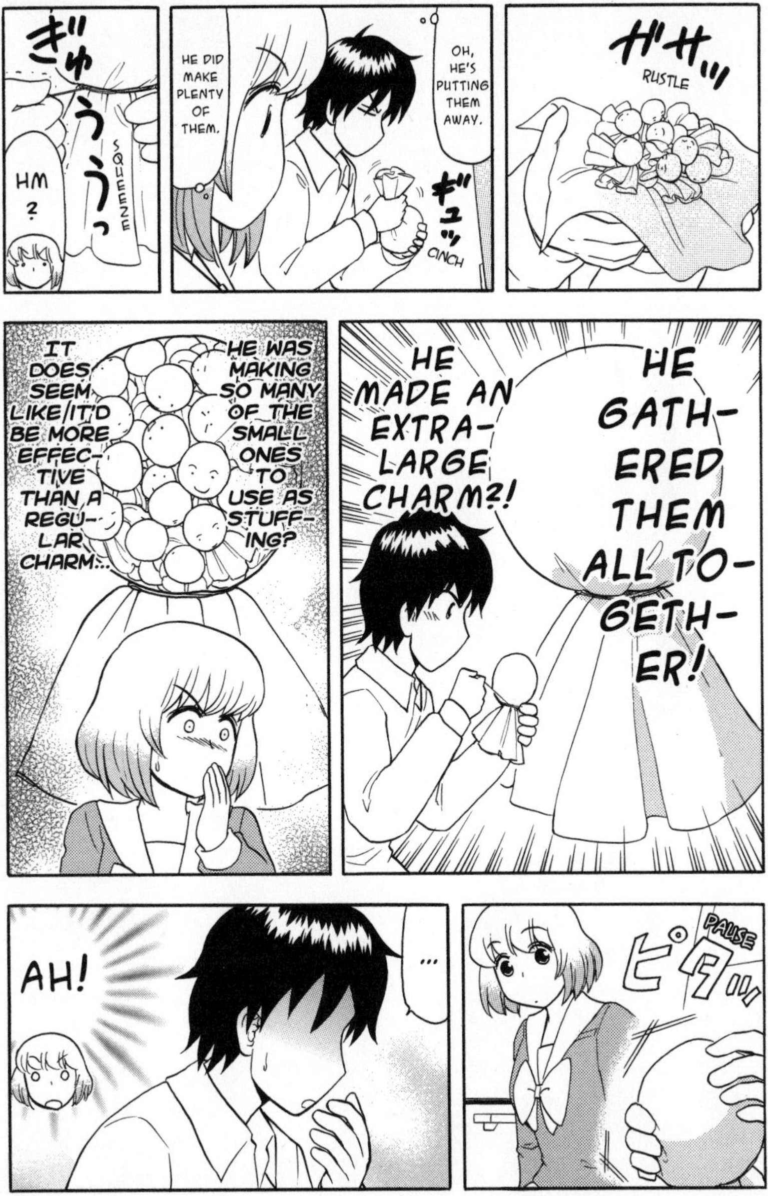
ザサッ
RUSTLE
OH, HE'S PUTTING THEM AWAY.
HE DID MAKE PLENTY OF THEM.
ギュッ
CINCH
ぎゅううっ
SQUEEZE
HM?
HE GATHERED THEM ALL TOGETHER!
HE MADE AN EXTRA-LARGE CHARM?!
HE WAS MAKING SO MANY OF THE SMALL ONES TO USE AS STUFFING?
IT DOES SEEM LIKE IT'D BE MORE EFFECTIVE THAN A REGULAR CHARM...
ピタッ
PAUSE
...
AH!

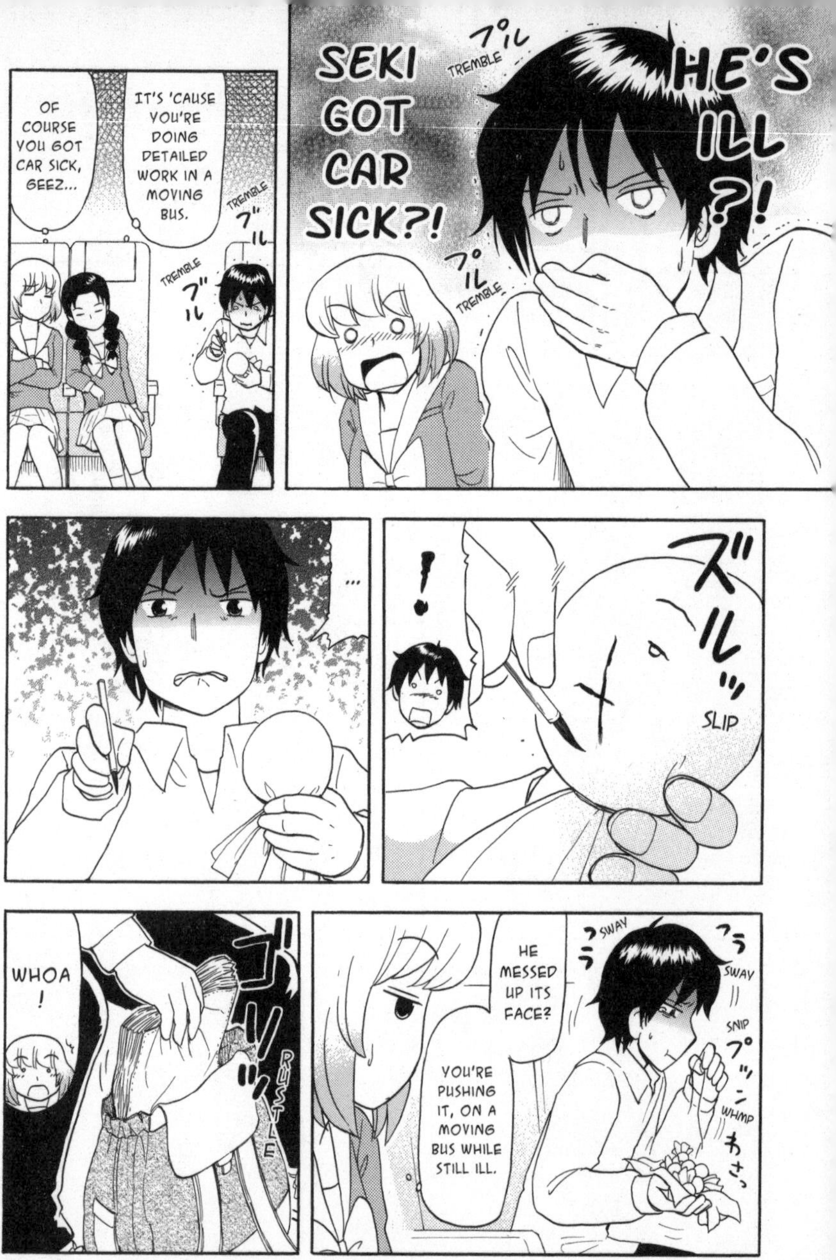
HE'S ILL?!
プル
TREMBLE
SEKI GOT CAR SICK?!
プル
TREMBLE
IT'S 'CAUSE YOU'RE DOING DETAILED WORK IN A MOVING BUS.
OF COURSE YOU GOT CAR SICK, GEEZ...
TREMBLE
ブル
TREMBLE
ブル
ズルッ
SLIP
!
...
HE MESSED UP ITS FACE?
YOU'RE PUSHING IT, ON A MOVING BUS WHILE STILL ILL.
フラ
SWAY
フラ
SWAY
SNIP
プツン
WHMP
わさっ
RUSTLE
WHOA!

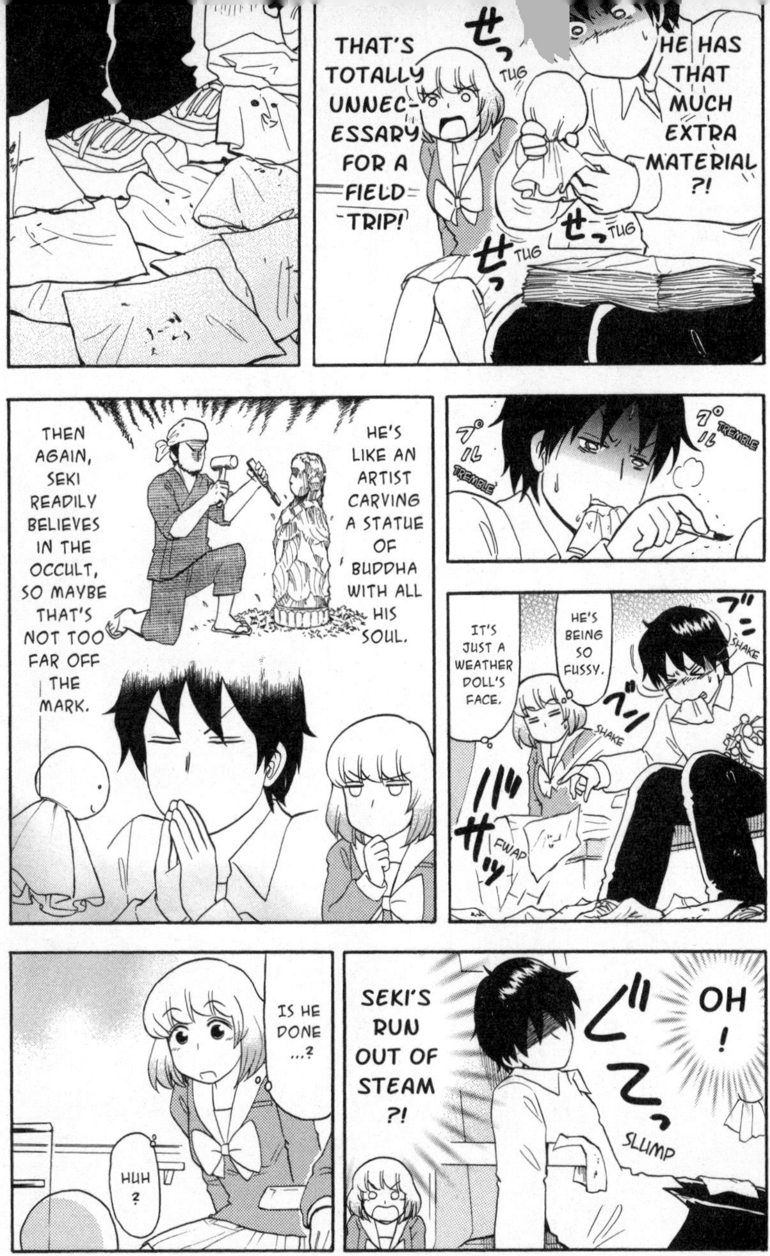
HE HAS THAT MUCH EXTRA MATERIAL?!
せっ
TUG
THAT'S TOTALLY UNNEC-ESSARY FOR A FIELD TRIP!
せっ
TUG
せっ
TUG
プル
TREMBLE
プル
TREMBLE
ブン
SHAKE
HE'S BEING SO FUSSY.
IT'S JUST A WEATHER DOLL'S FACE.
ブン
SHAKE
バサッ
FWAP
HE'S LIKE AN ARTIST CARVING A STATUE OF BUDDHA WITH ALL HIS SOUL.
THEN AGAIN, SEKI READILY BELIEVES IN THE OCCULT, SO MAYBE THAT'S NOT TOO FAR OFF THE MARK.
OH!
ぐてっ
SLUMP
SEKI'S RUN OUT OF STEAM?!
IS HE DONE...?
HUH?

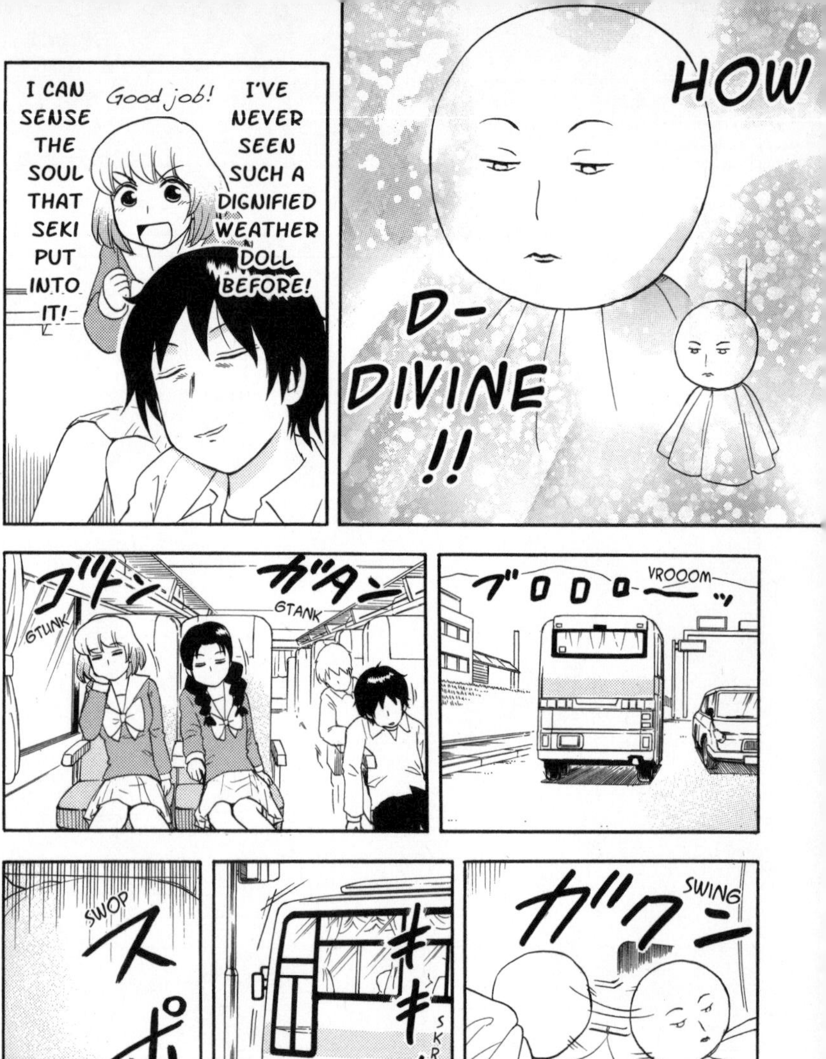
HOW
D-DIVINE!!
I'VE NEVER SEEN SUCH A DIGNIFIED WEATHER DOLL BEFORE!
Good job!
I CAN SENSE THE SOUL THAT SEKI PUT INTO IT!
ブロロロ～～ッ
VROOOM
ガタン
GTANK
ゴトン
GTUNK
ガクン
SWING
ガクン
SWING
キキーッ
SKREECH
スポッ
SWOP

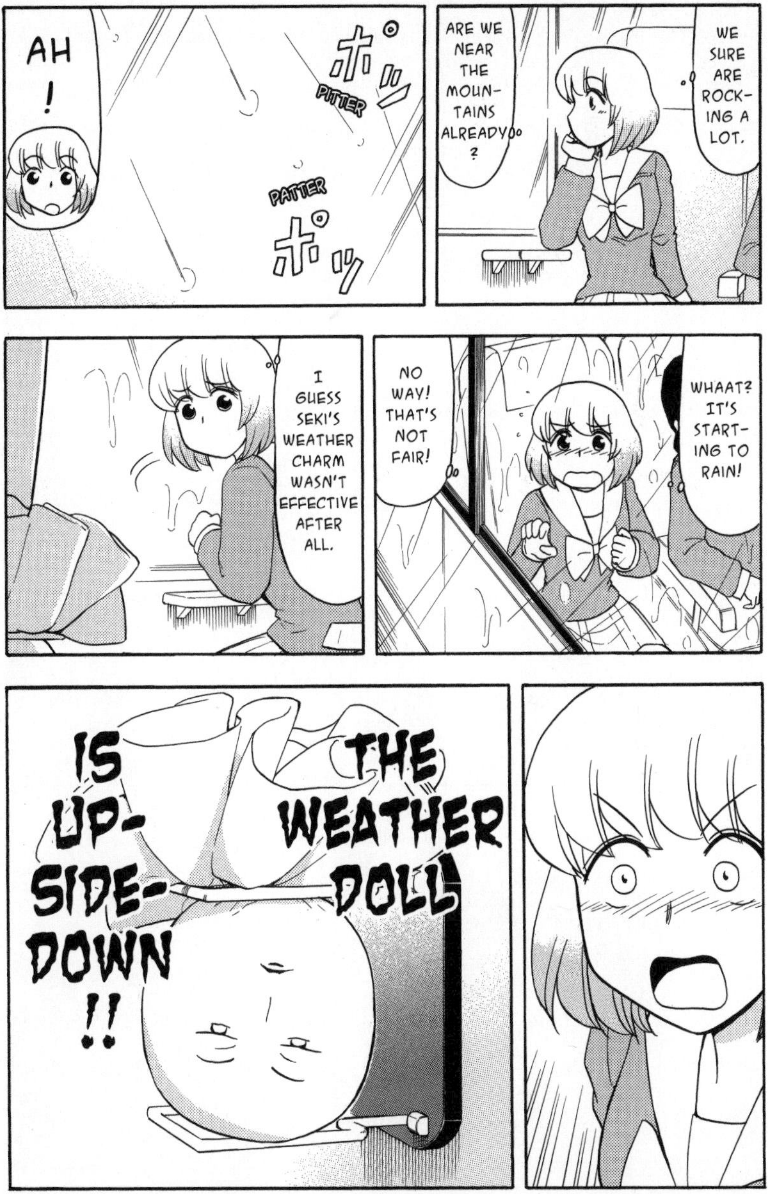
WE SURE ARE ROCKING A LOT.
ARE WE NEAR THE MOUNTAINS ALREADY?
PITTER
PATTER
AH!
WHAAT? IT'S STARTING TO RAIN!
NO WAY! THAT'S NOT FAIR!
I GUESS SEKI'S WEATHER CHARM WASN'T EFFECTIVE AFTER ALL.
THE WEATHER DOLL
IS UPSIDE-DOWN!!

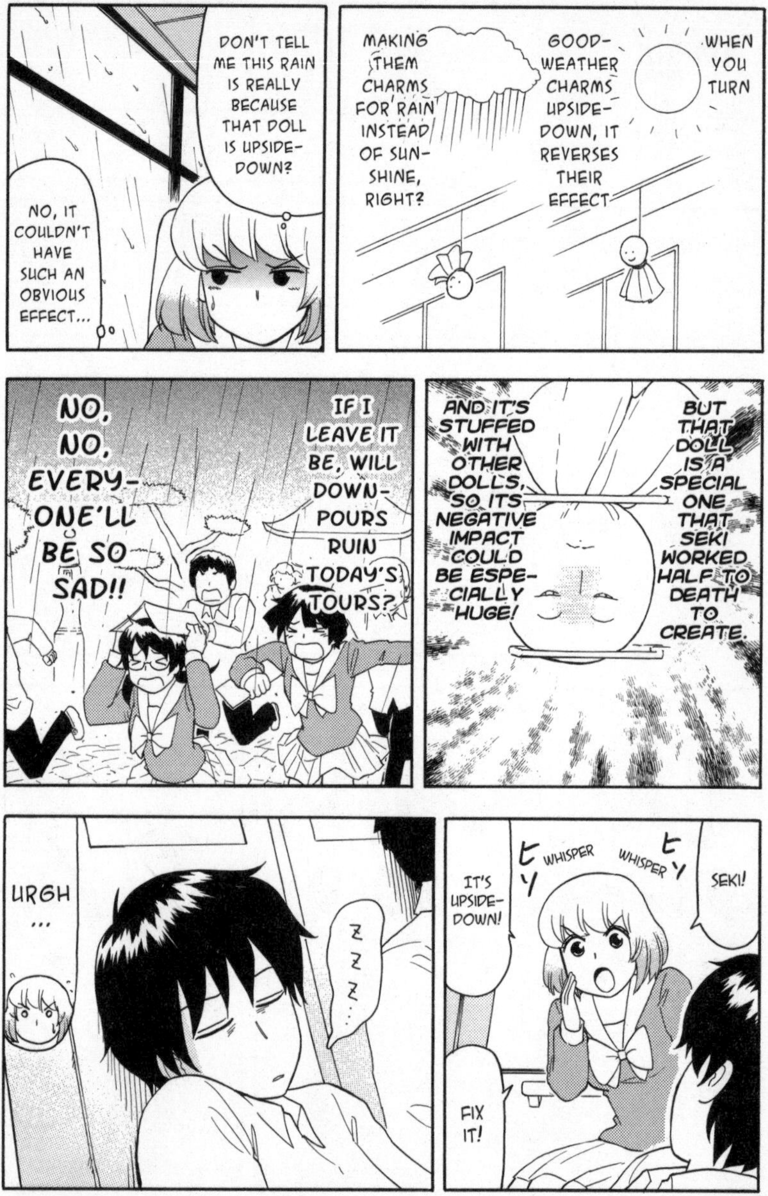
WHEN YOU TURN
GOOD-WEATHER CHARMS UPSIDE-DOWN, IT REVERSES THEIR EFFECT
MAKING THEM CHARMS FOR RAIN INSTEAD OF SUN-SHINE, RIGHT?
DON'T TELL ME THIS RAIN IS REALLY BECAUSE THAT DOLL IS UPSIDE-DOWN?
NO, IT COULDN'T HAVE SUCH AN OBVIOUS EFFECT...
BUT THAT DOLL IS A SPECIAL ONE THAT SEKI WORKED HALF TO DEATH TO CREATE.
AND IT'S STUFFED WITH OTHER DOLLS, SO ITS NEGATIVE IMPACT COULD BE ESPE-CIALLY HUGE!
IF I LEAVE IT BE, WILL DOWN-POURS RUIN TODAY'S TOURS?
NO, NO, EVERY-ONE'LL BE SO SAD!!
SEKI!
ヒソ WHISPER
ヒソ WHISPER
IT'S UPSIDE-DOWN!
FIX IT!
Z Z Z...
URGH ...

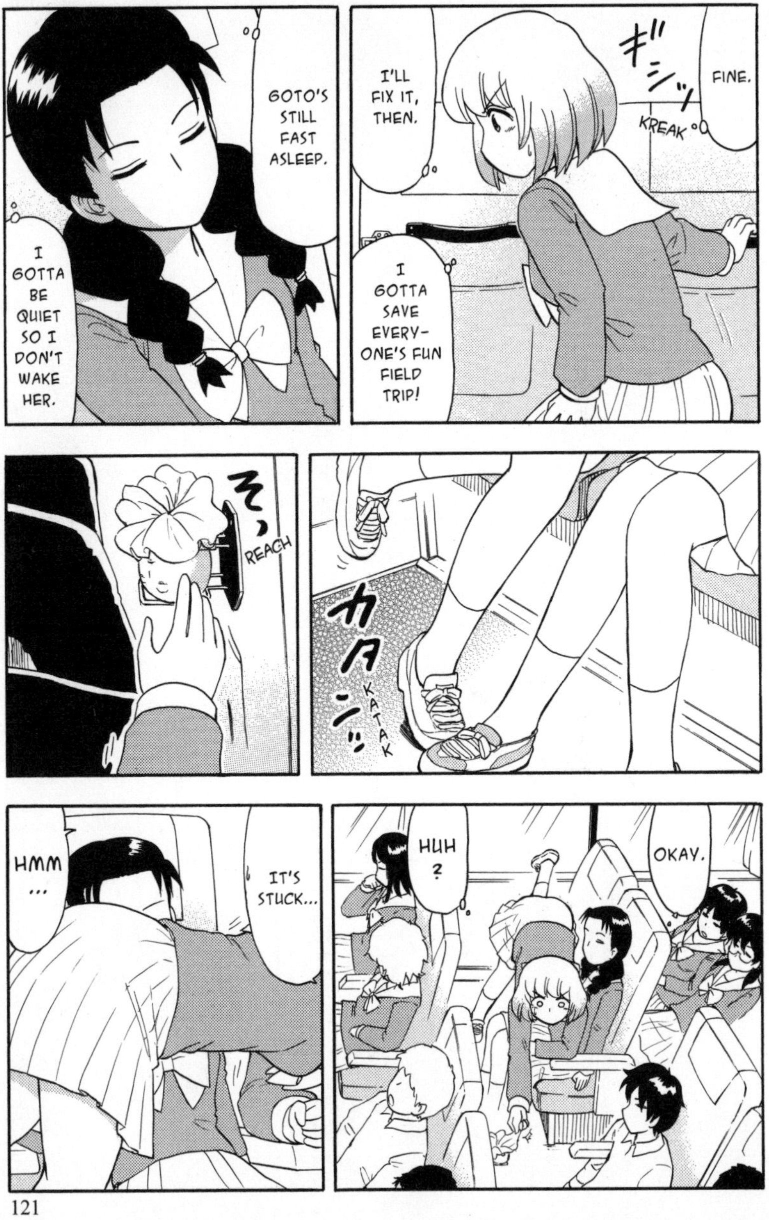
FINE.
ギシッ
KREAK
I'LL FIX IT, THEN.
I GOTTA SAVE EVERYONE'S FUN FIELD TRIP!
GOTO'S STILL FAST ASLEEP.
I GOTTA BE QUIET SO I DON'T WAKE HER.
カタン
KATAK
そっ
REACH
OKAY.
HUH?
IT'S STUCK...
HMM...

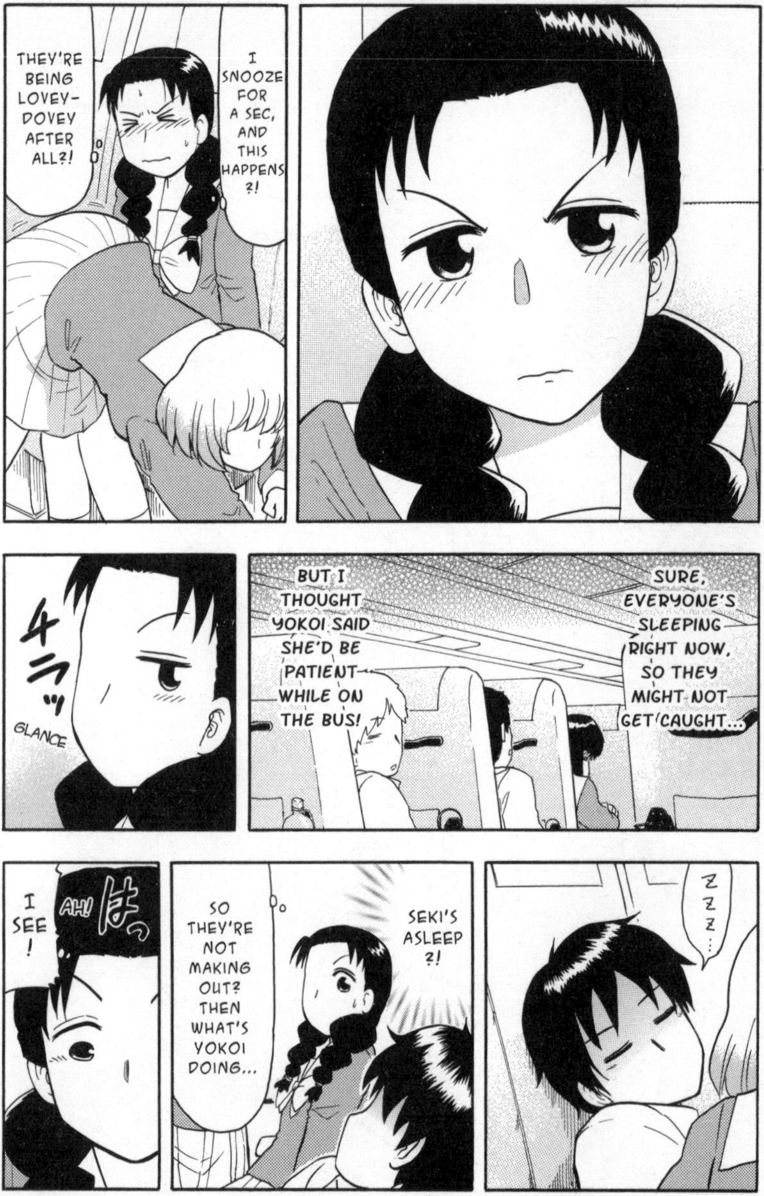
I SNOOZE FOR A SEC, AND THIS HAPPENS?!
THEY'RE BEING LOVEY-DOVEY AFTER ALL?!
SURE, EVERYONE'S SLEEPING RIGHT NOW, SO THEY MIGHT NOT GET CAUGHT...
BUT I THOUGHT YOKOI SAID SHE'D BE PATIENT WHILE ON THE BUS!
チラッ
GLANCE
Z Z Z...
SEKI'S ASLEEP?!
SO THEY'RE NOT MAKING OUT? THEN WHAT'S YOKOI DOING...
AH!
はっ
I SEE!

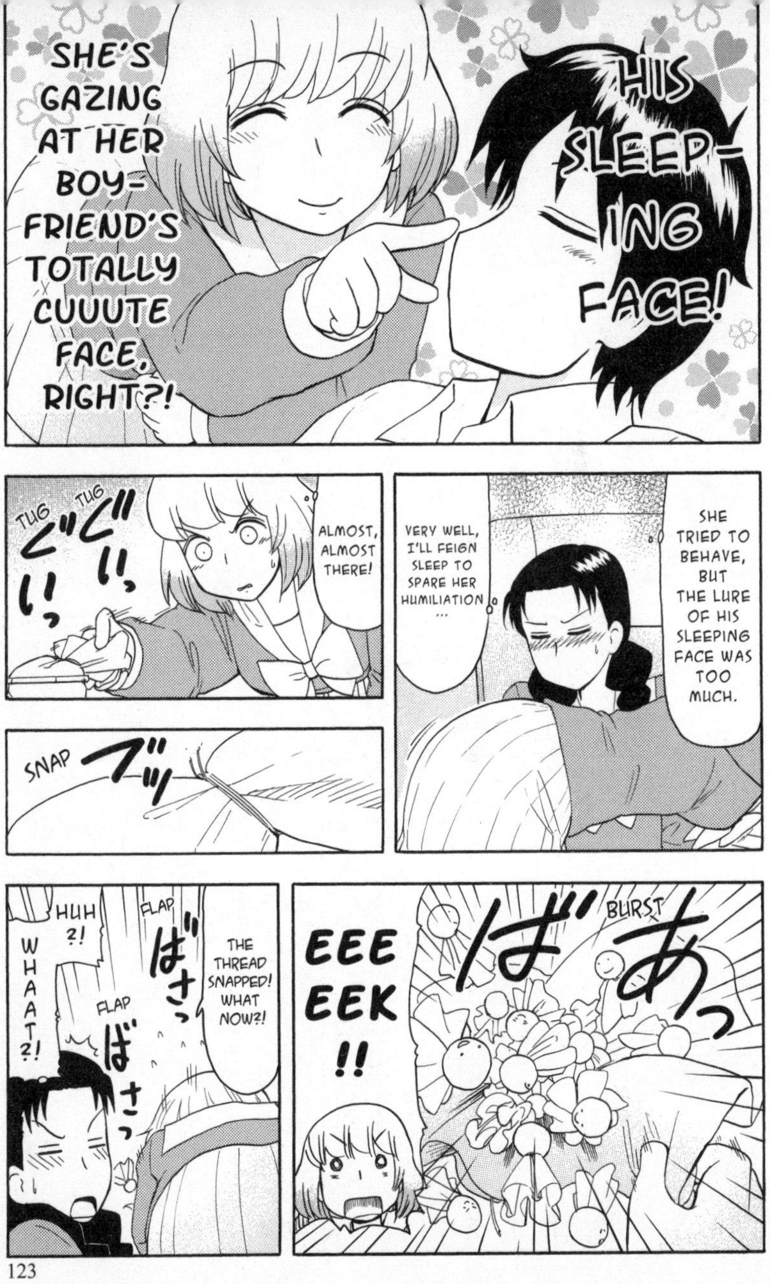
SHE'S GAZING AT HER BOY-FRIEND'S TOTALLY CUUUTE FACE, RIGHT?!
HIS SLEEP-ING FACE!
SHE TRIED TO BEHAVE, BUT THE LURE OF HIS SLEEPING FACE WAS TOO MUCH.
VERY WELL, I'LL FEIGN SLEEP TO SPARE HER HUMILIATION ...
ALMOST, ALMOST THERE!
TUG ぐいっ
TUG ぐいっ
SNAP ブツ
BURST ばあっ
EEEEEK!!
THE THREAD SNAPPED! WHAT NOW?!
FLAP ばさっ
FLAP ばさっ
HUH?!
WHAAAT?!

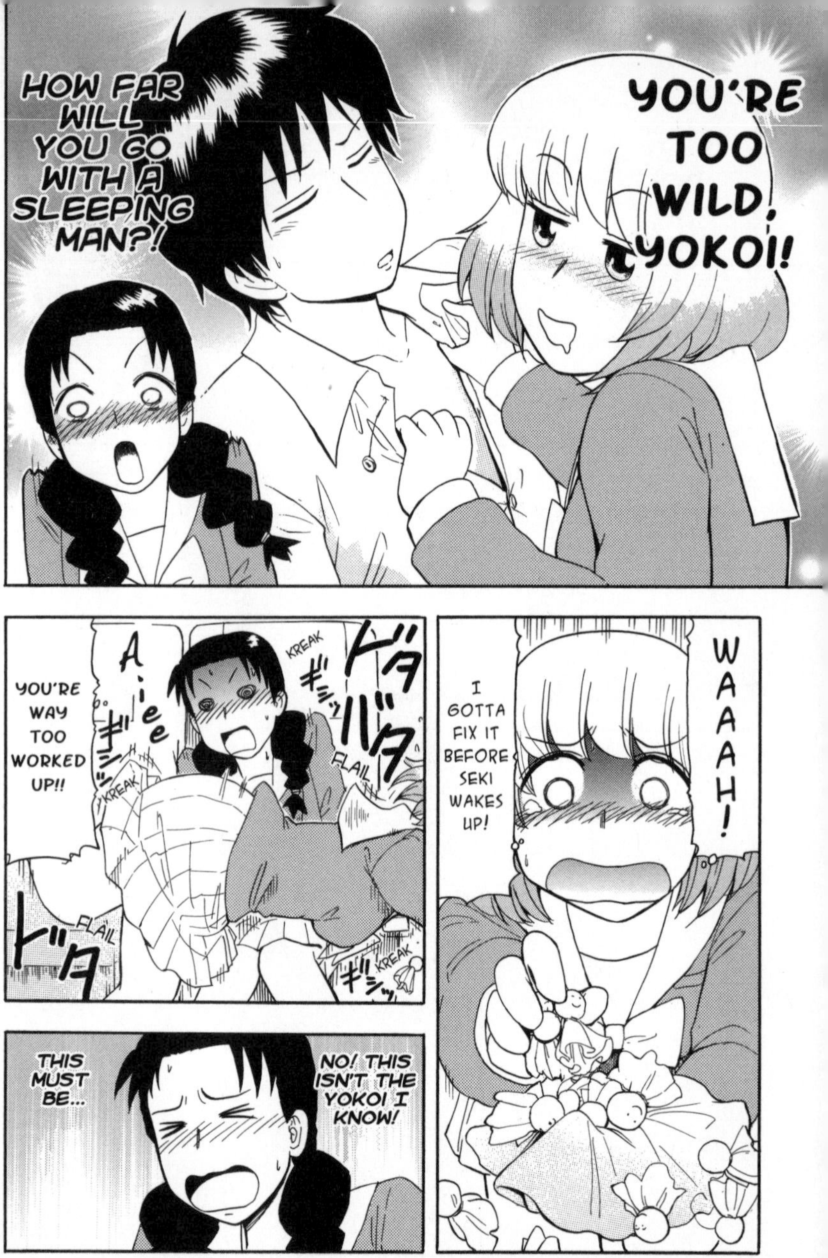
YOU'RE TOO WILD, YOKOI!
HOW FAR WILL YOU GO WITH A SLEEPING MAN?!
WAAAAH!
I GOTTA FIX IT BEFORE SEKI WAKES UP!
ドタバタ
ギシッ
KREAK
FLAIL
Aieee
ギシッ
KREAK
YOU'RE WAY TOO WORKED UP!!
ドタ
FLAIL
ギシッ
KREAK
NO! THIS ISN'T THE YOKOI I KNOW!
THIS MUST BE...

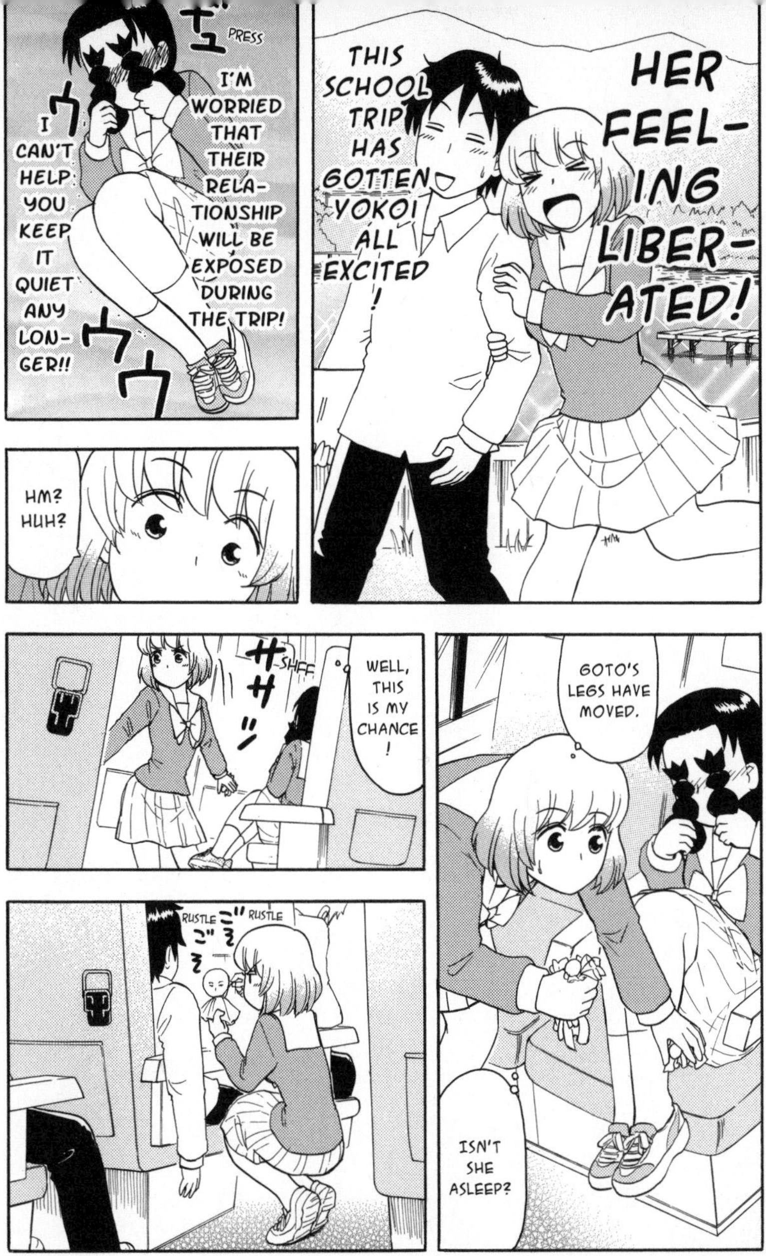
HER FEELING LIBERATED!
THIS SCHOOL TRIP HAS GOTTEN YOKOI ALL EXCITED!
PRESS
I'M WORRIED THAT THEIR RELATIONSHIP WILL BE EXPOSED DURING THE TRIP!
I CAN'T HELP YOU KEEP IT QUIET ANY LONGER!!
HM? HUH?
GOTO'S LEGS HAVE MOVED.
ISN'T SHE ASLEEP?
WELL, THIS IS MY CHANCE!
SHFF
RUSTLE
RUSTLE

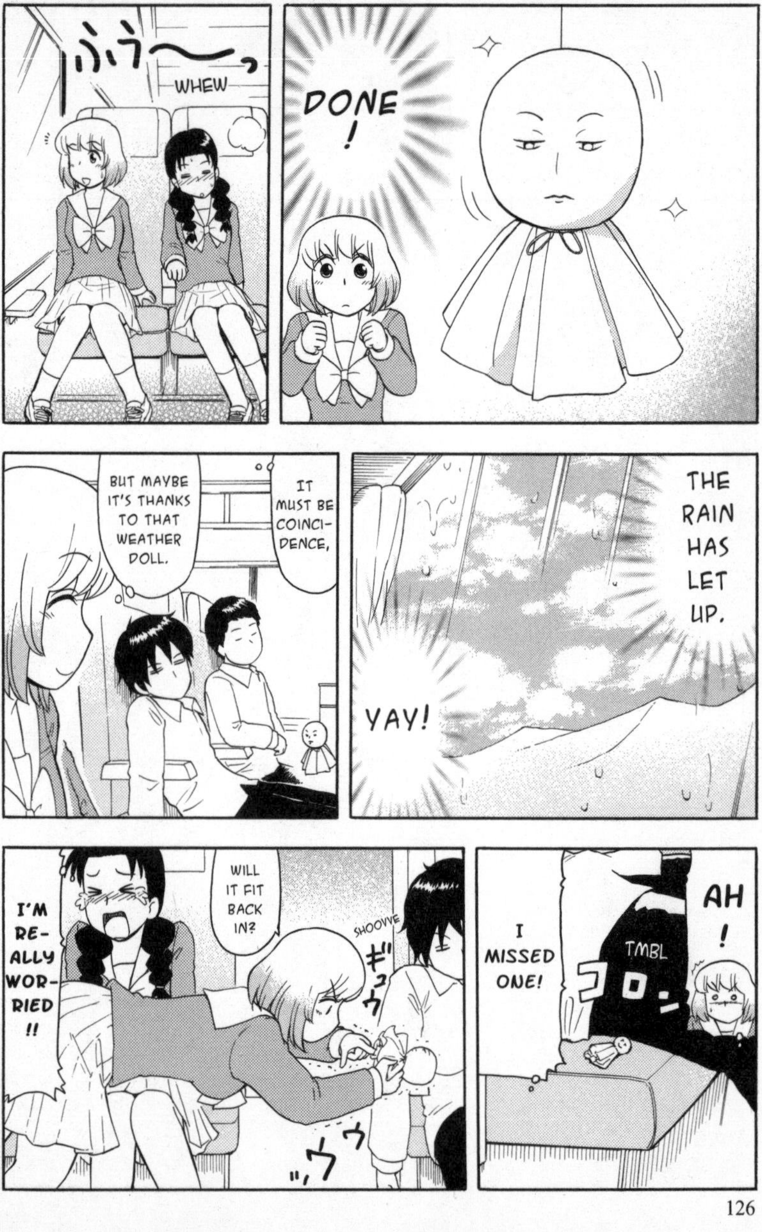
DONE!
ふう〜っ
WHEW
THE RAIN HAS LET UP.
YAY!
IT MUST BE COINCIDENCE,
BUT MAYBE IT'S THANKS TO THAT WEATHER DOLL.
AH!
I MISSED ONE!
コロン
TMBL
WILL IT FIT BACK IN?
ギュウウウッ
SHOOVVE
I'M REALLY WORRIED!!

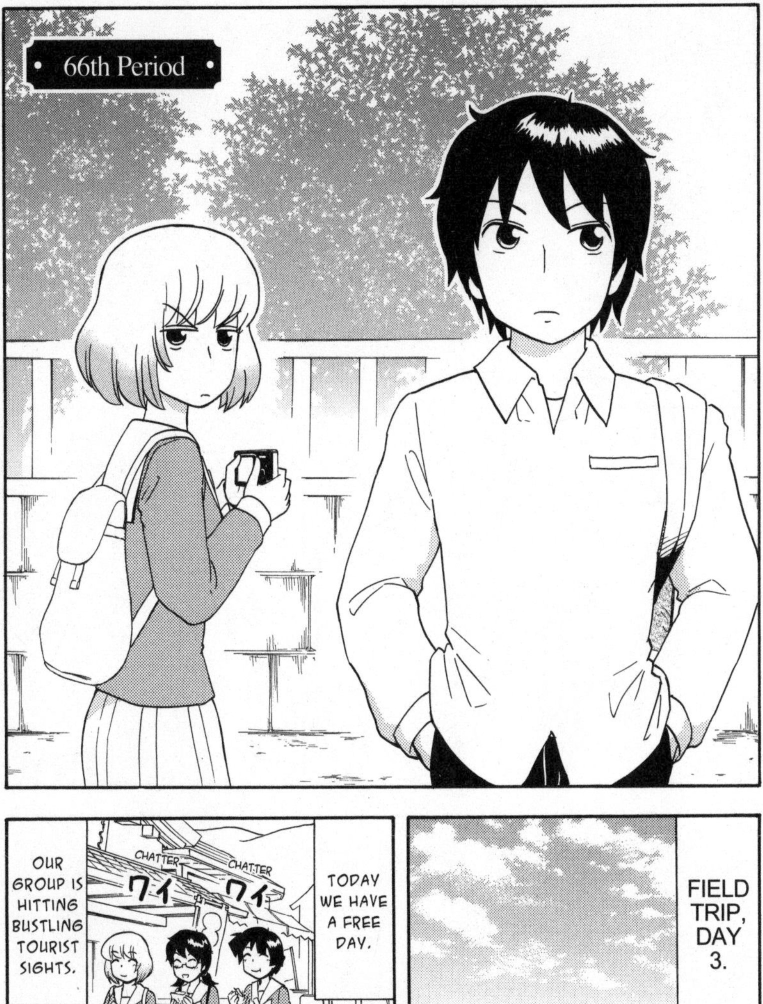
66th Period
FIELD TRIP, DAY 3.
TODAY WE HAVE A FREE DAY.
CHATTER
ワイ
CHATTER
ワイ
OUR GROUP IS HITTING BUSTLING TOURIST SIGHTS.

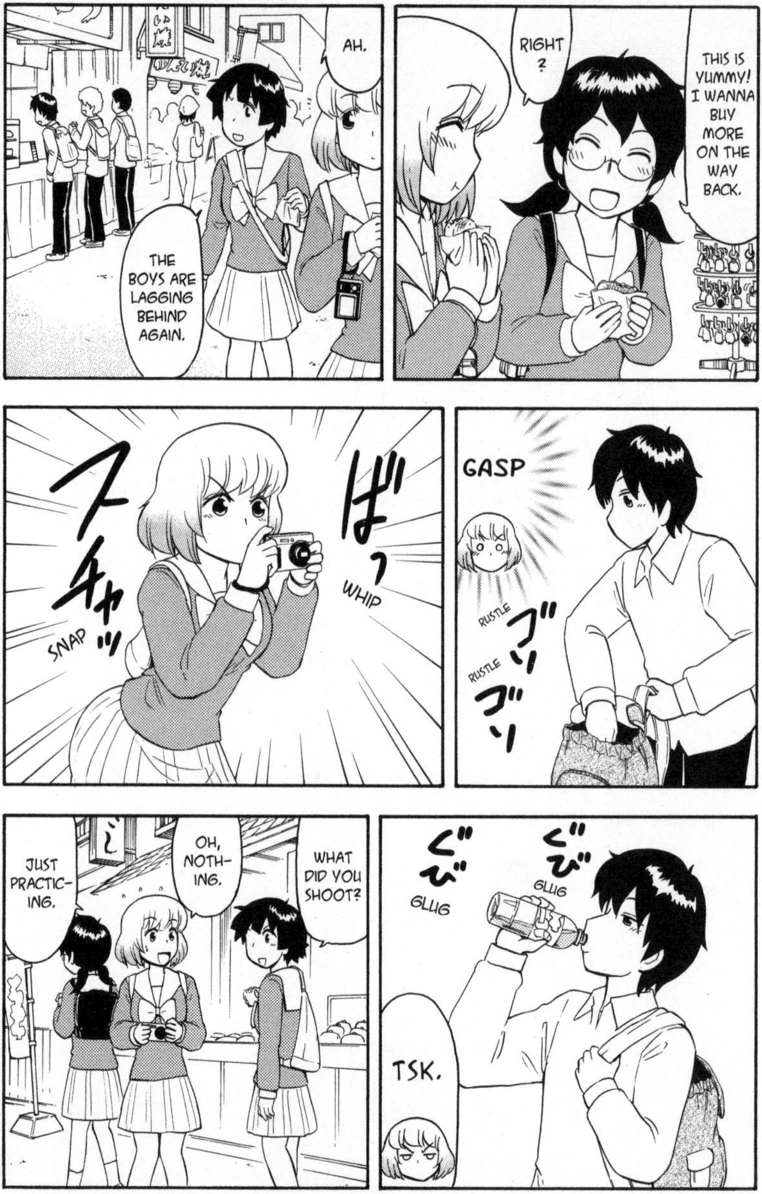
THIS IS YUMMY! I WANNA BUY MORE ON THE WAY BACK.
RIGHT?
AH.
THE BOYS ARE LAGGING BEHIND AGAIN.
GASP
ゴソ
RUSTLE
ゴソ
RUSTLE
ばっ
WHIP
スチャッ
SNAP
ぐび
GLUG
ぐび
GLUG
TSK.
WHAT DID YOU SHOOT?
OH, NOTHING.
JUST PRACTICING.

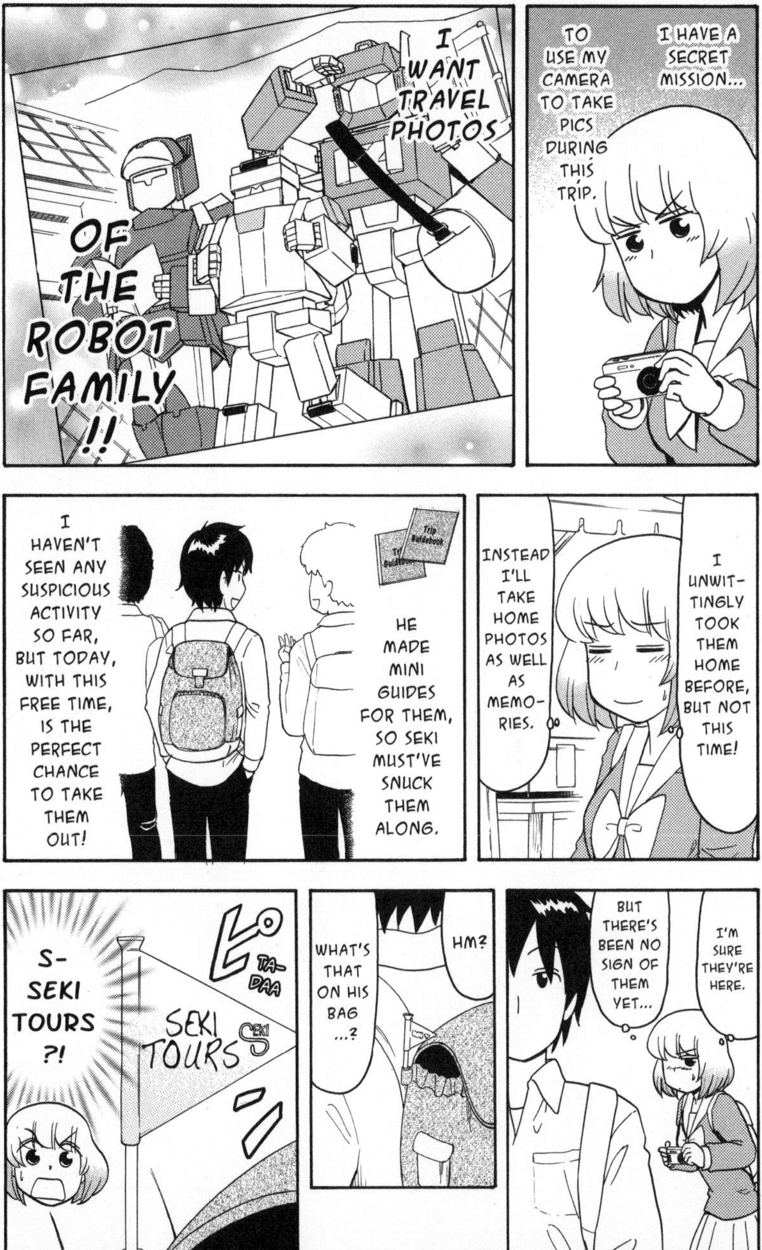
I HAVE A SECRET MISSION...
TO USE MY CAMERA TO TAKE PICS DURING THIS TRIP.
I WANT TRAVEL PHOTOS
OF THE ROBOT FAMILY !!
I UNWIT-TINGLY TOOK THEM HOME BEFORE, BUT NOT THIS TIME!
INSTEAD I'LL TAKE HOME PHOTOS AS WELL AS MEMO-RIES.
Trip Guidebook
Trip Guidebook
HE MADE MINI GUIDES FOR THEM, SO SEKI MUST'VE SNUCK THEM ALONG.
I HAVEN'T SEEN ANY SUSPICIOUS ACTIVITY SO FAR, BUT TODAY, WITH THIS FREE TIME, IS THE PERFECT CHANCE TO TAKE THEM OUT!
I'M SURE THEY'RE HERE.
BUT THERE'S BEEN NO SIGN OF THEM YET...
HM?
WHAT'S THAT ON HIS BAG ...?
TA-DAA
SEKI TOURS
SEKI
S-SEKI TOURS ?!

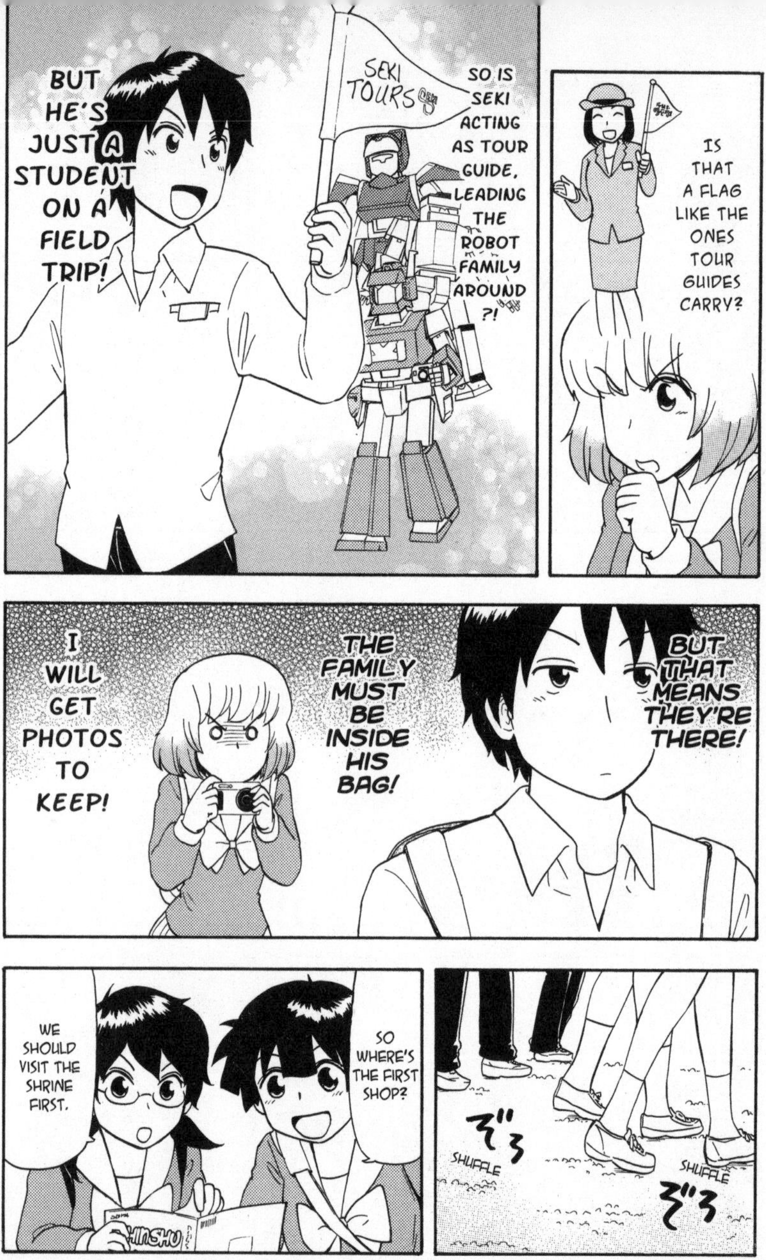
IS THAT A FLAG LIKE THE ONES TOUR GUIDES CARRY?
SO IS SEKI ACTING AS TOUR GUIDE, LEADING THE ROBOT FAMILY AROUND ?!
SEKI TOURS
BUT HE'S JUST A STUDENT ON A FIELD TRIP!
BUT THAT MEANS THEY'RE THERE!
THE FAMILY MUST BE INSIDE HIS BAG!
I WILL GET PHOTOS TO KEEP!
ぞろ
SHUFFLE
SHUFFLE
ぞろ
SO WHERE'S THE FIRST SHOP?
WE SHOULD VISIT THE SHRINE FIRST.
SHINSHU

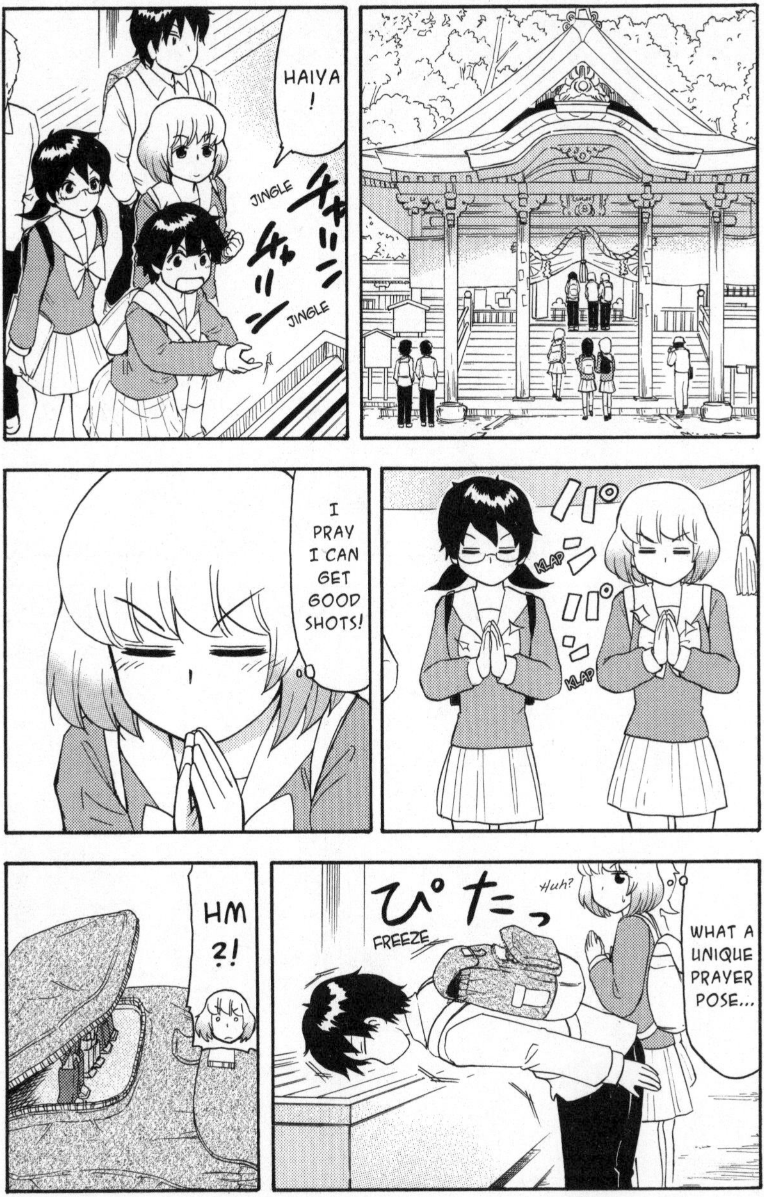
HAIYA !
JINGLE
チャリン
チャリン
JINGLE
パン
KLAP
パン
KLAP
I PRAY I CAN GET GOOD SHOTS!
ぴたっ
FREEZE
Huh?
WHAT A UNIQUE PRAYER POSE...
HM ?!

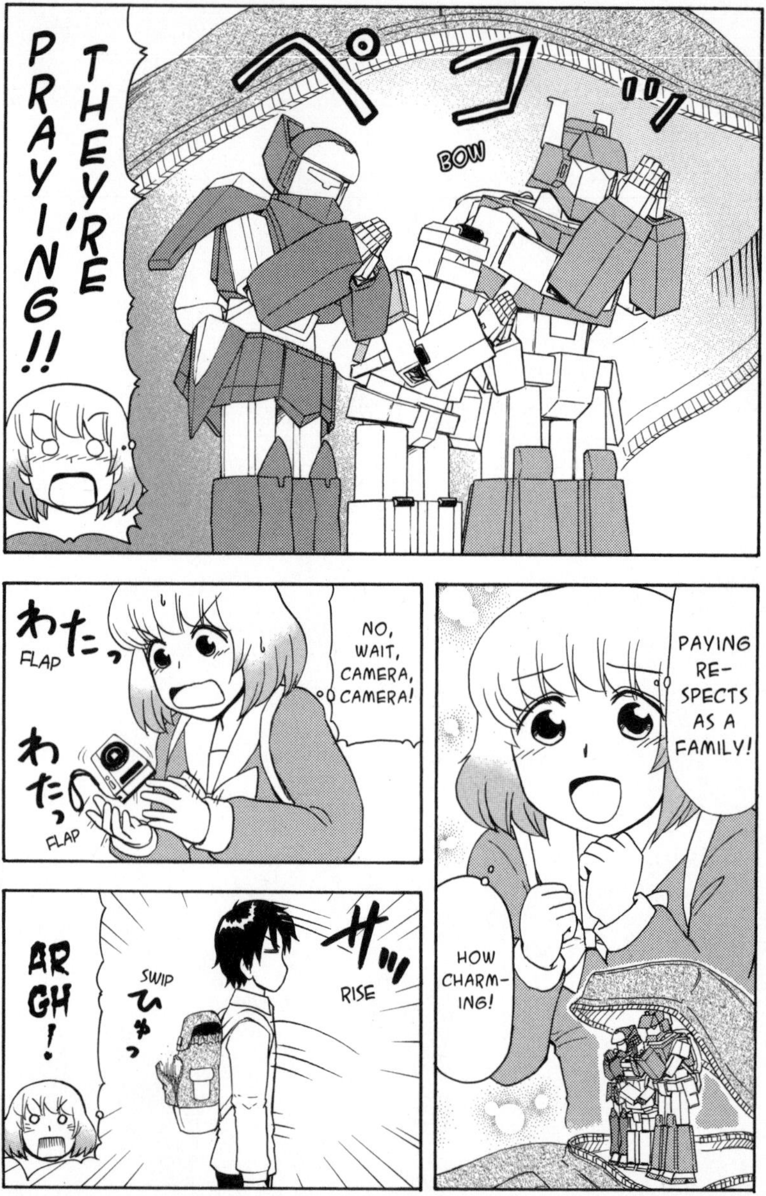

ペコッ
BOW
THEY'RE PRAYING!!
PAYING RE-SPECTS AS A FAMILY!
HOW CHARM-ING!
NO, WAIT, CAMERA, CAMERA!
わたっ
FLAP
わたっ
FLAP
ザッ
RISE
ひゅっ
SWIP
ARGH!

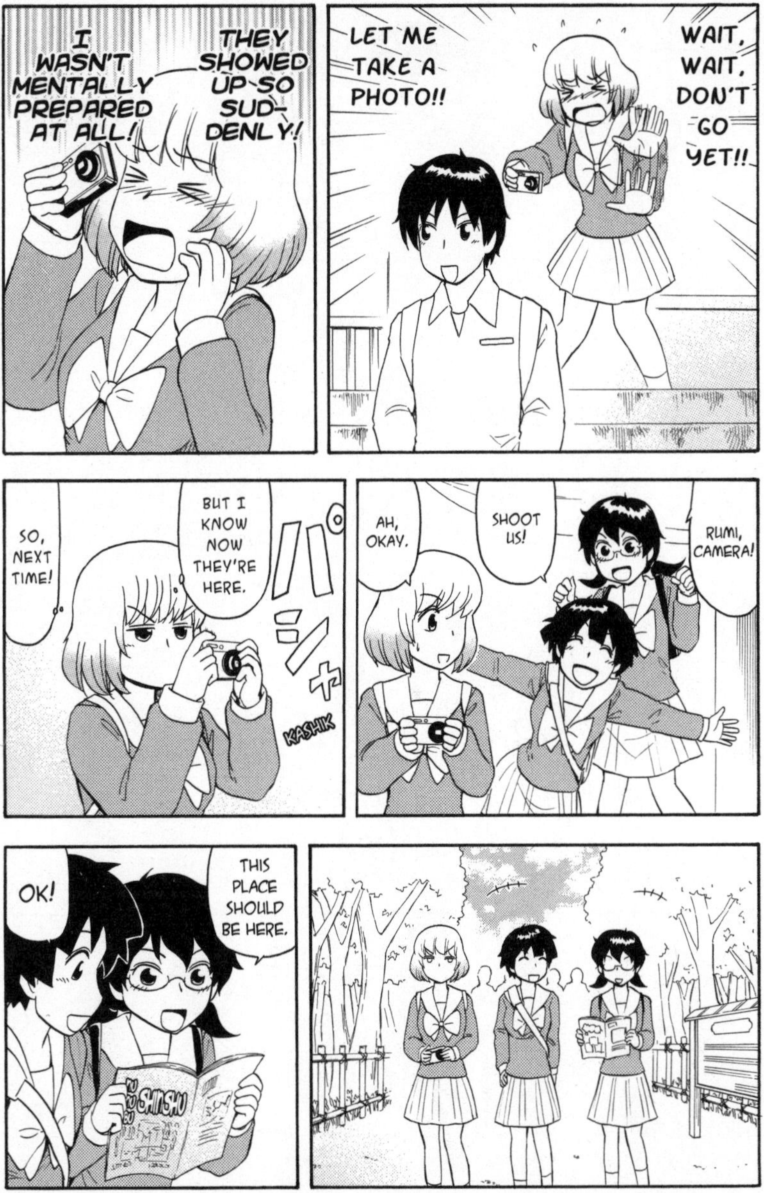
WAIT, WAIT, DON'T GO YET!!
LET ME TAKE A PHOTO!!
THEY SHOWED UP SO SUD-DENLY!
I WASN'T MENTALLY PREPARED AT ALL!
RUMI, CAMERA!
SHOOT US!
AH, OKAY.
BUT I KNOW NOW THEY'RE HERE.
パシャ
KASHIK
SO, NEXT TIME!
THIS PLACE SHOULD BE HERE.
OK!
SHINSHU

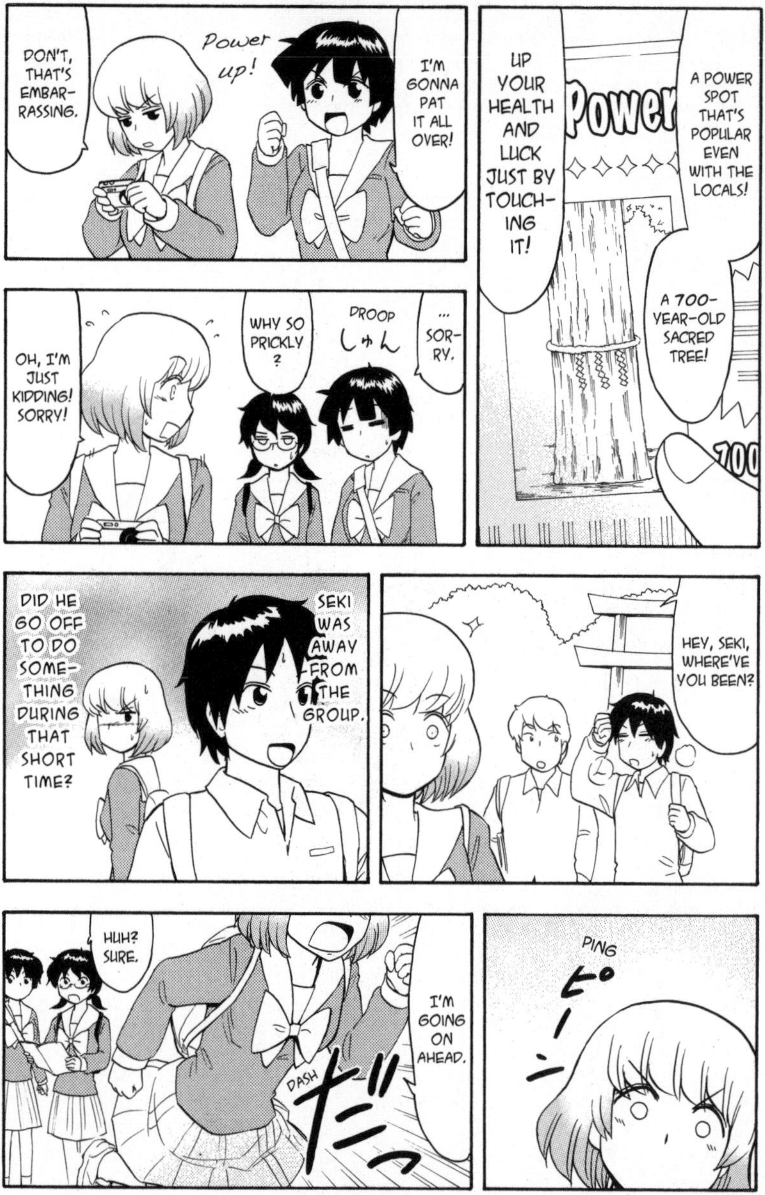
A POWER SPOT THAT'S POPULAR EVEN WITH THE LOCALS!
UP YOUR HEALTH AND LUCK JUST BY TOUCHING IT!
Power
A 700-YEAR-OLD SACRED TREE!
700
I'M GONNA PAT IT ALL OVER!
Power up!
DON'T, THAT'S EMBARRASSING.
... SORRY.
DROOP
しゅん
WHY SO PRICKLY?
OH, I'M JUST KIDDING! SORRY!
HEY, SEKI, WHERE'VE YOU BEEN?
SEKI WAS AWAY FROM THE GROUP.
DID HE GO OFF TO DO SOMETHING DURING THAT SHORT TIME?
PING
ピーン
I'M GOING ON AHEAD.
DASH
ダッ
HUH? SURE.

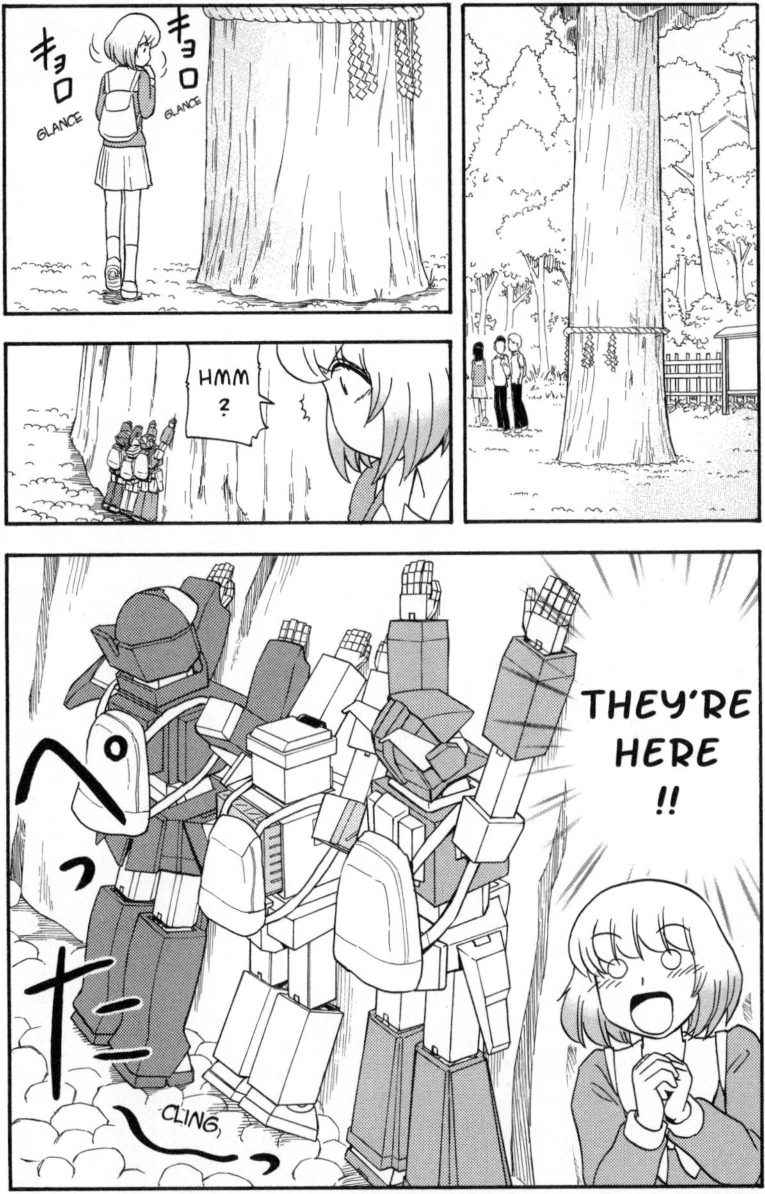
キョロ
GLANCE
キョロ
GLANCE
HMM ?
THEY'RE HERE !!
ぺった〜っ
CLING,

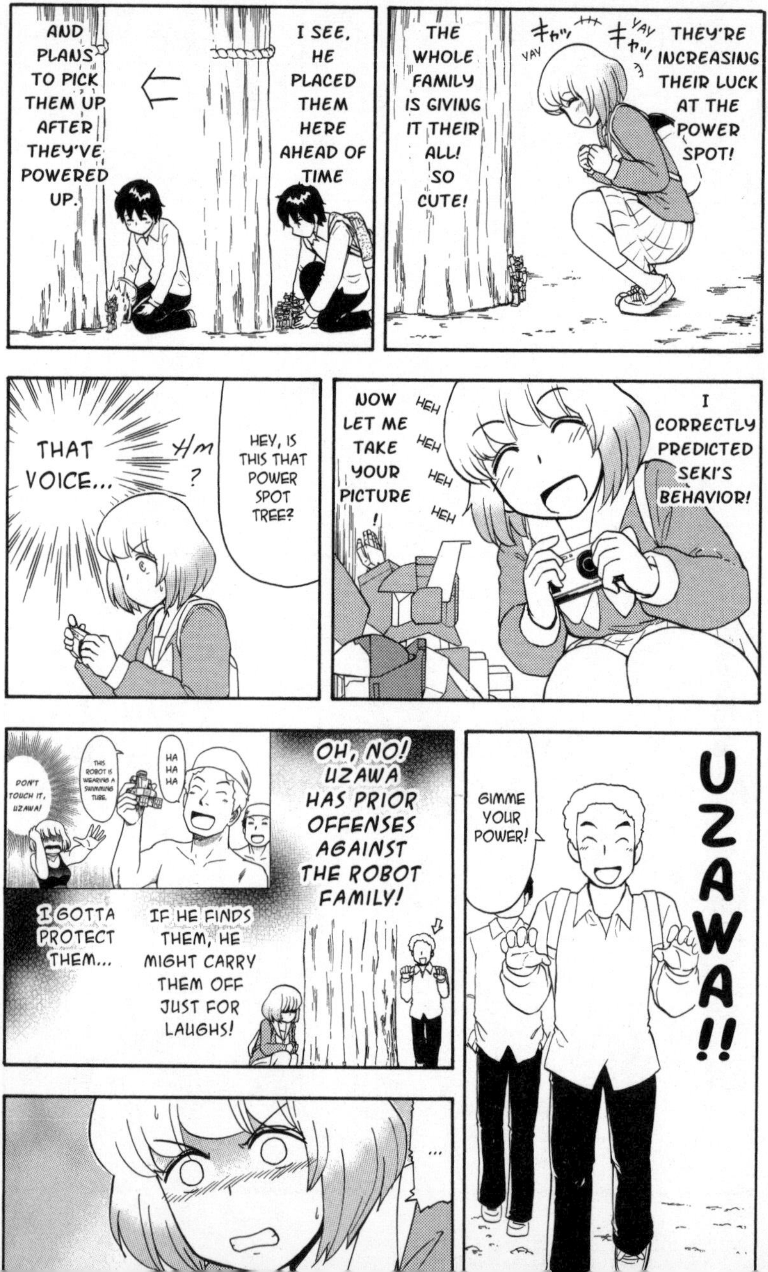
THEY'RE INCREASING THEIR LUCK AT THE POWER SPOT!
キャッ キャッ
YAY YAY
THE WHOLE FAMILY IS GIVING IT THEIR ALL! SO CUTE!
I SEE, HE PLACED THEM HERE AHEAD OF TIME
AND PLANS TO PICK THEM UP AFTER THEY'VE POWERED UP.
I CORRECTLY PREDICTED SEKI'S BEHAVIOR!
HEH HEH HEH HEH
NOW LET ME TAKE YOUR PICTURE!
HEY, IS THIS THAT POWER SPOT TREE?
Hm?
THAT VOICE...
UZAWA!!
GIMME YOUR POWER!
OH, NO! UZAWA HAS PRIOR OFFENSES AGAINST THE ROBOT FAMILY!
HA HA HA
THIS ROBOT IS WEARING A SWIMMING TUBE.
DON'T TOUCH IT, UZAWA!
IF HE FINDS THEM, HE MIGHT CARRY THEM OFF JUST FOR LAUGHS!
I GOTTA PROTECT THEM...
...

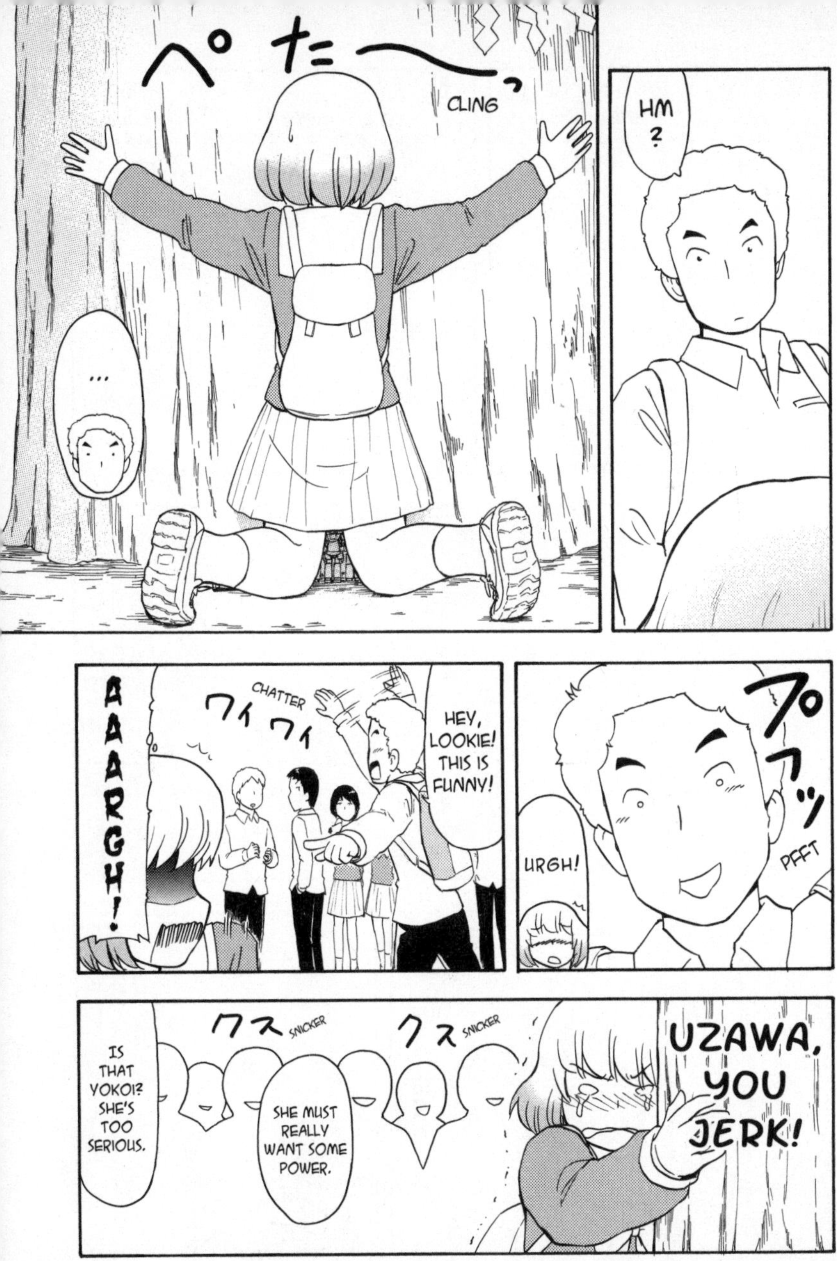
HM?
ぺたーっ
CLING
...
プフッ
PFFT
URGH!
HEY, LOOKIE! THIS IS FUNNY!
ワイワイ
CHATTER
AAAARGH!
UZAWA, YOU JERK!
クス
SNICKER
クス
SNICKER
SHE MUST REALLY WANT SOME POWER.
IS THAT YOKOI? SHE'S TOO SERIOUS.

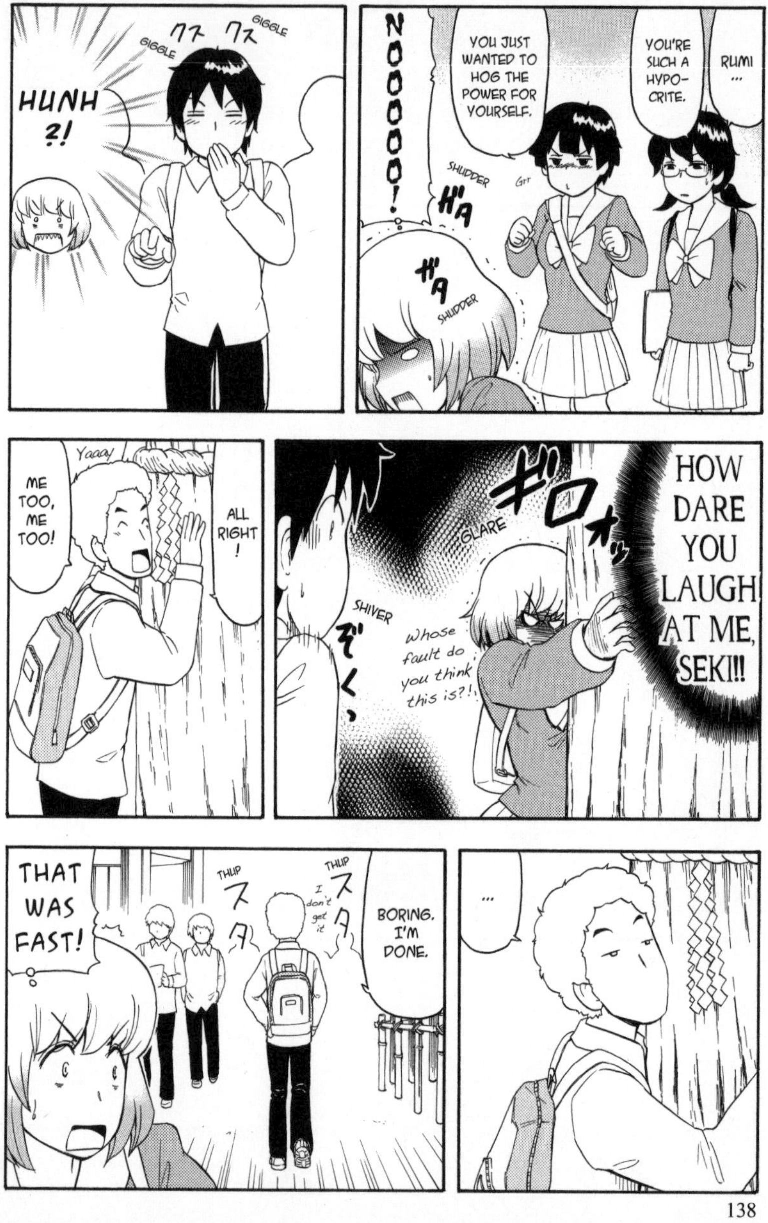
RUMI ...
YOU'RE SUCH A HYPO-CRITE.
YOU JUST WANTED TO HOG THE POWER FOR YOURSELF.
Grr
NOOOOOO!
SHUDDER
ガタ
SHUDDER
ガタ
GIGGLE
クス クス
GIGGLE
HUNH ?!
HOW DARE YOU LAUGH AT ME, SEKI!!
ギロォッ
GLARE
Whose fault do you think this is?!
SHIVER
ぞくっ
ALL RIGHT!
Yaaay
ME TOO, ME TOO!
...
BORING. I'M DONE.
THUP
スタ
I don't get it
THUP
スタ
THAT WAS FAST!

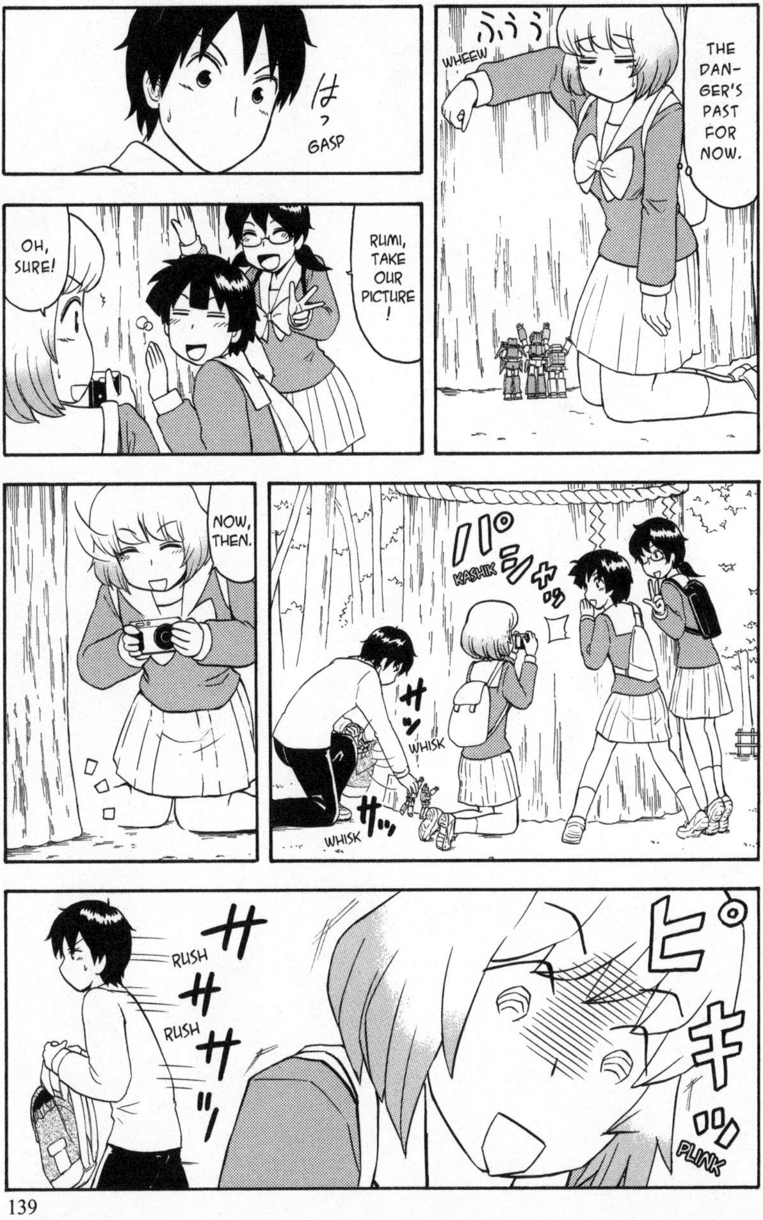

THE DAN-GER'S PAST FOR NOW.
ふうう
WHEEW
はっ
GASP
RUMI, TAKE OUR PICTURE!
OH, SURE!
パシャッ
KASHIK
サッ
WHISK
サッ
WHISK
NOW, THEN.
ピキーン
PLINK
ササササッ
RUSH
RUSH

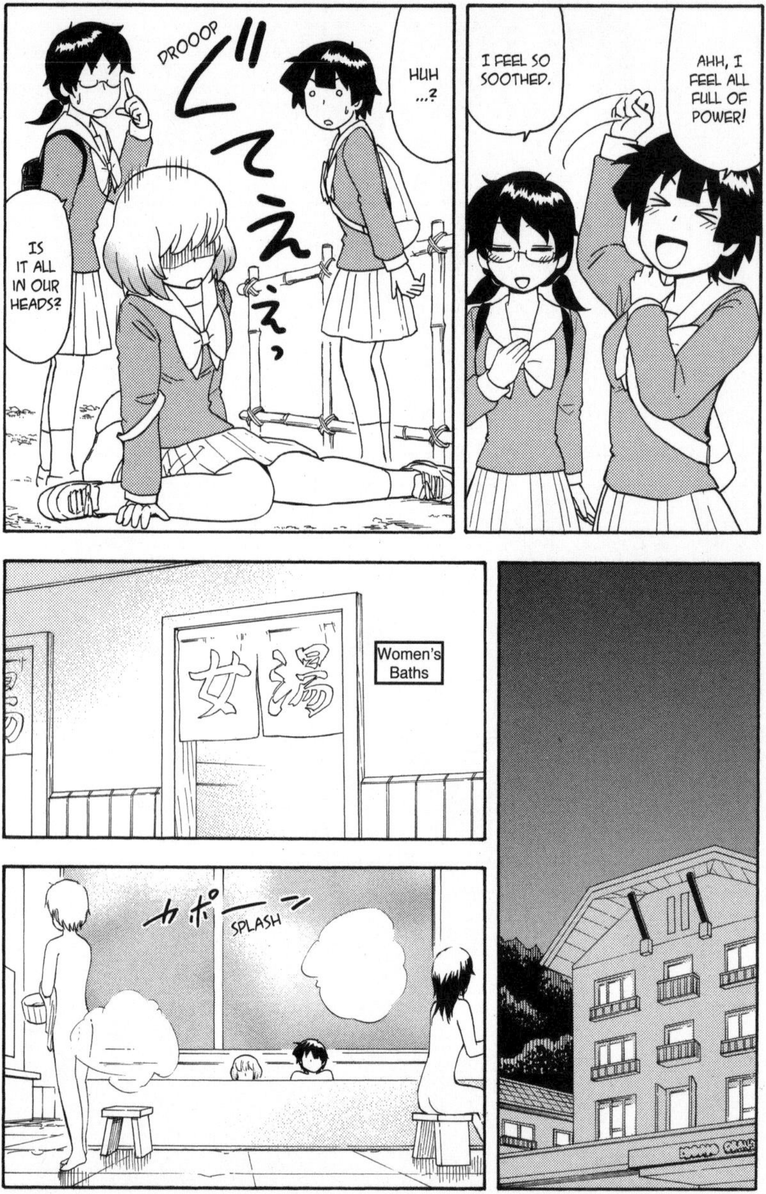
AHH, I FEEL ALL FULL OF POWER!
I FEEL SO SOOTHED.
HUH ...?
ぐてえぇ
DROOOP
IS IT ALL IN OUR HEADS?
女湯
Women's Baths
カポーン
SPLASH

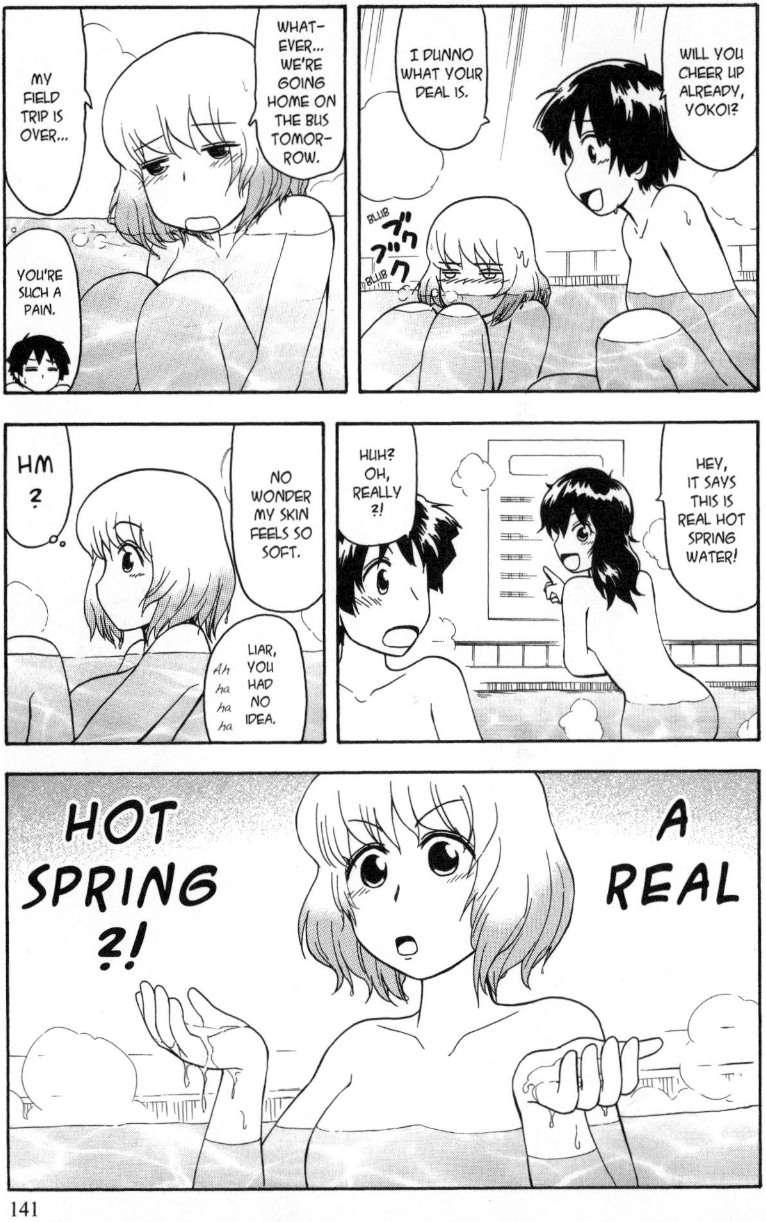
WILL YOU CHEER UP ALREADY, YOKOI?
I DUNNO WHAT YOUR DEAL IS.
BLUB BLUB
WHATEVER... WE'RE GOING HOME ON THE BUS TOMORROW.
MY FIELD TRIP IS OVER...
YOU'RE SUCH A PAIN.
HEY, IT SAYS THIS IS REAL HOT SPRING WATER!
HUH? OH, REALLY?!
NO WONDER MY SKIN FEELS SO SOFT.
HM?
LIAR, YOU HAD NO IDEA.
Ah ha ha ha
A REAL HOT SPRING?!

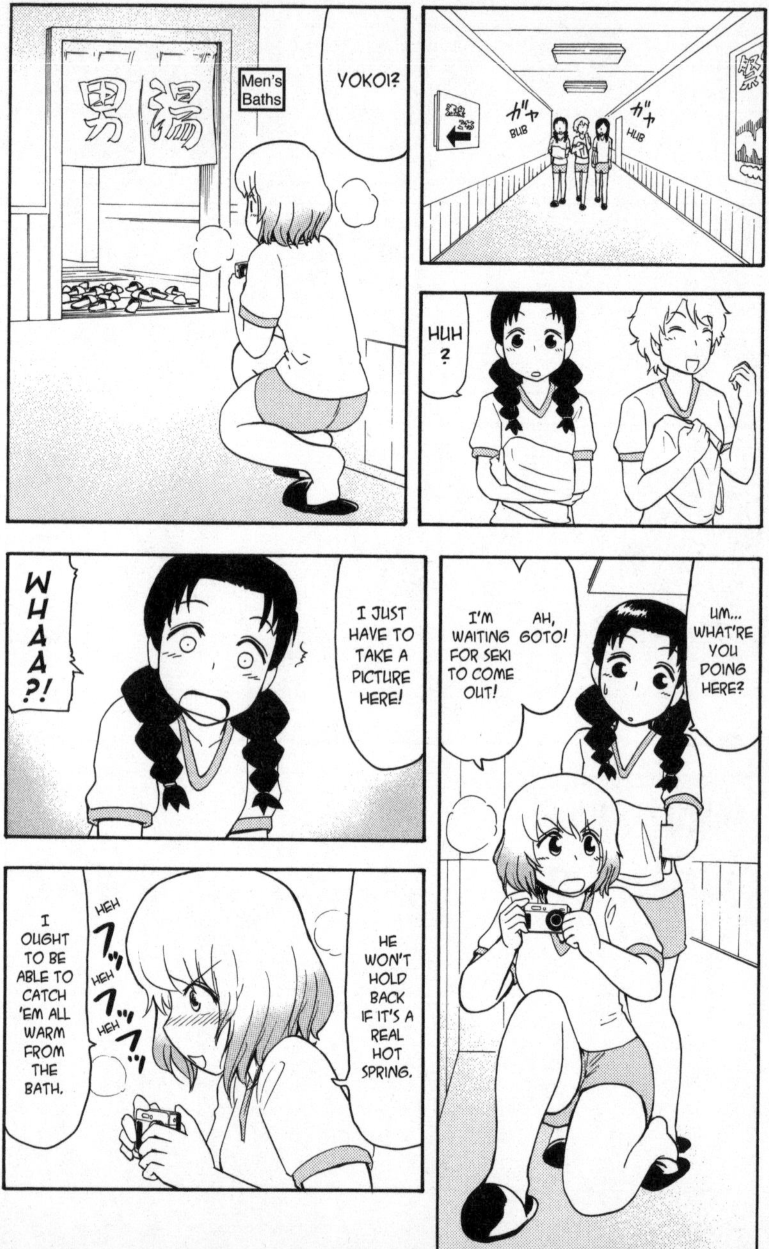
ガヤ
BUB
ガヤ
HUB
HUH?
YOKOI!?
男湯
Men's Baths
UM... WHAT'RE YOU DOING HERE?
AH, GOTO!
I'M WAITING FOR SEKI TO COME OUT!
I JUST HAVE TO TAKE A PICTURE HERE!
WHAAA?!
HE WON'T HOLD BACK IF IT'S A REAL HOT SPRING.
HEH
フッ
HEH
フッ
HEH
フッ
I OUGHT TO BE ABLE TO CATCH 'EM ALL WARM FROM THE BATH.

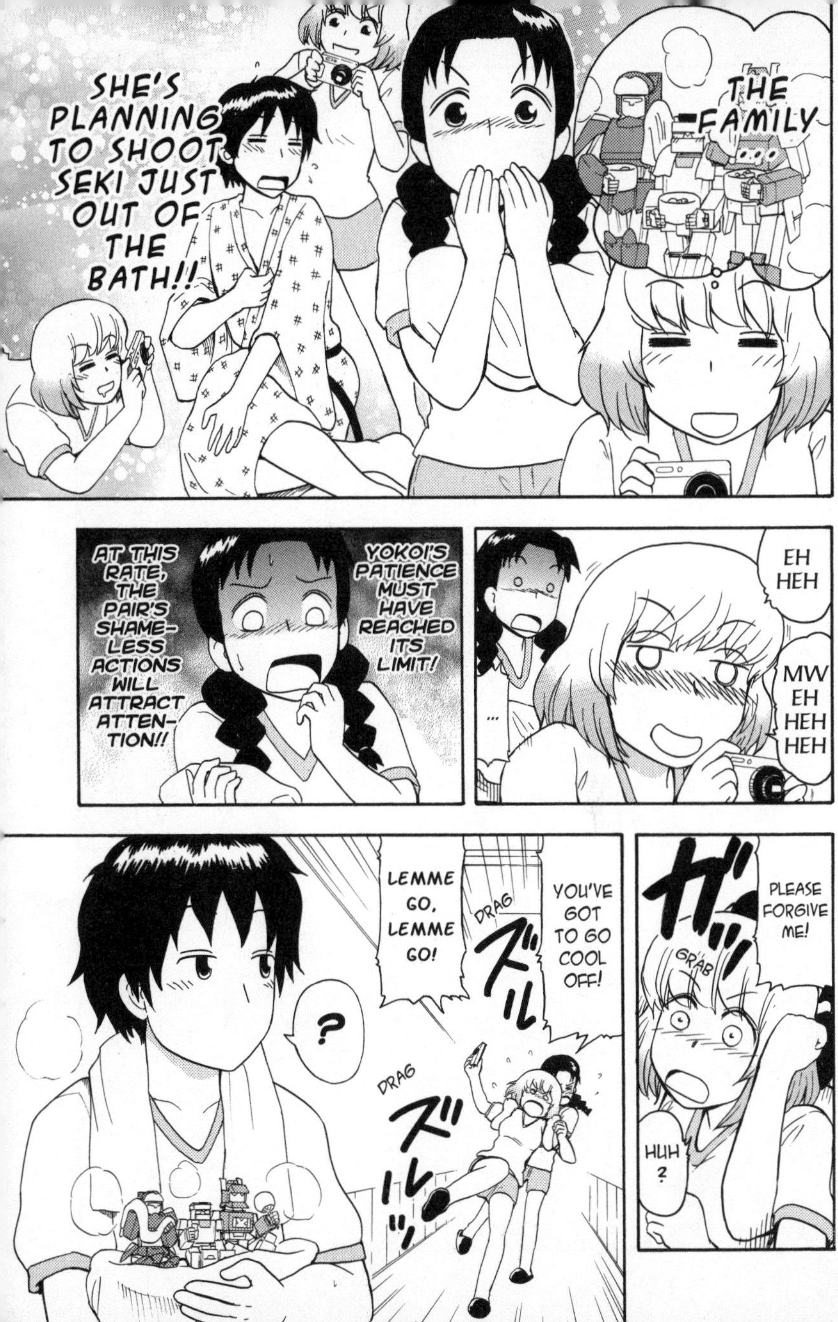
THE FAMILY
SHE'S PLANNING TO SHOOT SEKI JUST OUT OF THE BATH!!
EH HEH
MW EH HEH HEH HEH
...
YOKOI'S PATIENCE MUST HAVE REACHED ITS LIMIT!
AT THIS RATE, THE PAIR'S SHAME-LESS ACTIONS WILL ATTRACT ATTEN-TION!!
ガッ
PLEASE FORGIVE ME!
GRAB
HUH?
YOU'VE GOT TO GO COOL OFF!
LEMME GO, LEMME GO!
DRAG
ズル
DRAG
ズルッ
?

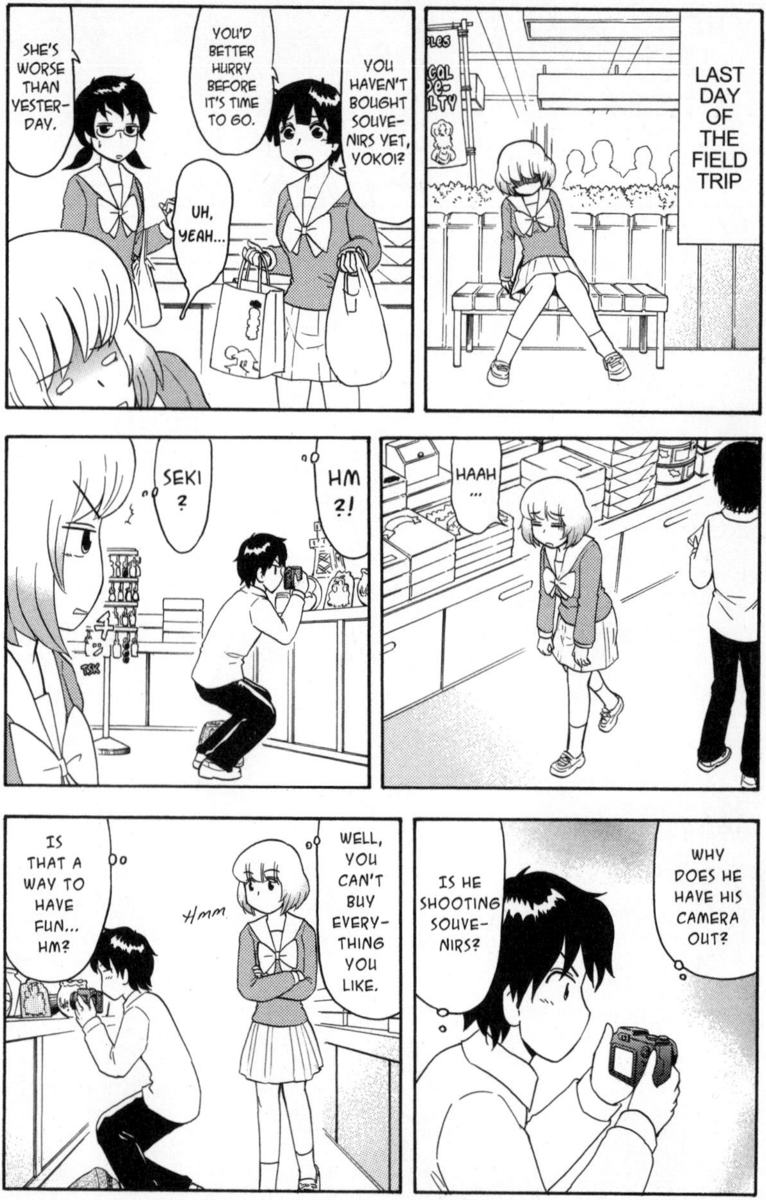
LAST DAY OF THE FIELD TRIP
YOU HAVEN'T BOUGHT SOUVE-NIRS YET, YOKOI?
YOU'D BETTER HURRY BEFORE IT'S TIME TO GO.
UH, YEAH...
SHE'S WORSE THAN YESTER-DAY.
HAAH ...
HM ?!
SEKI ?
TSK
WHY DOES HE HAVE HIS CAMERA OUT?
IS HE SHOOTING SOUVE-NIRS?
WELL, YOU CAN'T BUY EVERY-THING YOU LIKE.
Hmm
IS THAT A WAY TO HAVE FUN... HM?

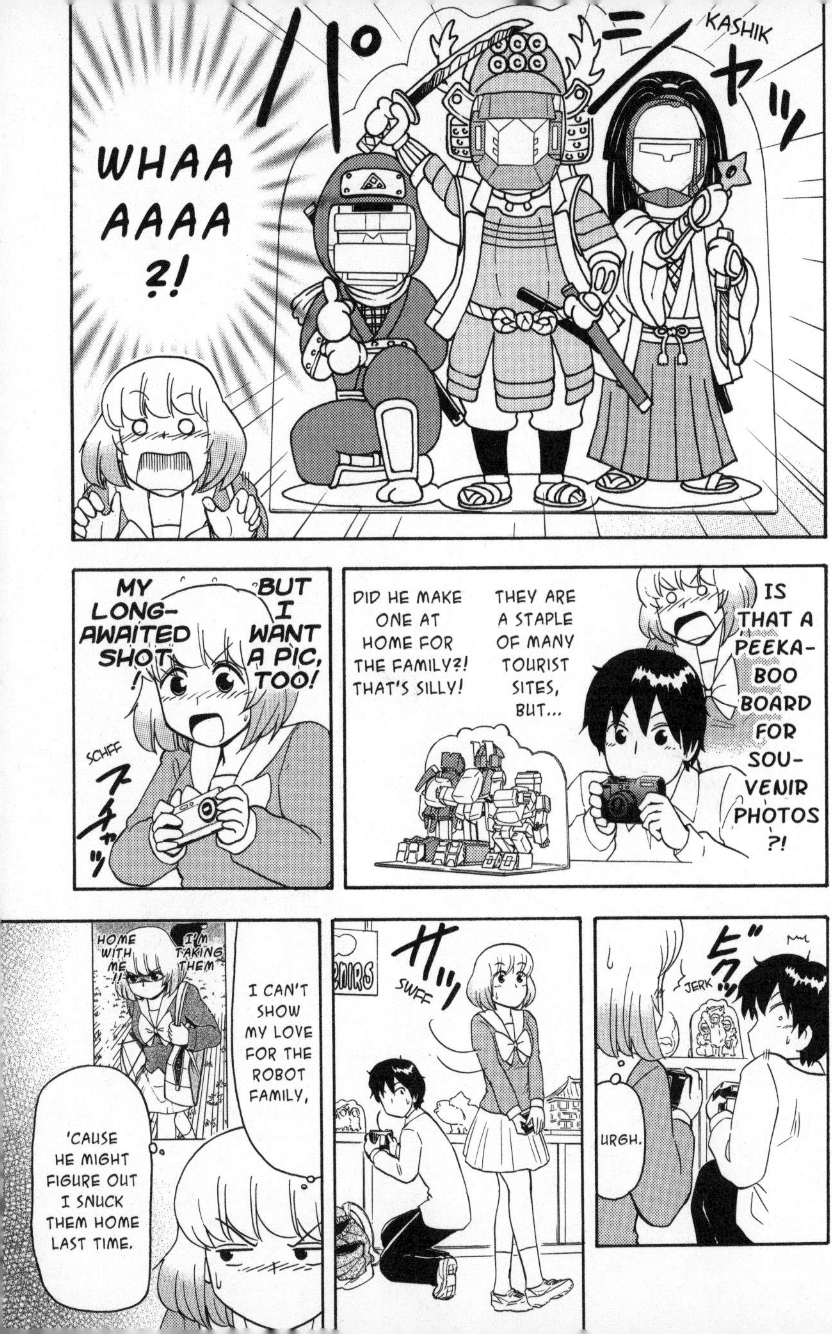
KASHIK
WHAA AAAA ?!
IS THAT A PEEKA-BOO BOARD FOR SOU-VENIR PHOTOS ?!
THEY ARE A STAPLE OF MANY TOURIST SITES, BUT...
DID HE MAKE ONE AT HOME FOR THE FAMILY?! THAT'S SILLY!
BUT I WANT A PIC, TOO!
MY LONG-AWAITED SHOT!
SCHFF
JERK
URGH.
SWFF
I CAN'T SHOW MY LOVE FOR THE ROBOT FAMILY,
'CAUSE HE MIGHT FIGURE OUT I SNUCK THEM HOME LAST TIME.
I'M TAKING THEM HOME WITH ME!!

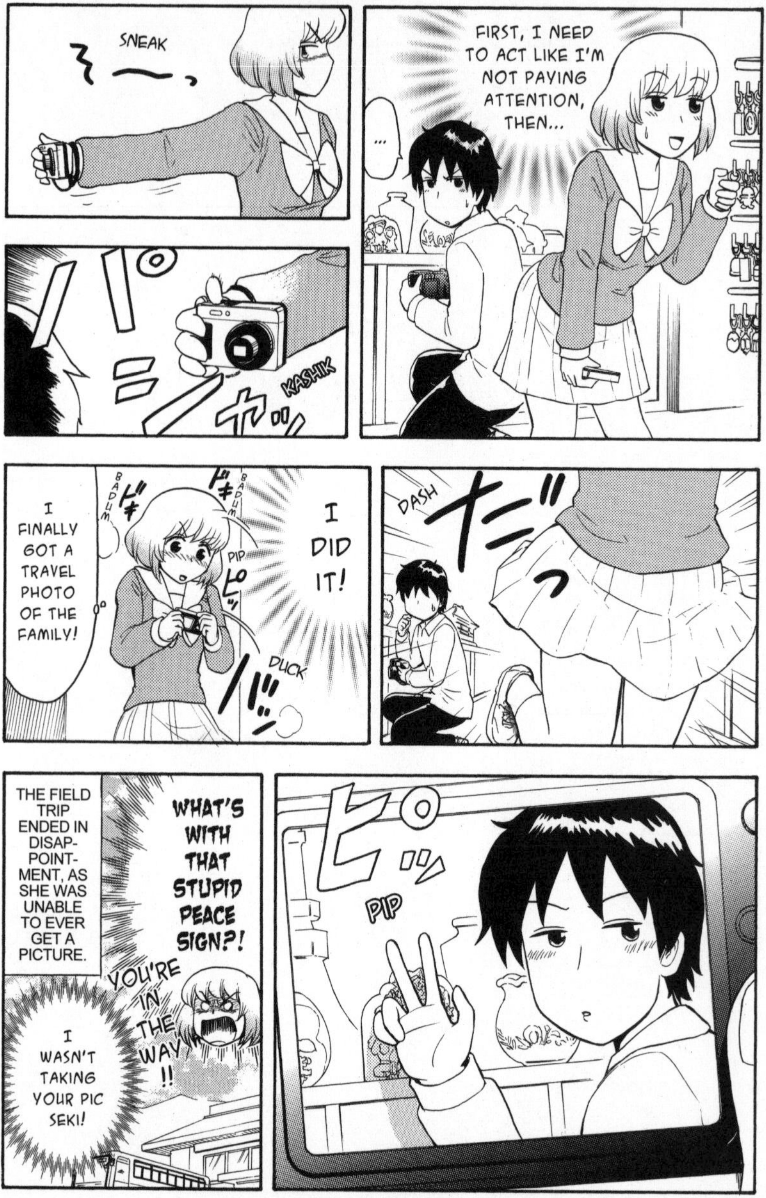

FIRST, I NEED TO ACT LIKE I'M NOT PAYING ATTENTION, THEN...
...
SNEAK
KASHIK
DASH
I DID IT!
BADUM
BADUM
PIP
I FINALLY GOT A TRAVEL PHOTO OF THE FAMILY!
DUCK
PIP
WHAT'S WITH THAT STUPID PEACE SIGN?!
THE FIELD TRIP ENDED IN DISAPPOINTMENT, AS SHE WAS UNABLE TO EVER GET A PICTURE.
YOU'RE IN THE WAY!!
I WASN'T TAKING YOUR PIC SEKI!

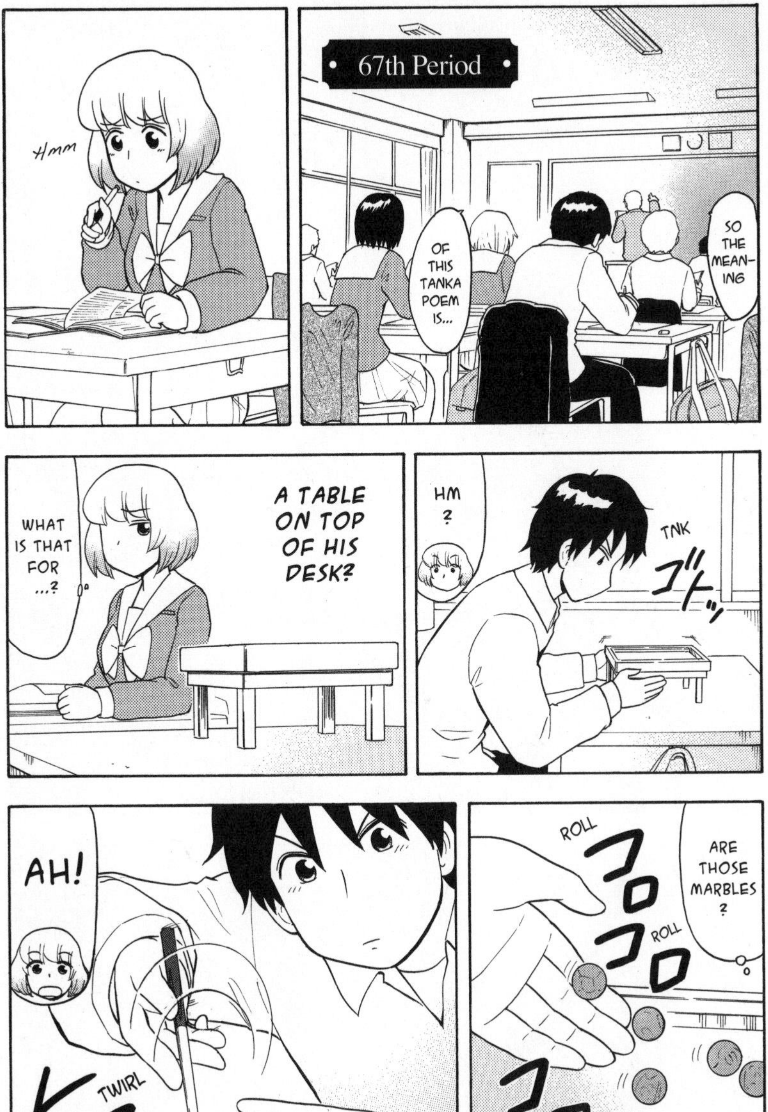

• 67th Period •
SO THE MEAN-ING
OF THIS TANKA POEM IS...
HMM
HM ?
TNK
ゴトッ
A TABLE ON TOP OF HIS DESK?
WHAT IS THAT FOR ...?
ARE THOSE MARBLES ?
ROLL
コロ
ROLL
コロ
ROLL
コローン
AH!
TWIRL
ヒュン

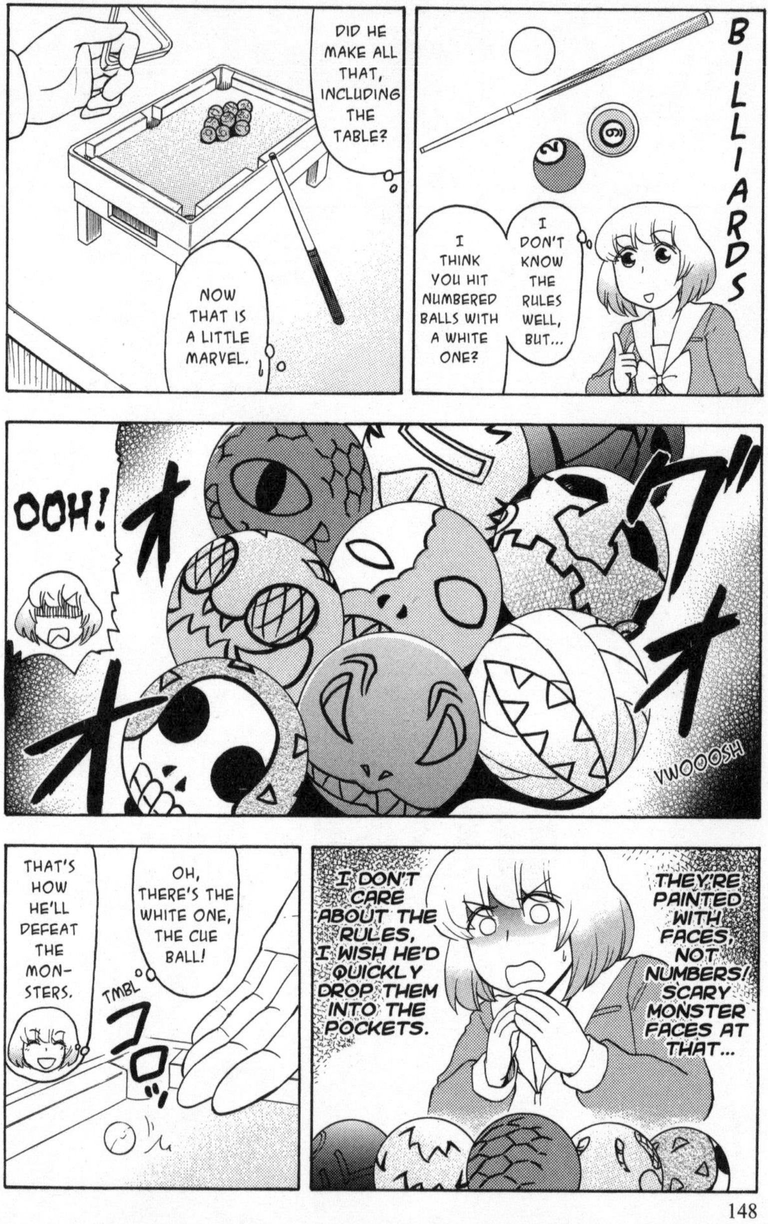
BILLIARDS
I DON'T KNOW THE RULES WELL, BUT...
I THINK YOU HIT NUMBERED BALLS WITH A WHITE ONE?
DID HE MAKE ALL THAT, INCLUDING THE TABLE?
NOW THAT IS A LITTLE MARVEL.
VWOOOSH
OOH!
THEY'RE PAINTED WITH FACES, NOT NUMBERS! SCARY MONSTER FACES AT THAT...
I DON'T CARE ABOUT THE RULES, I WISH HE'D QUICKLY DROP THEM INTO THE POCKETS.
OH, THERE'S THE WHITE ONE, THE CUE BALL!
THAT'S HOW HE'LL DEFEAT THE MON-STERS.
TMBL

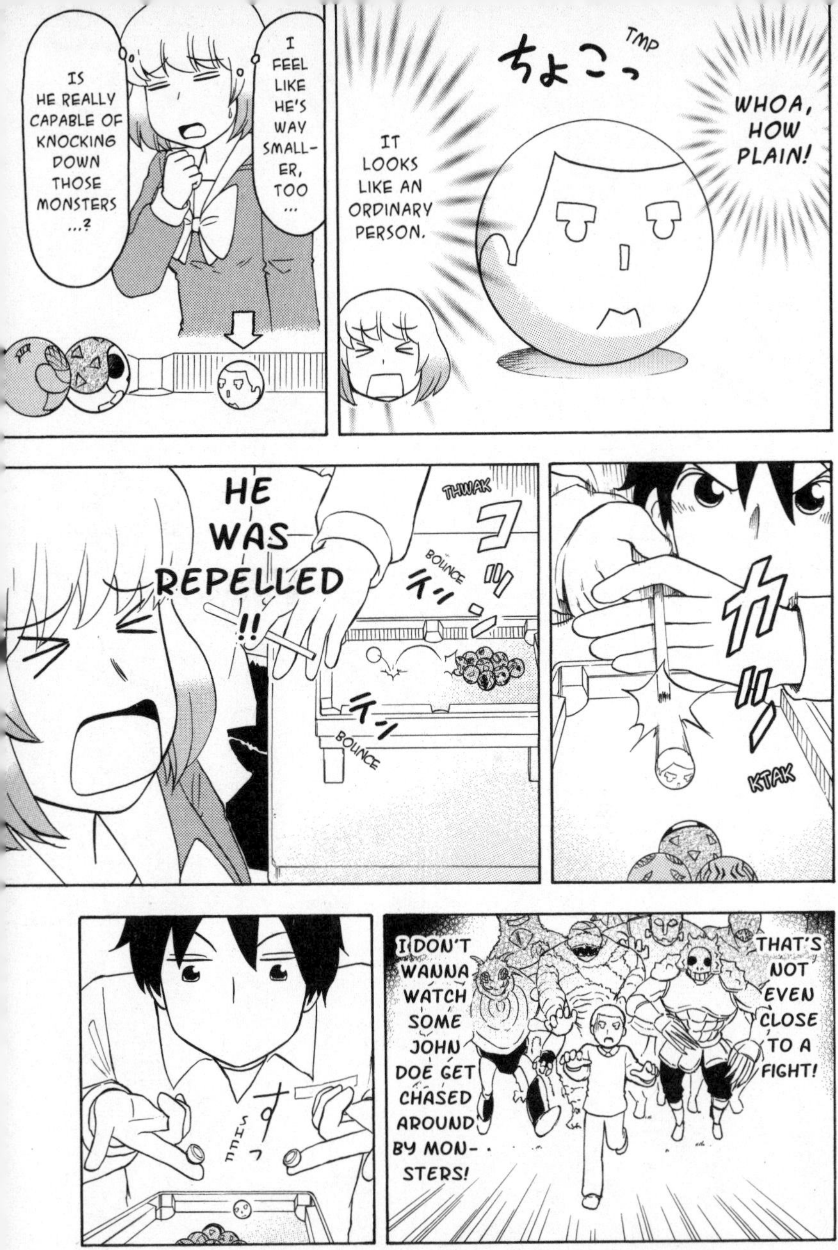
ちょこっ
TMP
WHOA, HOW PLAIN!
IT LOOKS LIKE AN ORDINARY PERSON.
I FEEL LIKE HE'S WAY SMALLER, TOO ...
IS HE REALLY CAPABLE OF KNOCKING DOWN THOSE MONSTERS ...?
カッ
KTAK
THWAK
コツン
BOUNCE
テン
テン
BOUNCE
HE WAS REPELLED!!
THAT'S NOT EVEN CLOSE TO A FIGHT!
I DON'T WANNA WATCH SOME JOHN DOE GET CHASED AROUND BY MONSTERS!
SHFF

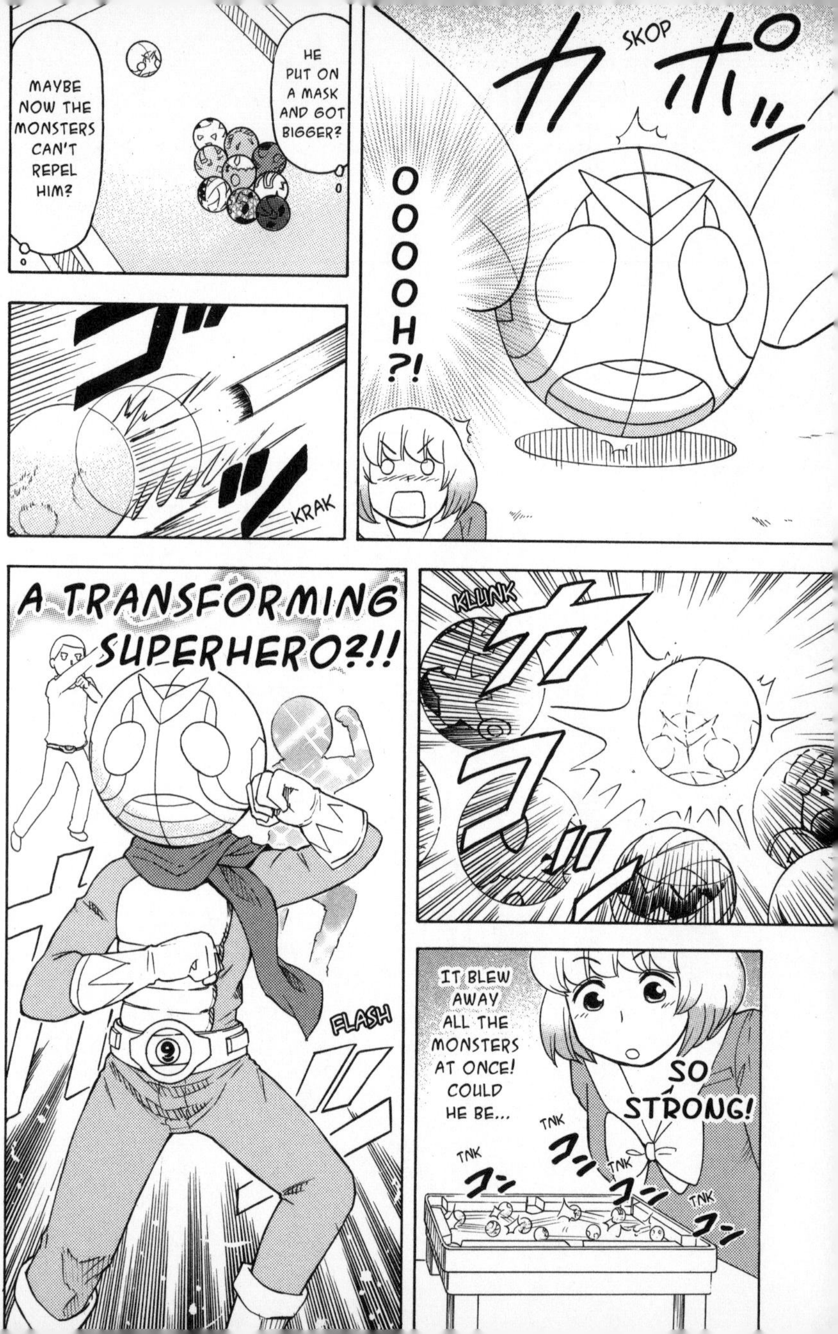
SKOP
カポッ
OOOOOH?!
HE PUT ON A MASK AND GOT BIGGER?
MAYBE NOW THE MONSTERS CAN'T REPEL HIM?
ゴッ
KRAK
KLUNK
カコッ
IT BLEW AWAY ALL THE MONSTERS AT ONCE! COULD HE BE...
SO STRONG!
TNK
コン
TNK
コン
TNK
コン
TNK
コン
A TRANSFORMING SUPERHERO?!!
FLASH

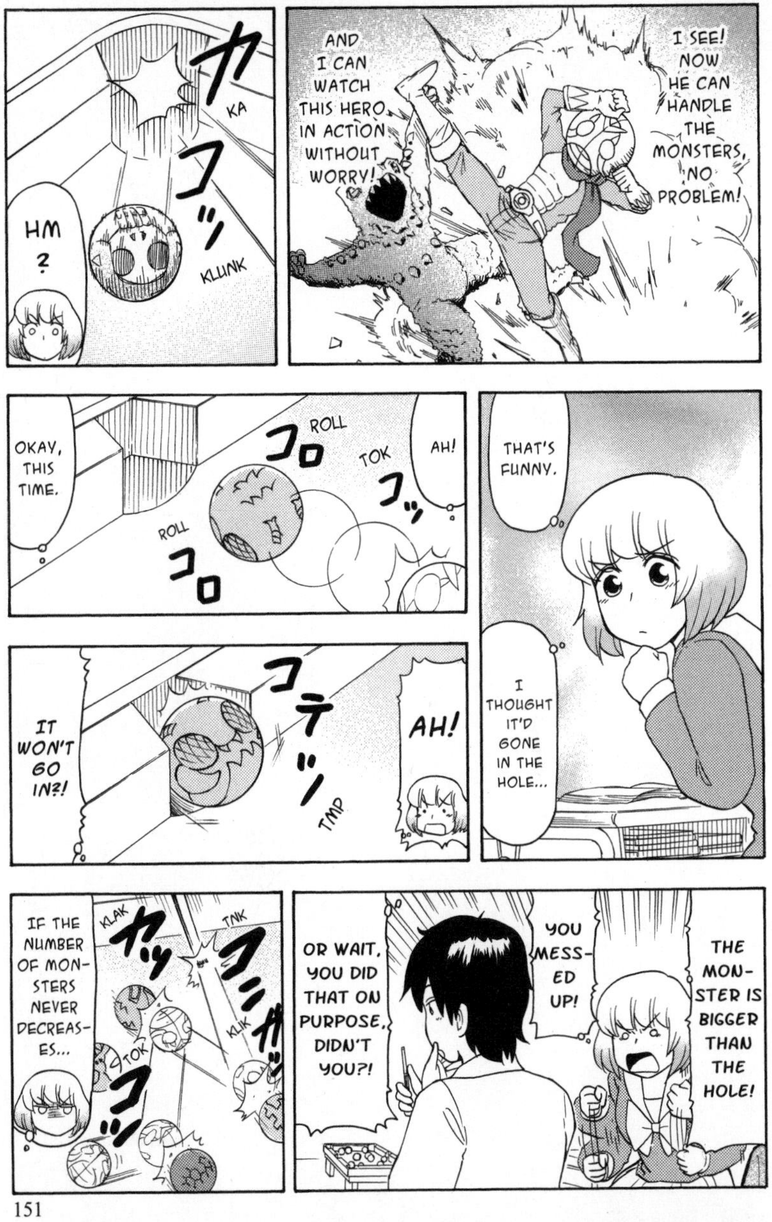
I SEE! NOW HE CAN HANDLE THE MONSTERS, NO PROBLEM!
AND I CAN WATCH THIS HERO IN ACTION WITHOUT WORRY!
KA
KLUNK
HM?
THAT'S FUNNY.
I THOUGHT IT'D GONE IN THE HOLE...
AH!
ROLL
TOK
ROLL
OKAY, THIS TIME.
AH!
TMP
IT WON'T GO IN?!
THE MONSTER IS BIGGER THAN THE HOLE!
YOU MESSED UP!
OR WAIT, YOU DID THAT ON PURPOSE, DIDN'T YOU?!
TNK
KLIK
KLAK
TOK
IF THE NUMBER OF MONSTERS NEVER DECREASES...

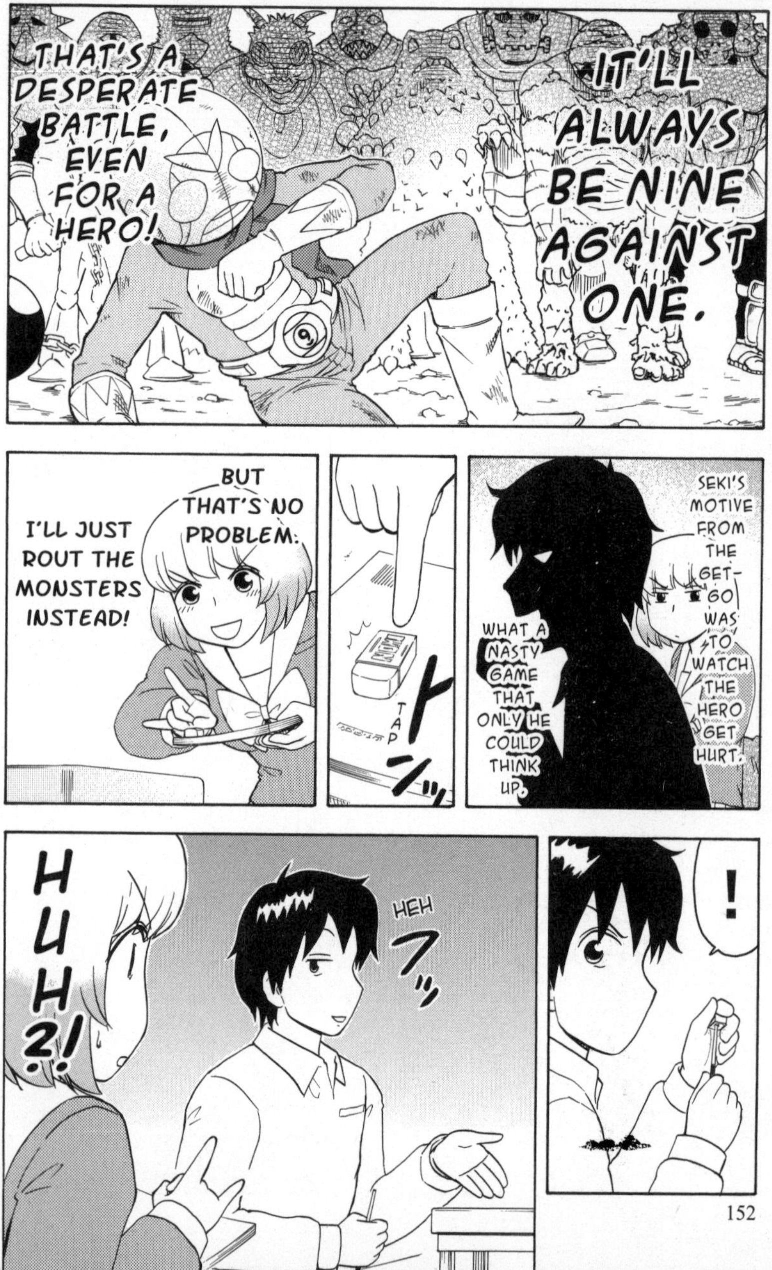
IT'LL ALWAYS BE NINE AGAINST ONE.
THAT'S A DESPERATE BATTLE, EVEN FOR A HERO!
SEKI'S MOTIVE FROM THE GET-GO WAS TO WATCH THE HERO GET HURT.
WHAT A NASTY GAME THAT ONLY HE COULD THINK UP.
TAP
トッ
BUT THAT'S NO PROBLEM.
I'LL JUST ROUT THE MONSTERS INSTEAD!
!
HEH
フッ
HUH?!

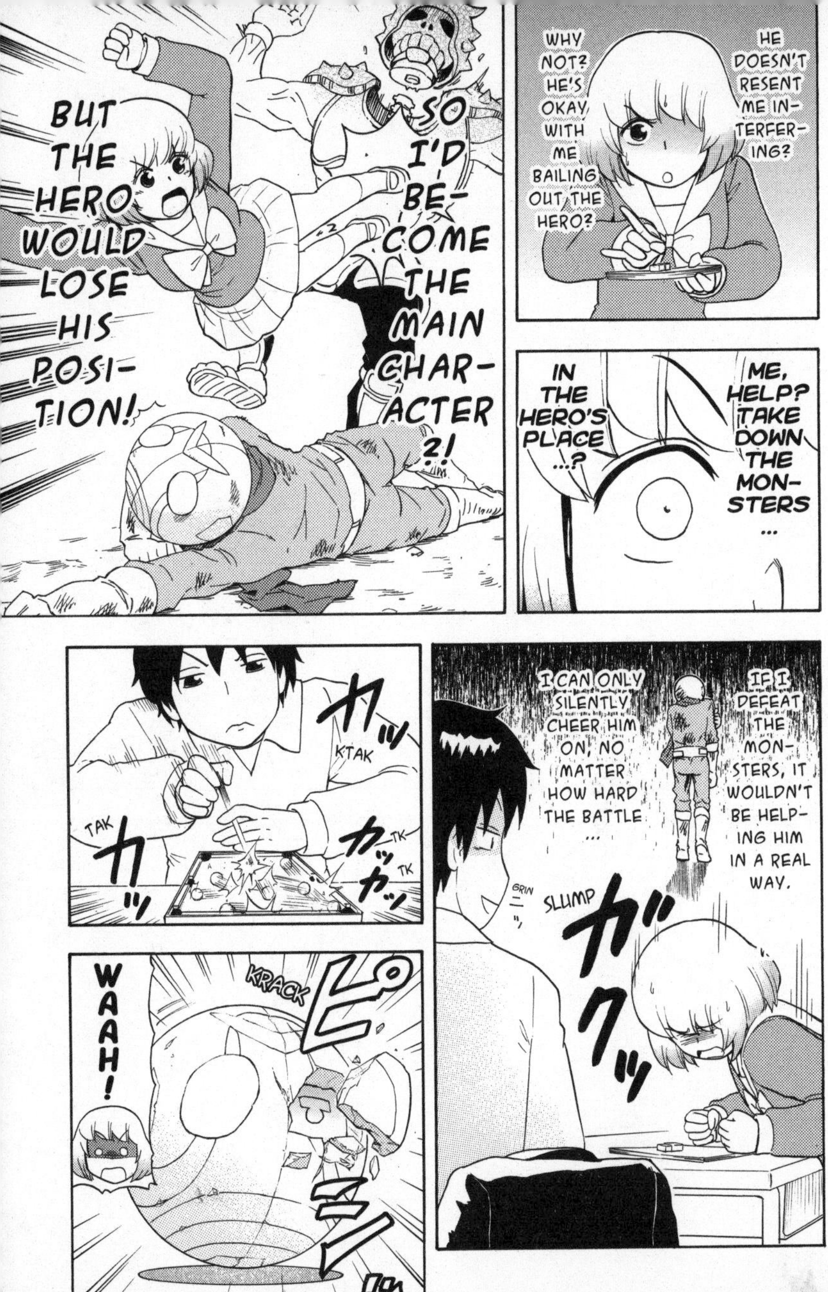
HE DOESN'T RESENT ME INTERFERING?
WHY NOT? HE'S OKAY WITH ME BAILING OUT THE HERO?
ME, HELP? TAKE DOWN THE MONSTERS ...
IN THE HERO'S PLACE ...?
SO I'D BECOME THE MAIN CHARACTER?!
BUT THE HERO WOULD LOSE HIS POSITION!
IF I DEFEAT THE MONSTERS, IT WOULDN'T BE HELPING HIM IN A REAL WAY.
I CAN ONLY SILENTLY CHEER HIM ON, NO MATTER HOW HARD THE BATTLE ...
SLUMP
GRIN
KTAK
TK
TK
TAK
KRACK
WAAAH!

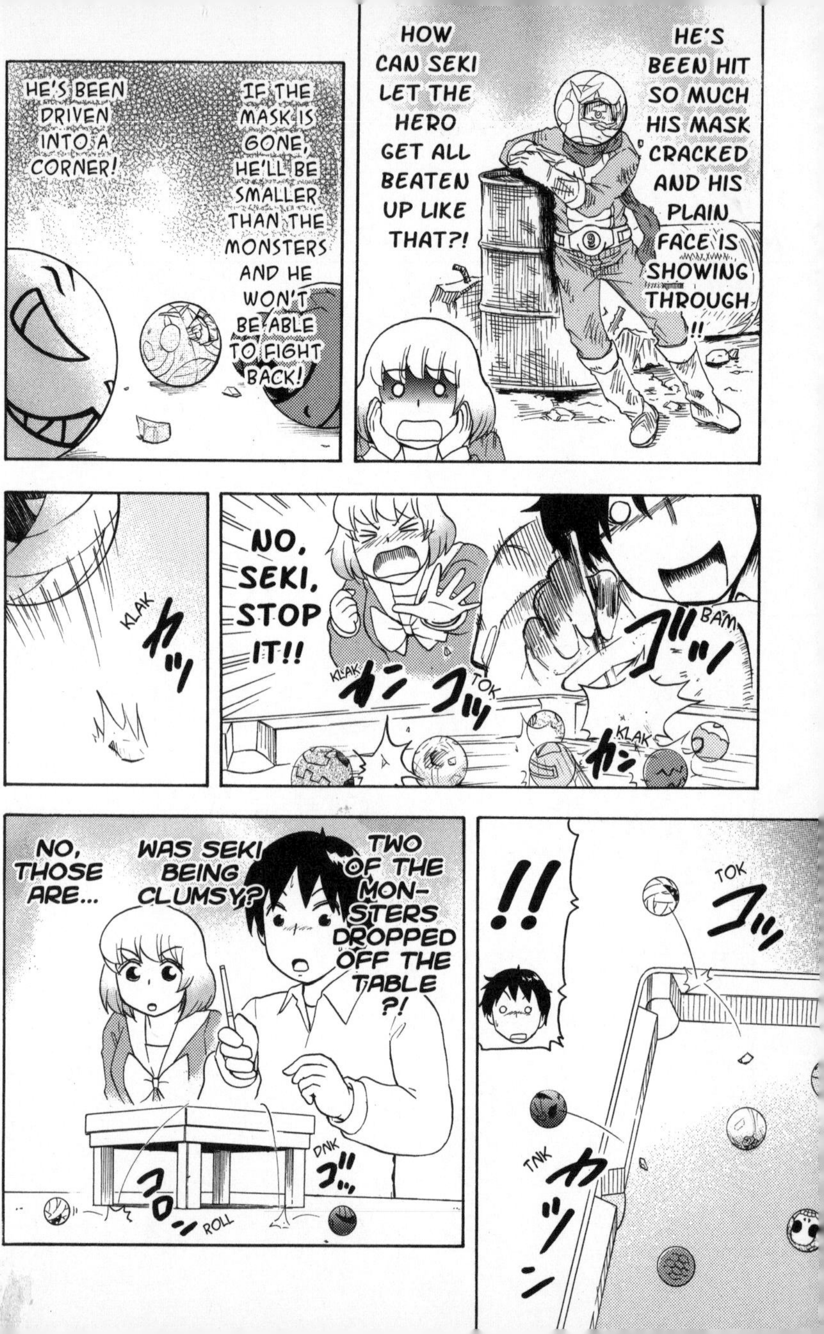

HE'S BEEN HIT SO MUCH HIS MASK CRACKED AND HIS PLAIN FACE IS SHOWING THROUGH!!
HOW CAN SEKI LET THE HERO GET ALL BEATEN UP LIKE THAT?!
IF THE MASK IS GONE, HE'LL BE SMALLER THAN THE MONSTERS AND HE WON'T BE ABLE TO FIGHT BACK!
HE'S BEEN DRIVEN INTO A CORNER!
BAM
NO, SEKI, STOP IT!!
TOK
KLAK
KLAK
KLAK
!!
TOK
TNK
TWO OF THE MON-STERS DROPPED OFF THE TABLE?!
WAS SEKI BEING CLUMSY?
NO, THOSE ARE...
DNK
ROLL

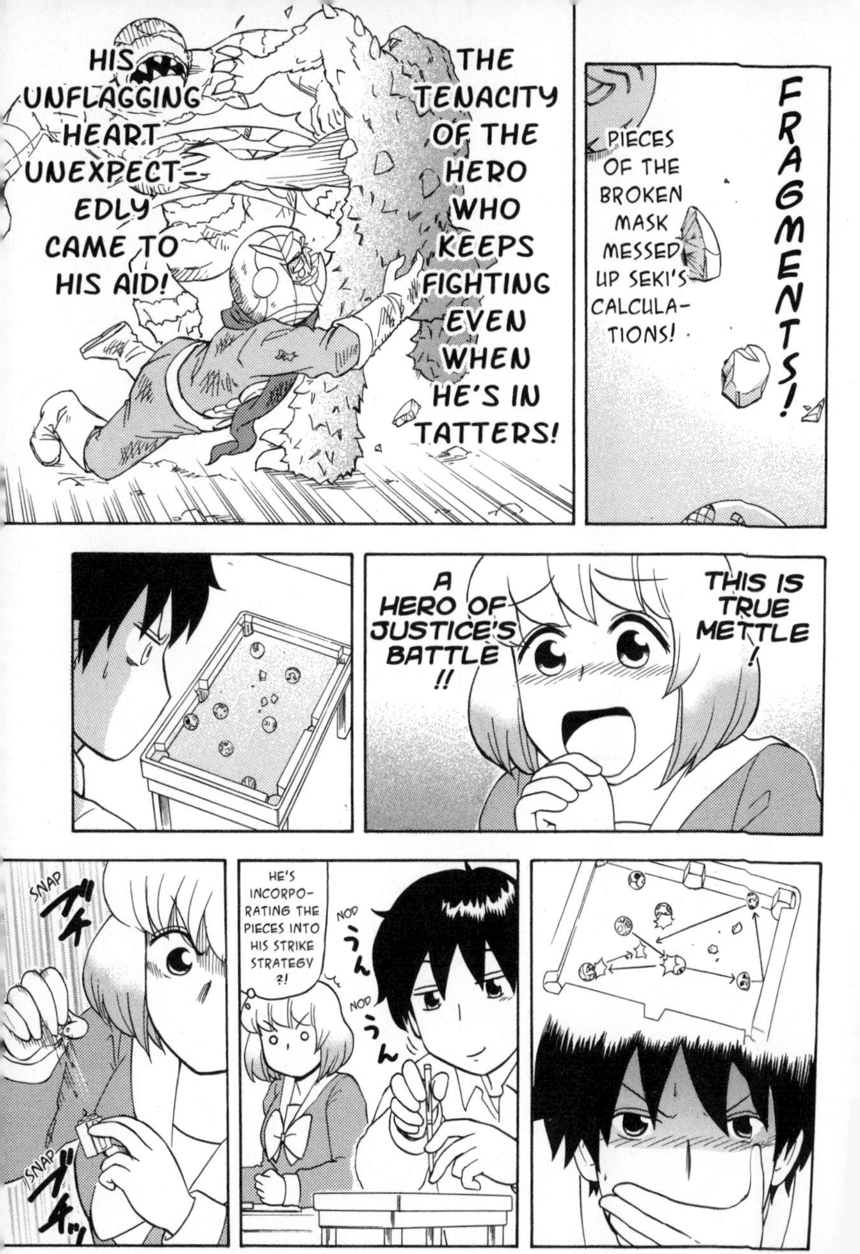
FRAGMENTS!
PIECES OF THE BROKEN MASK MESSED UP SEKI'S CALCULA- TIONS!
THE TENACITY OF THE HERO WHO KEEPS FIGHTING EVEN WHEN HE'S IN TATTERS!
HIS UNFLAGGING HEART UNEXPECT- EDLY CAME TO HIS AID!
THIS IS TRUE METTLE !
A HERO OF JUSTICE'S BATTLE !!
NOD うん
NOD うん
HE'S INCORPO- RATING THE PIECES INTO HIS STRIKE STRATEGY ?!
SNAP ブチ
SNAP ブチッ

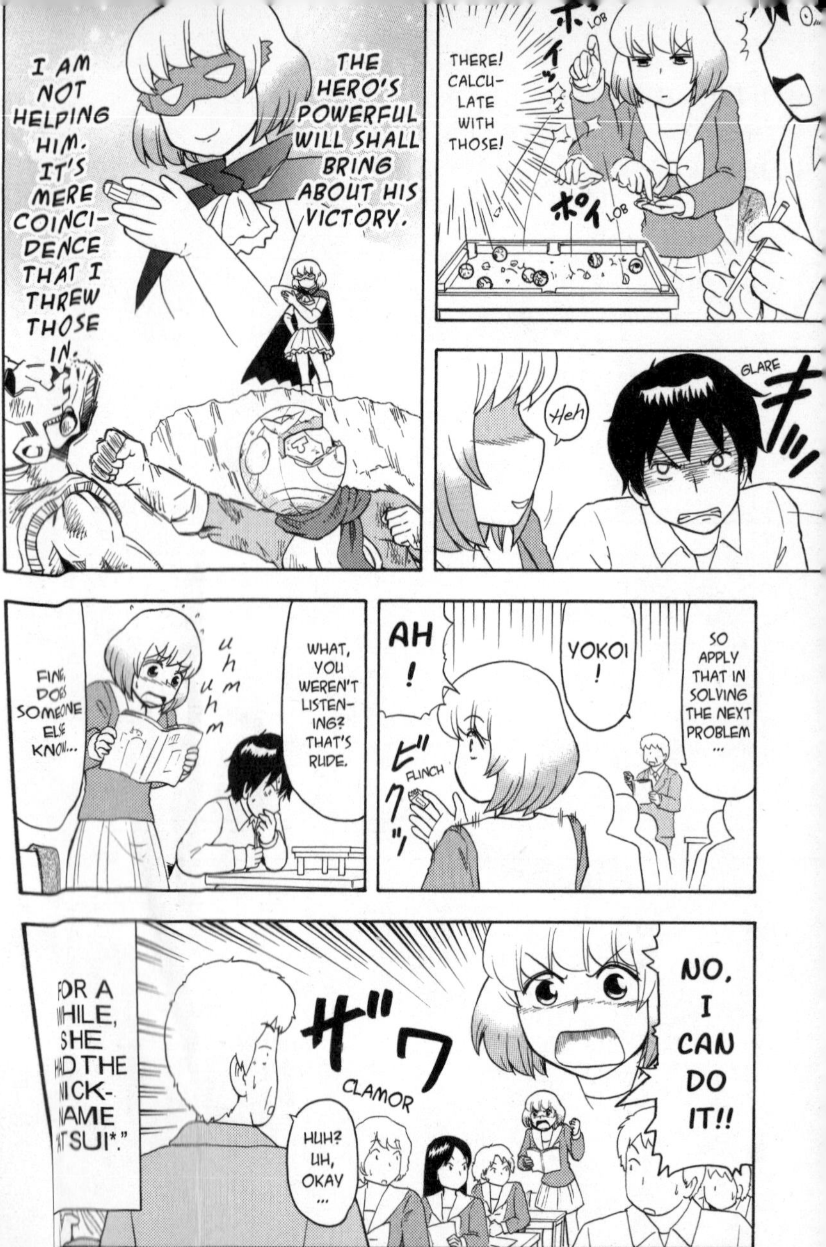
LOB
THERE! CALCULATE WITH THOSE!
LOB
GLARE
Heh
THE HERO'S POWERFUL WILL SHALL BRING ABOUT HIS VICTORY.
I AM NOT HELPING HIM. IT'S MERE COINCIDENCE THAT I THREW THOSE IN.
SO APPLY THAT IN SOLVING THE NEXT PROBLEM ...
YOKOI!
AH!
FLINCH
WHAT, YOU WEREN'T LISTENING? THAT'S RUDE.
uhm uhm
FINE, DOES SOMEONE ELSE KNOW...
NO, I CAN DO IT!!
CLAMOR
HUH? UH, OKAY ...
FOR A WHILE, SHE HAD THE NICKNAME "ATSUI*."

*Atsui: Hot / Intense

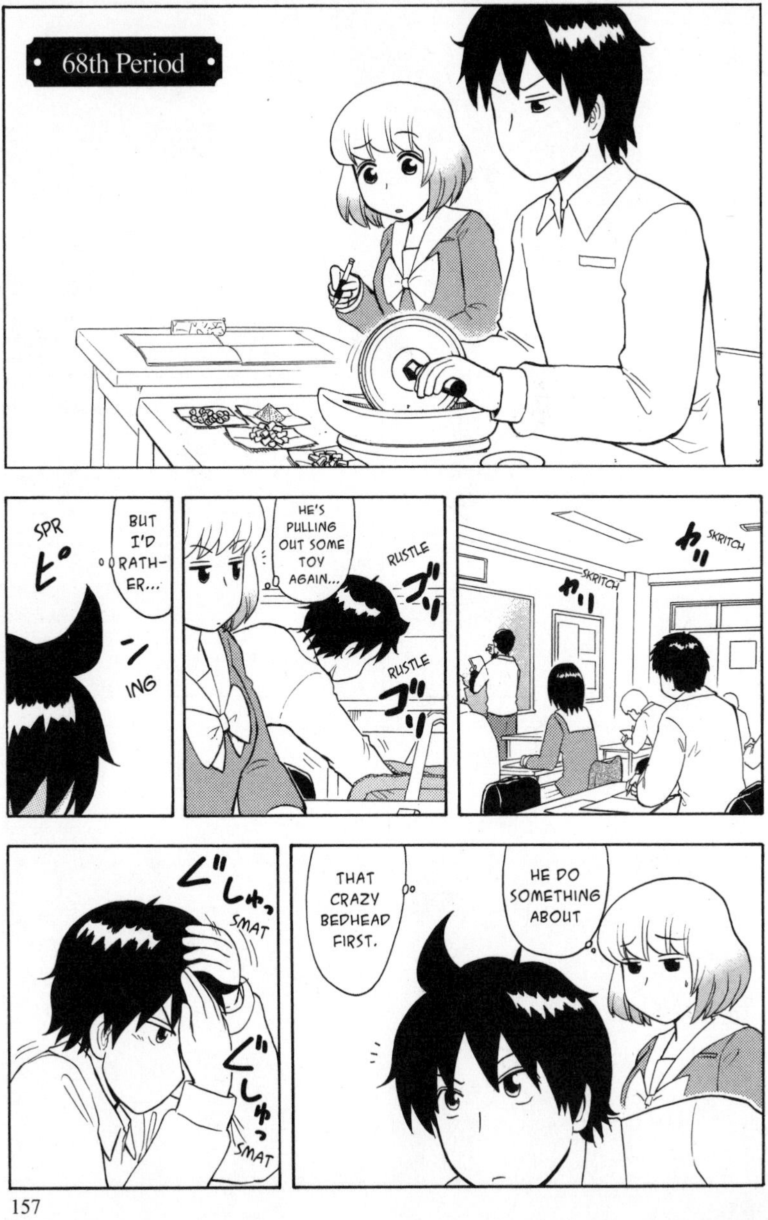
68th Period
SKRITCH
SKRITCH
HE'S PULLING OUT SOME TOY AGAIN...
RUSTLE
RUSTLE
SPR
BUT I'D RATHER...
ING
HE DO SOMETHING ABOUT
THAT CRAZY BEDHEAD FIRST.
SMAT
SMAT

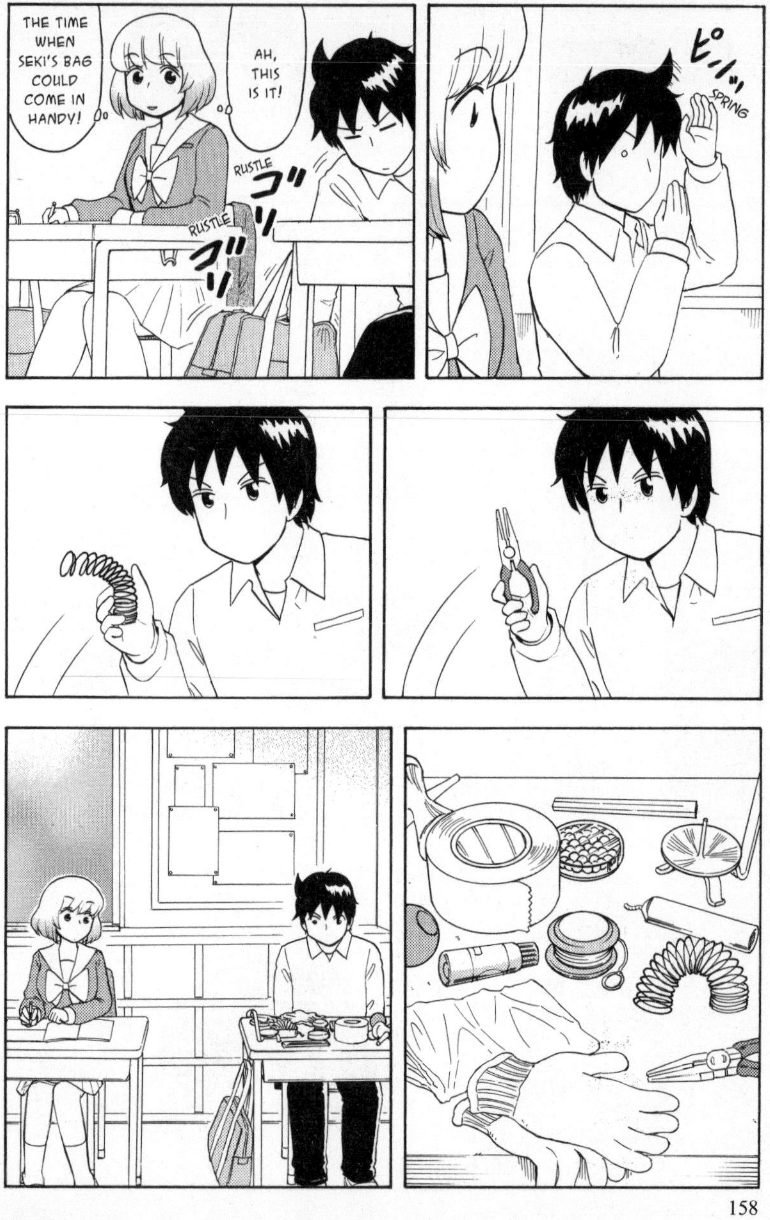
SPRING
AH, THIS IS IT!
THE TIME WHEN SEKI'S BAG COULD COME IN HANDY!
RUSTLE
ゴソ
RUSTLE
ゴソ

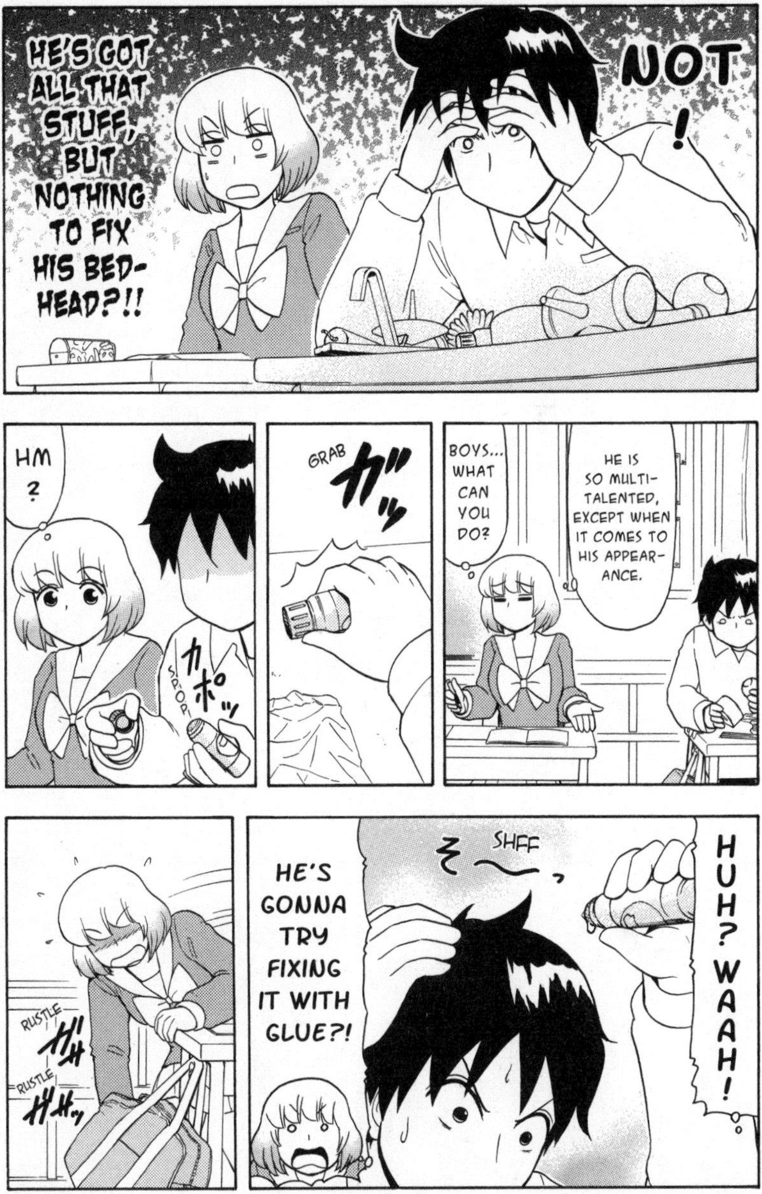
NOT!
HE'S GOT ALL THAT STUFF, BUT NOTHING TO FIX HIS BED-HEAD?!!
HE IS SO MULTI-TALENTED, EXCEPT WHEN IT COMES TO HIS APPEARANCE.
BOYS... WHAT CAN YOU DO?
GRAB
HM?
SPOP
HUH? WAAH!
SHFF
HE'S GONNA TRY FIXING IT WITH GLUE?!
RUSTLE
RUSTLE

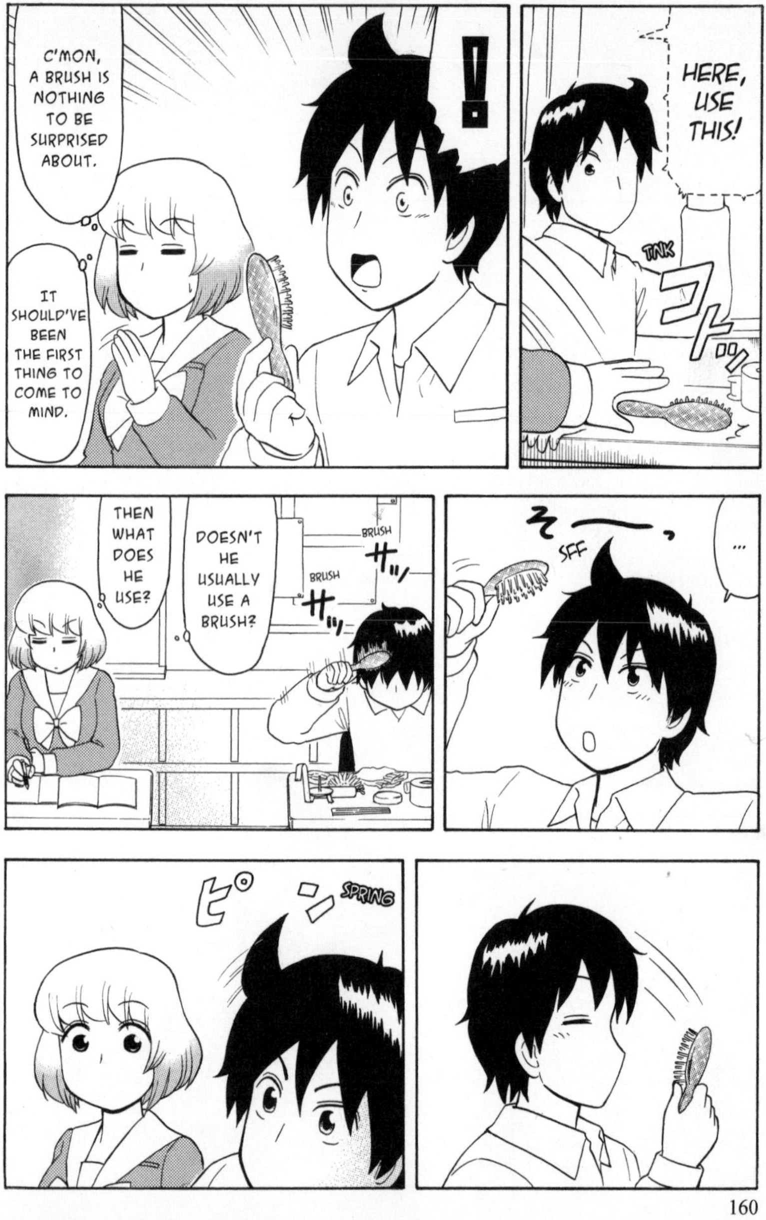
HERE, USE THIS!
TNK
!
C'MON, A BRUSH IS NOTHING TO BE SURPRISED ABOUT.
IT SHOULD'VE BEEN THE FIRST THING TO COME TO MIND.
...
SFF
DOESN'T HE USUALLY USE A BRUSH?
BRUSH
BRUSH
THEN WHAT DOES HE USE?
SPRING

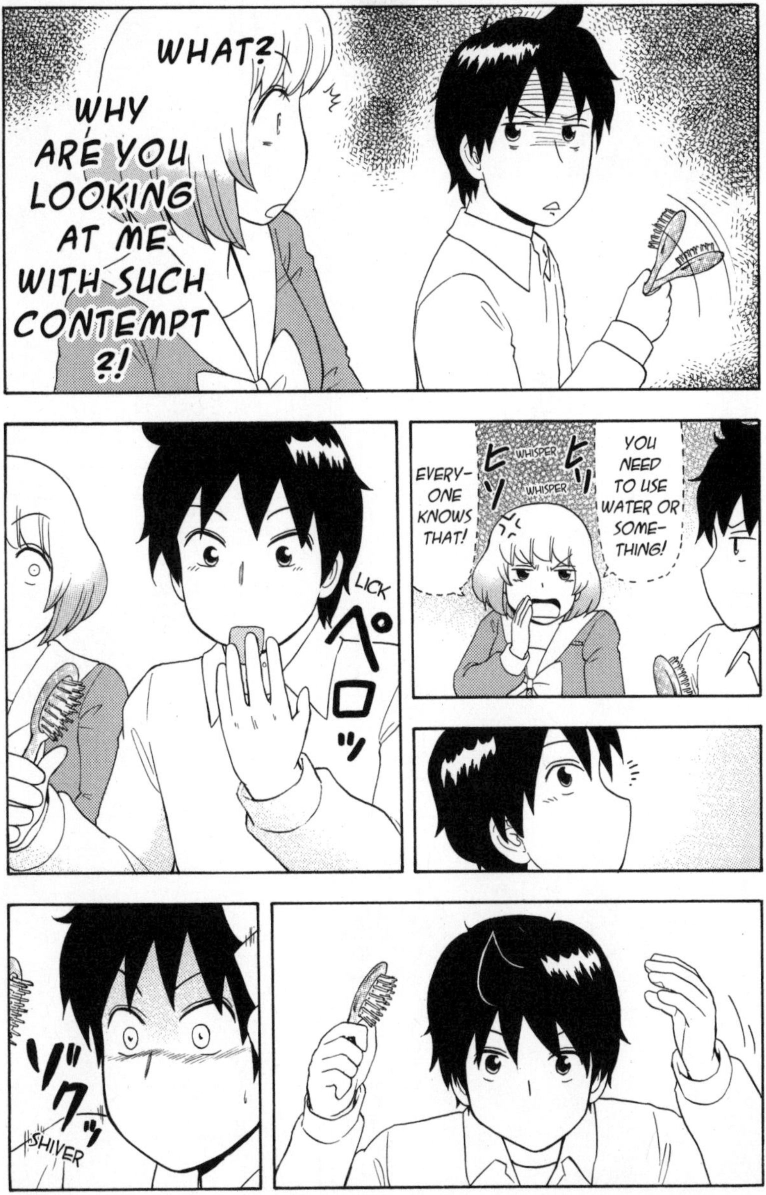
WHAT?
WHY ARE YOU LOOKING AT ME WITH SUCH CONTEMPT ?!
ヒソ
WHISPER
ヒソ
WHISPER
YOU NEED TO USE WATER OR SOME-THING!
EVERY-ONE KNOWS THAT!
LICK
ペロッ
ゾクッ
SHIVER

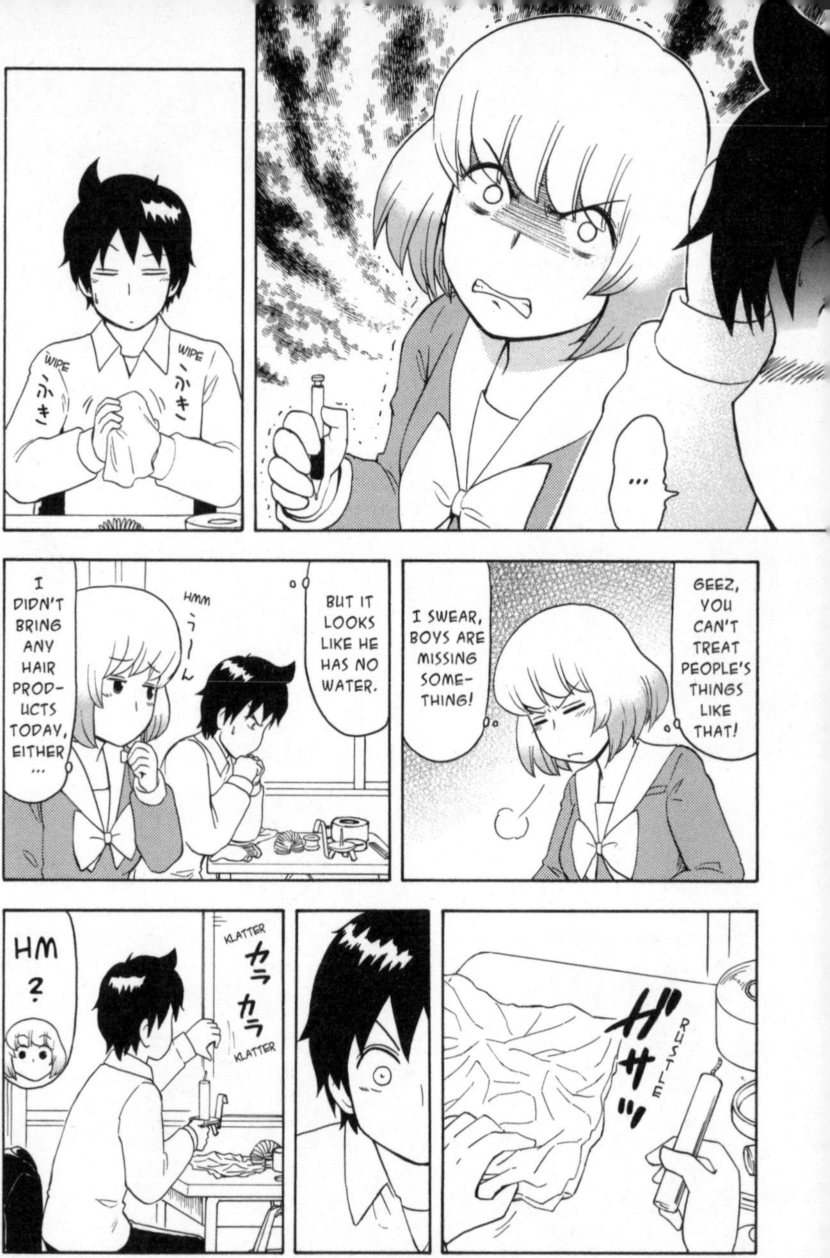
...
WIPE ふき
WIPE ふき
GEEZ, YOU CAN'T TREAT PEOPLE'S THINGS LIKE THAT!
I SWEAR, BOYS ARE MISSING SOME-THING!
BUT IT LOOKS LIKE HE HAS NO WATER.
HMM うーん
I DIDN'T BRING ANY HAIR PROD-UCTS TODAY, EITHER ...
ガサッ RUSTLE
KLATTER カラ
カラ KLATTER
HM ?

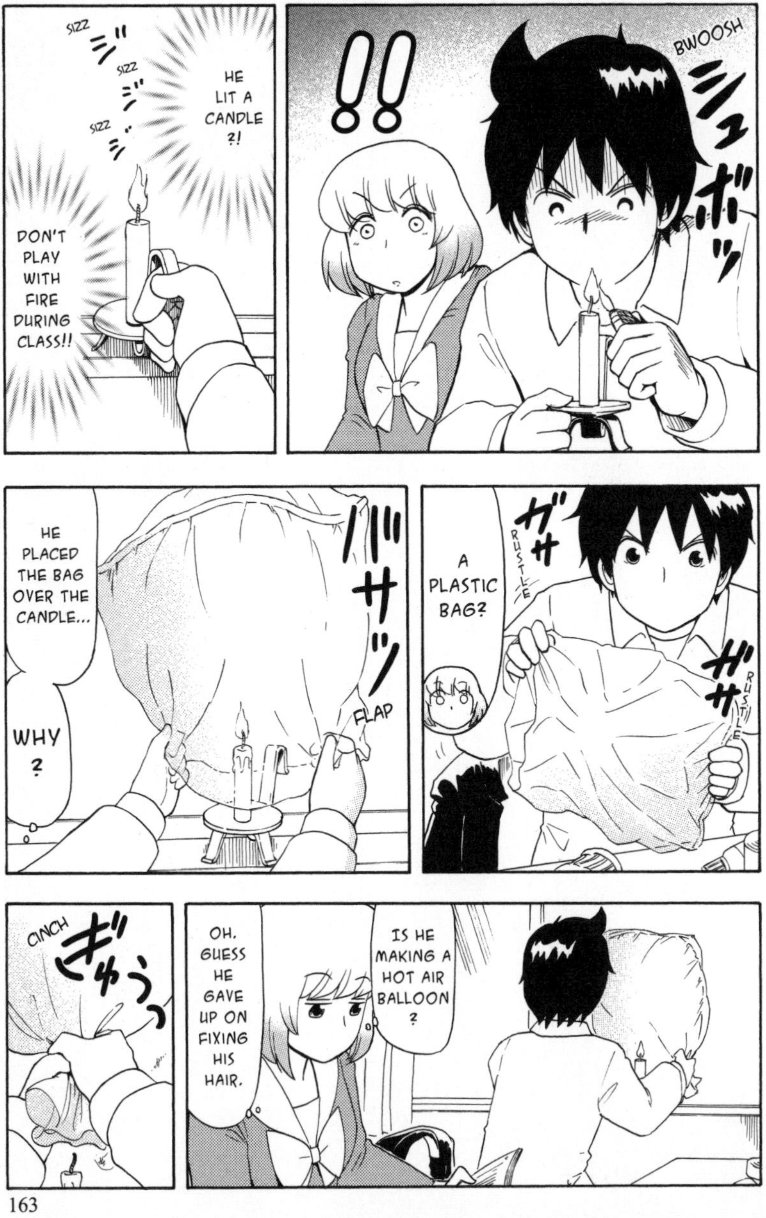

BWOOSH
シュボッ
!!
SIZZ
ジ
SIZZ
ジ
SIZZ
ジ
HE LIT A CANDLE?!
DON'T PLAY WITH FIRE DURING CLASS!!
ガサ
RUSTLE
A PLASTIC BAG?
ガサ
RUSTLE
バサッ
FLAP
HE PLACED THE BAG OVER THE CANDLE...
WHY?
IS HE MAKING A HOT AIR BALLOON?
OH. GUESS HE GAVE UP ON FIXING HIS HAIR.
CINCH
ぎゅうっ

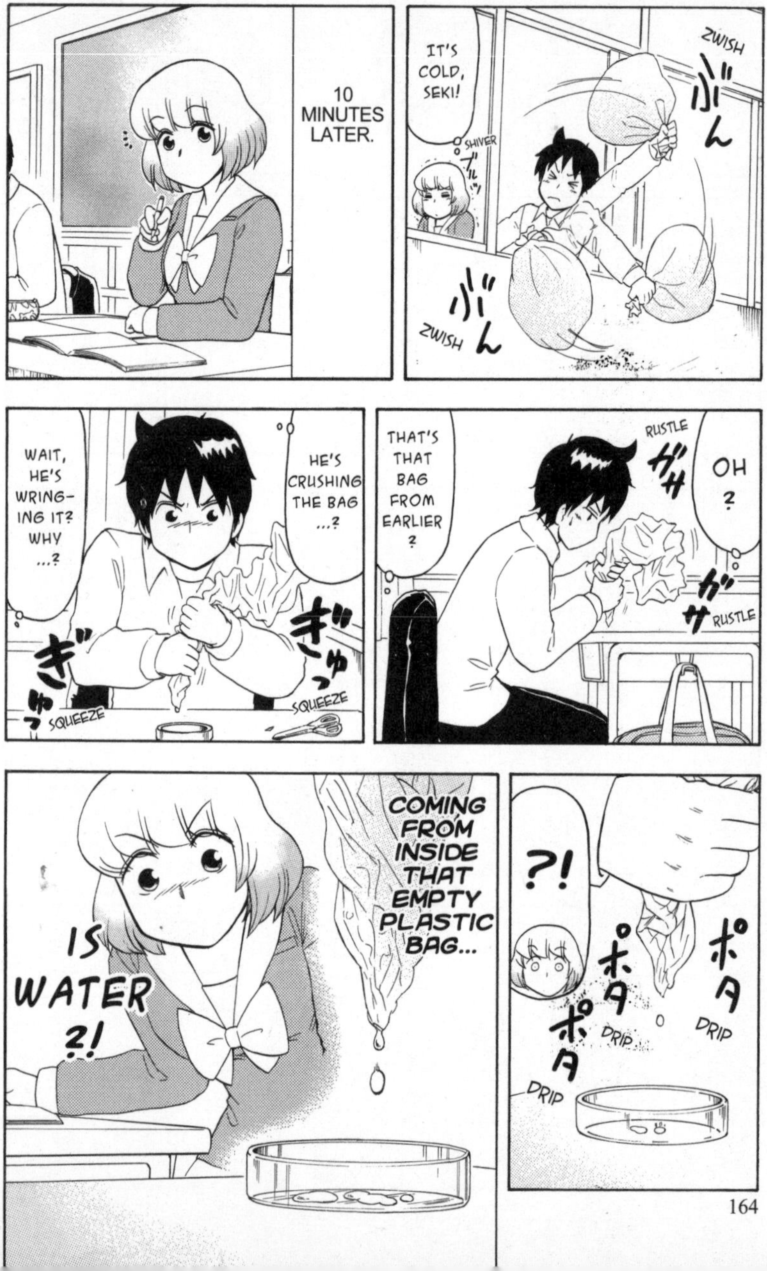
ZWISH
ぶん
IT'S COLD, SEKI!
SHIVER
ブルッ
ぶん
ZWISH
10 MINUTES LATER.
RUSTLE
ガサ
OH?
THAT'S THAT BAG FROM EARLIER?
ガサ
RUSTLE
HE'S CRUSHING THE BAG ...?
WAIT, HE'S WRING-ING IT? WHY ...?
ぎゅっ
SQUEEZE
ぎゅっ
SQUEEZE
?!
ポタ
DRIP
ポタ
DRIP
ポタ
DRIP
COMING FROM INSIDE THAT EMPTY PLASTIC BAG...
IS WATER ?!

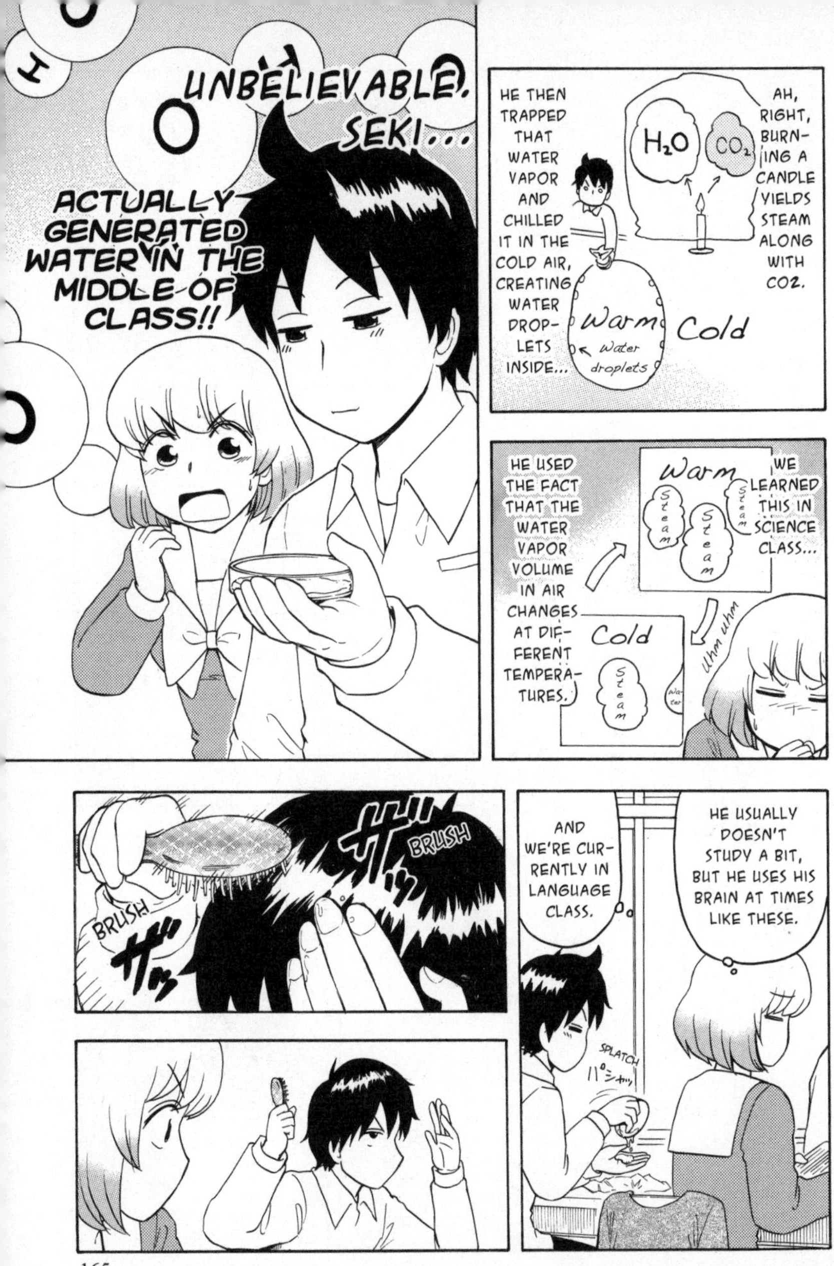
AH, RIGHT, BURNING A CANDLE YIELDS STEAM ALONG WITH CO2.
HE THEN TRAPPED THAT WATER VAPOR AND CHILLED IT IN THE COLD AIR, CREATING WATER DROPLETS INSIDE...
H_2O
CO_2
Warm
Water droplets
Cold
WE LEARNED THIS IN SCIENCE CLASS...
HE USED THE FACT THAT THE WATER VAPOR VOLUME IN AIR CHANGES AT DIFFERENT TEMPERATURES.
Warm
Steam
Steam
Steam
Cold
Steam
Water
Uhm uhm
UNBELIEVABLE, SEKI...
ACTUALLY GENERATED WATER IN THE MIDDLE OF CLASS!!
HE USUALLY DOESN'T STUDY A BIT, BUT HE USES HIS BRAIN AT TIMES LIKE THESE.
AND WE'RE CURRENTLY IN LANGUAGE CLASS.
SPLATCH
BRUSH
BRUSH

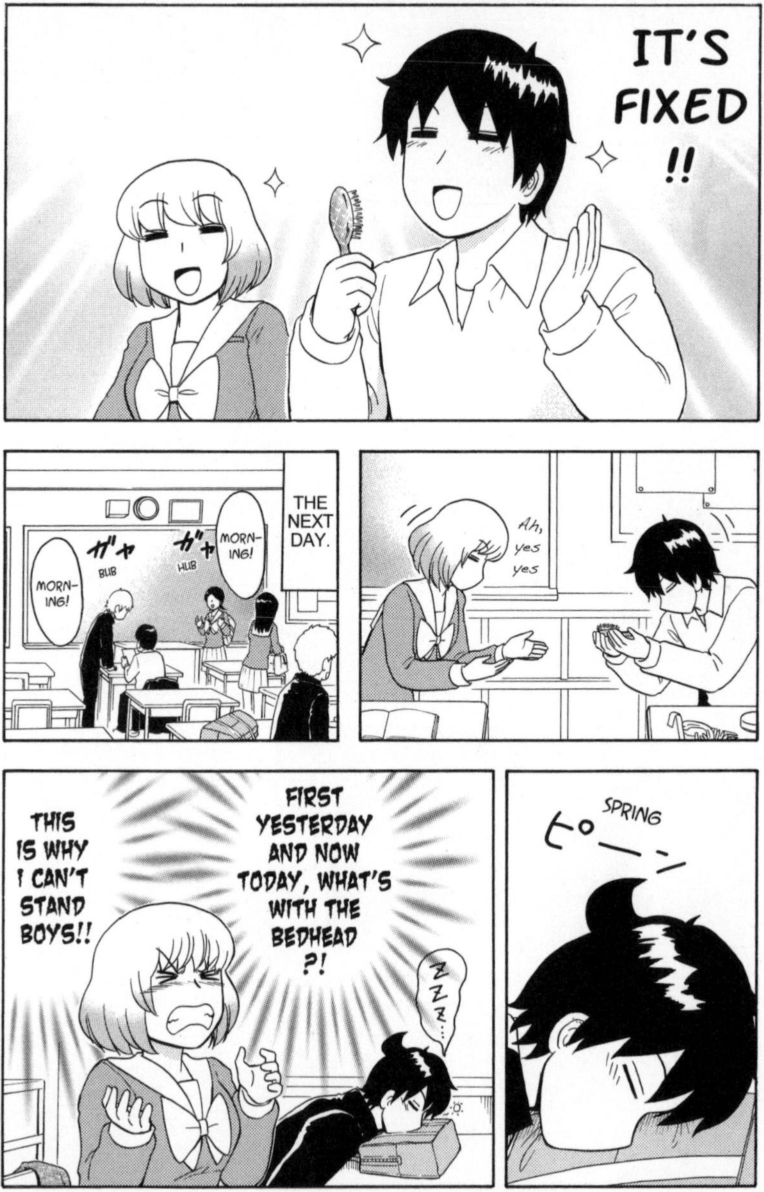
IT'S FIXED !!
Ah, yes yes
THE NEXT DAY.
MORN-ING!
ガヤ
HUB
ガヤ
BUB
MORN-ING!
ピーン
SPRING
FIRST YESTERDAY AND NOW TODAY, WHAT'S WITH THE BEDHEAD ?!
THIS IS WHY I CAN'T STAND BOYS!!
ZZZ...

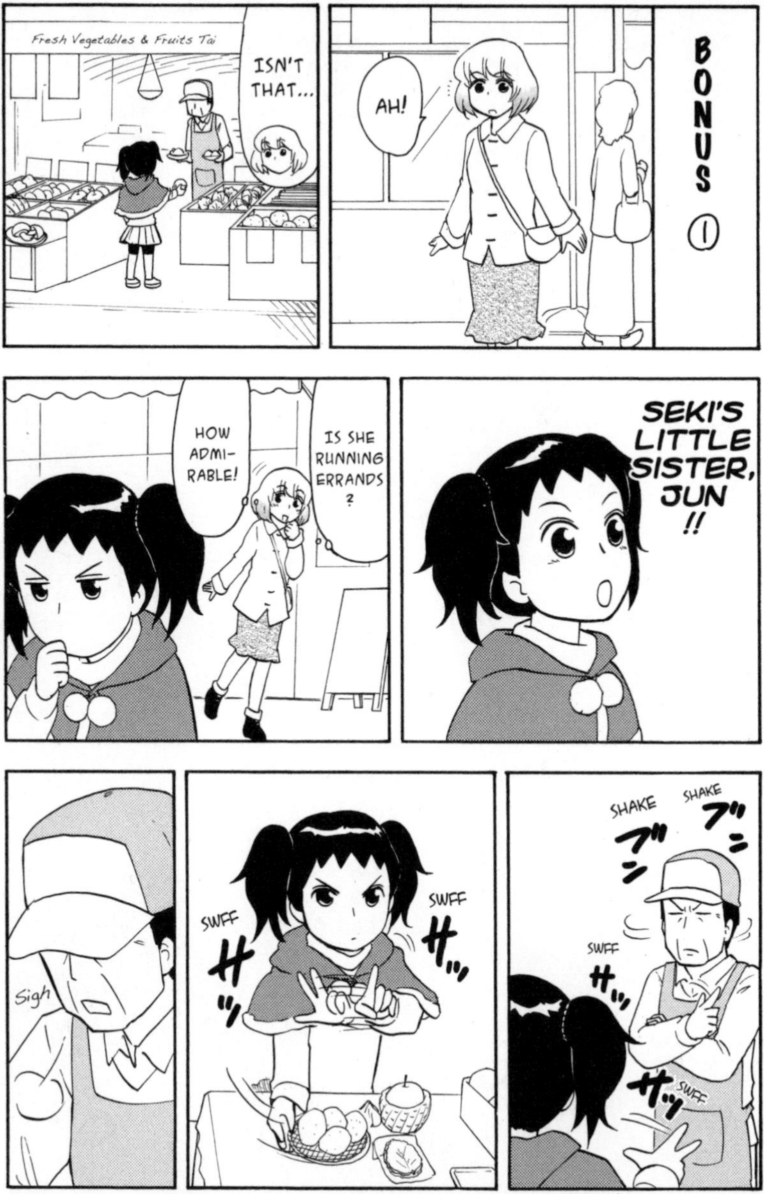
BONUS ①
AH!
ISN'T THAT...
Fresh Vegetables & Fruits Tai
SEKI'S LITTLE SISTER, JUN!!
IS SHE RUNNING ERRANDS?
HOW ADMIRABLE!
SHAKE
SHAKE
SWFF
SWFF
SWFF
SWFF
Sigh

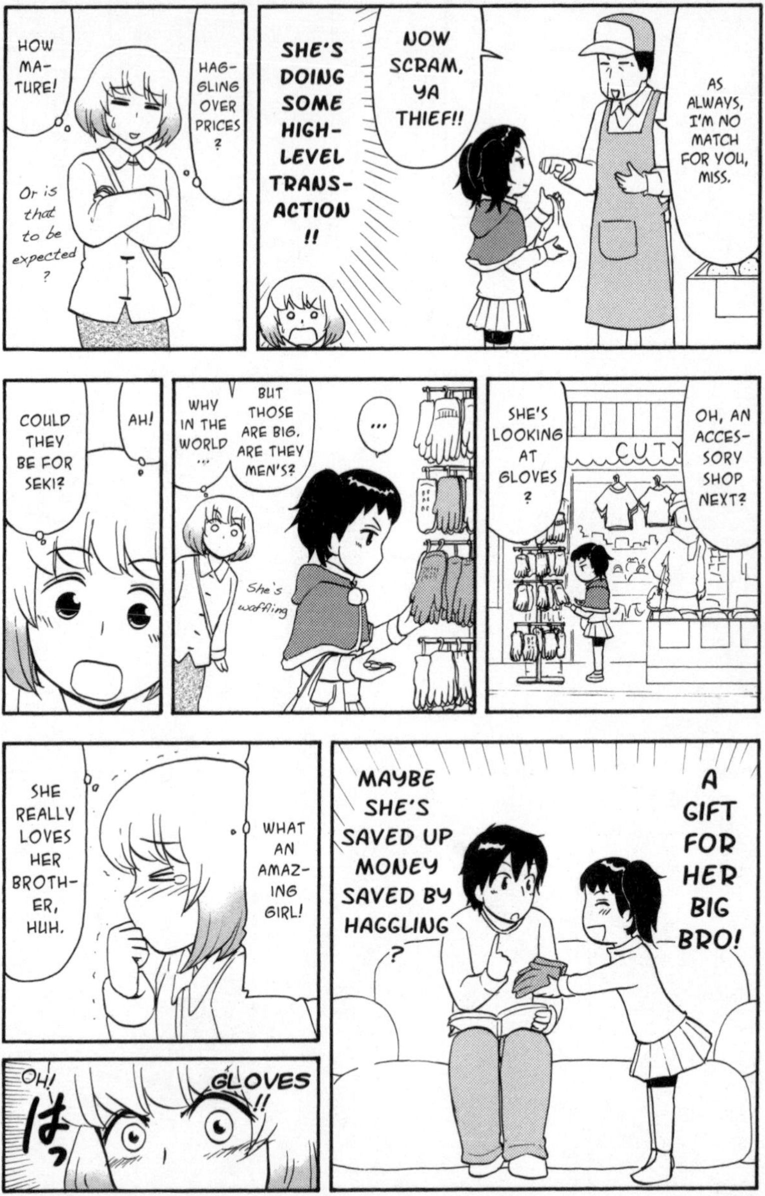
AS ALWAYS, I'M NO MATCH FOR YOU, MISS.
NOW SCRAM, YA THIEF!!
SHE'S DOING SOME HIGH-LEVEL TRANSACTION!!
HAGGLING OVER PRICES?
HOW MATURE!
Or is that to be expected?
OH, AN ACCESSORY SHOP NEXT?
CUTY
SHE'S LOOKING AT GLOVES?
...
BUT THOSE ARE BIG. ARE THEY MEN'S?
WHY IN THE WORLD...
She's waffling
AH!
COULD THEY BE FOR SEKI?
A GIFT FOR HER BIG BRO!
MAYBE SHE'S SAVED UP MONEY SAVED BY HAGGLING?
WHAT AN AMAZING GIRL!
SHE REALLY LOVES HER BROTHER, HUH.
GLOVES!!
OH!
はっ

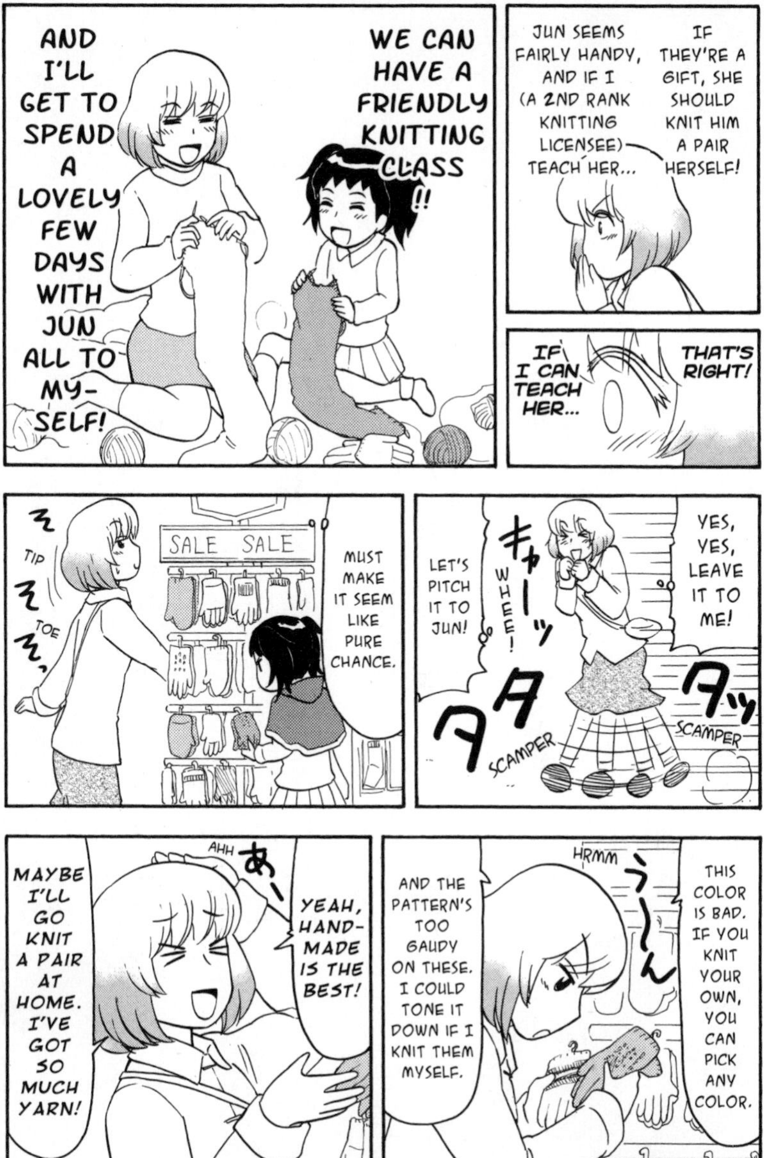
IF THEY'RE A GIFT, SHE SHOULD KNIT HIM A PAIR HERSELF!
JUN SEEMS FAIRLY HANDY, AND IF I (A 2ND RANK KNITTING LICENSEE) TEACH HER...
THAT'S RIGHT!
IF I CAN TEACH HER...
WE CAN HAVE A FRIENDLY KNITTING CLASS!!
AND I'LL GET TO SPEND A LOVELY FEW DAYS WITH JUN ALL TO MY-SELF!
YES, YES, LEAVE IT TO ME!
キャーッ
WHEE!
LET'S PITCH IT TO JUN!
タッ
SCAMPER
タタ
SCAMPER
MUST MAKE IT SEEM LIKE PURE CHANCE.
SALE SALE
TIP
TOE
THIS COLOR IS BAD. IF YOU KNIT YOUR OWN, YOU CAN PICK ANY COLOR.
うーん
HRMM
AND THE PATTERN'S TOO GAUDY ON THESE. I COULD TONE IT DOWN IF I KNIT THEM MYSELF.
YEAH, HAND-MADE IS THE BEST!
あ、
AHH
MAYBE I'LL GO KNIT A PAIR AT HOME. I'VE GOT SO MUCH YARN!

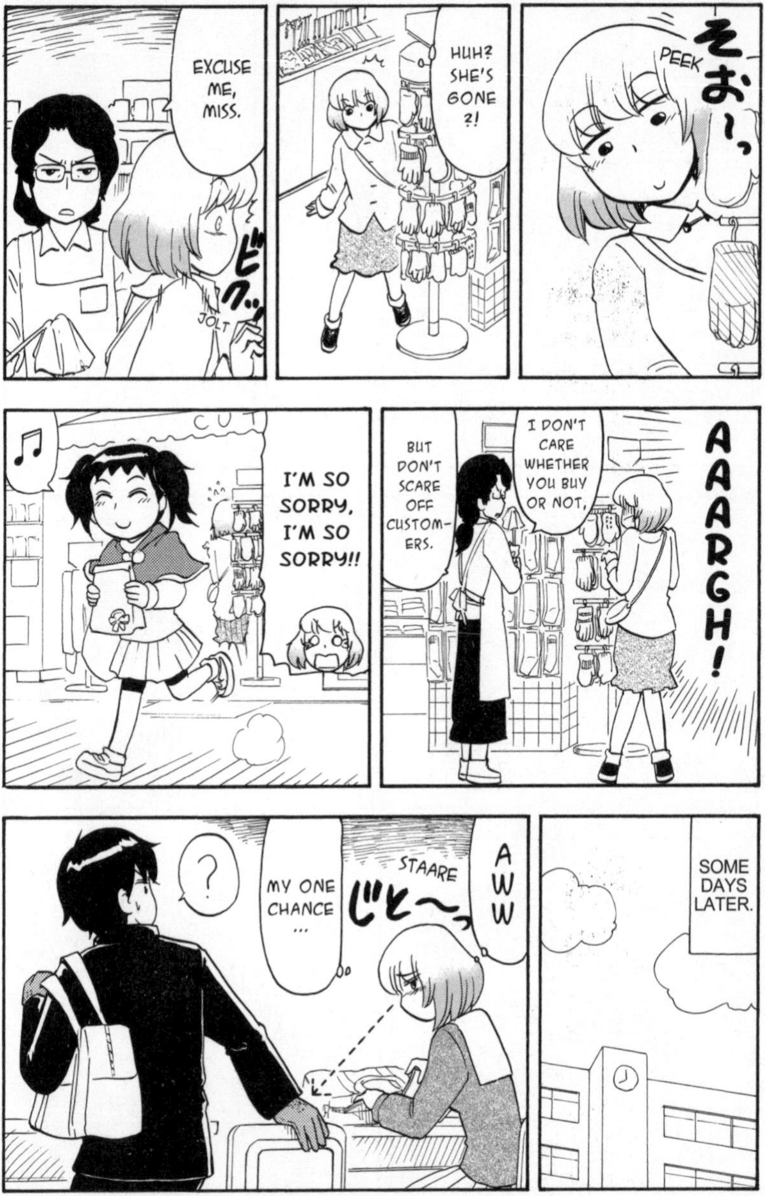
そお～っ
PEEK
HUH? SHE'S GONE?!
EXCUSE ME, MISS.
ビクッ
JOLT
AAAARGH!
I DON'T CARE WHETHER YOU BUY OR NOT,
BUT DON'T SCARE OFF CUSTOM-ERS.
I'M SO SORRY, I'M SO SORRY!!
♪
SOME DAYS LATER.
AWW
じとーっ
STAARE
MY ONE CHANCE ...
?

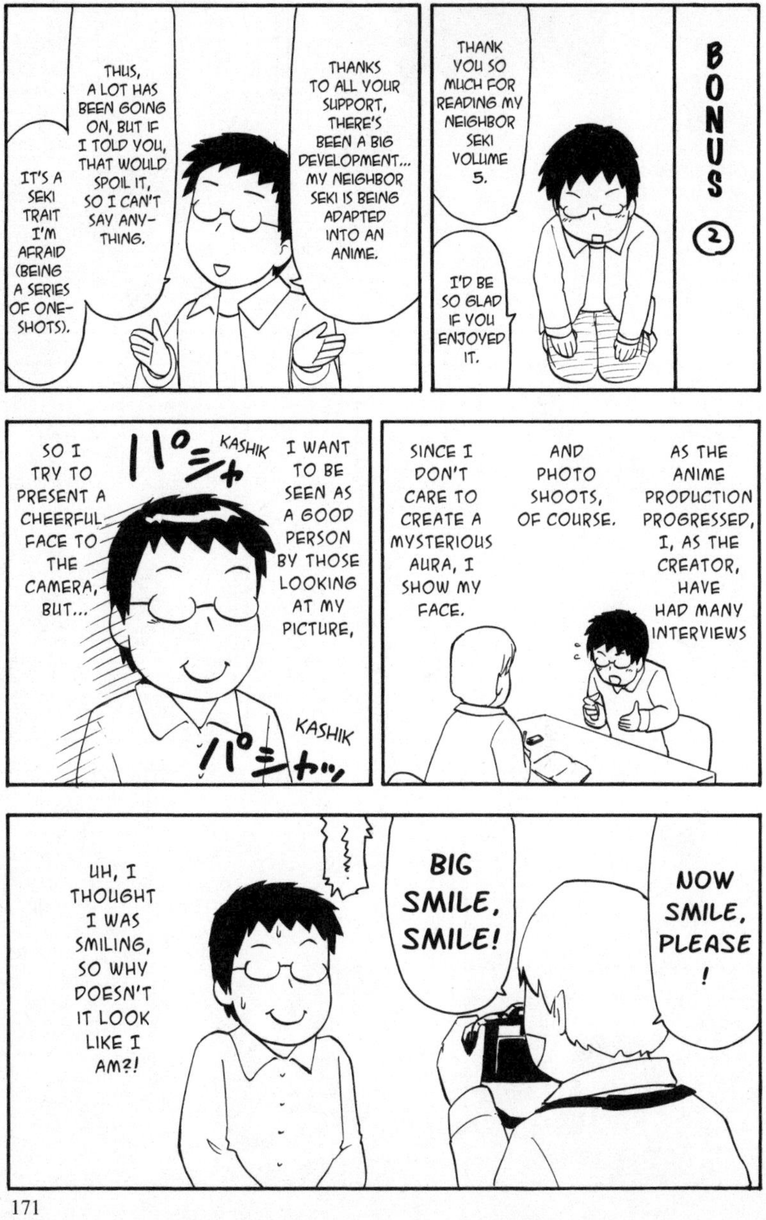
BONUS ②
THANK YOU SO MUCH FOR READING MY NEIGHBOR SEKI VOLUME 5.
I'D BE SO GLAD IF YOU ENJOYED IT.
THANKS TO ALL YOUR SUPPORT, THERE'S BEEN A BIG DEVELOPMENT... MY NEIGHBOR SEKI IS BEING ADAPTED INTO AN ANIME.
THUS, A LOT HAS BEEN GOING ON, BUT IF I TOLD YOU, THAT WOULD SPOIL IT, SO I CAN'T SAY ANY-THING.
IT'S A SEKI TRAIT I'M AFRAID (BEING A SERIES OF ONE-SHOTS).
AS THE ANIME PRODUCTION PROGRESSED, I, AS THE CREATOR, HAVE HAD MANY INTERVIEWS
AND PHOTO SHOOTS, OF COURSE.
SINCE I DON'T CARE TO CREATE A MYSTERIOUS AURA, I SHOW MY FACE.
I WANT TO BE SEEN AS A GOOD PERSON BY THOSE LOOKING AT MY PICTURE,
パシャ
KASHIK
SO I TRY TO PRESENT A CHEERFUL FACE TO THE CAMERA, BUT...
パシャッ
KASHIK
NOW SMILE, PLEASE!
BIG SMILE, SMILE!
UH, I THOUGHT I WAS SMILING, SO WHY DOESN'T IT LOOK LIKE I AM?!

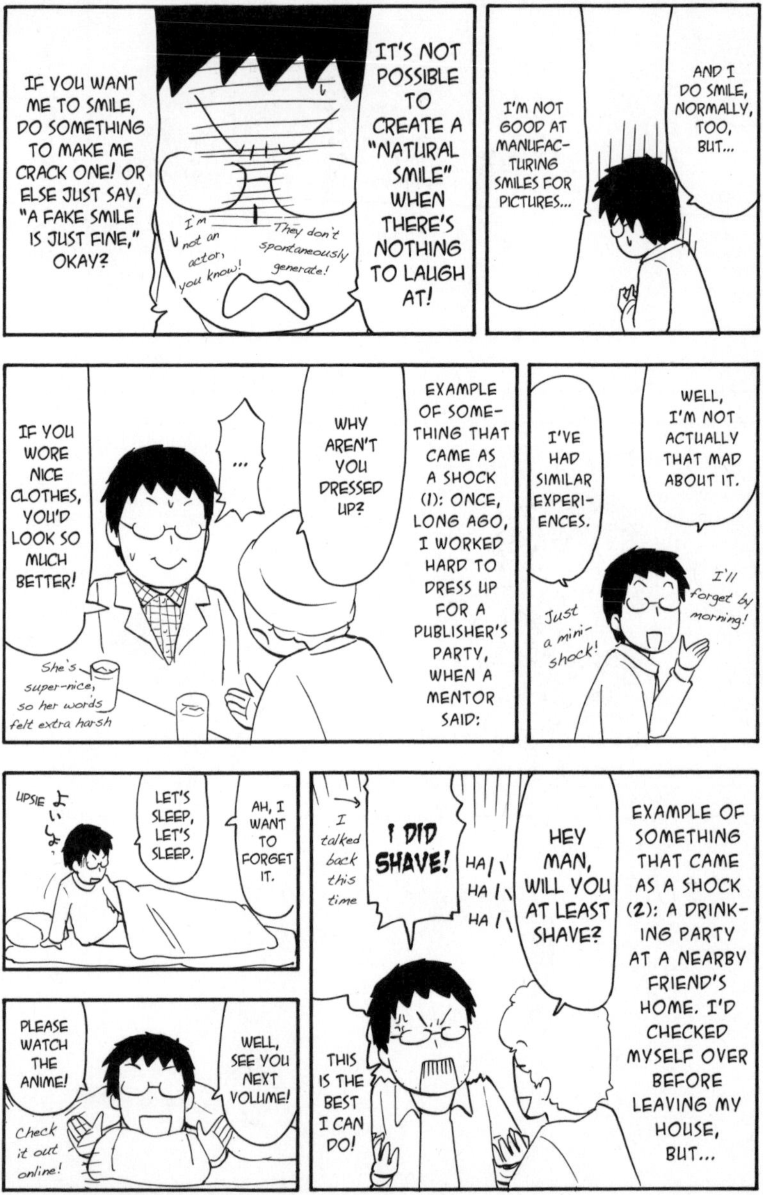
AND I DO SMILE, NORMALLY, TOO, BUT...
I'M NOT GOOD AT MANUFACTURING SMILES FOR PICTURES...
IT'S NOT POSSIBLE TO CREATE A "NATURAL SMILE" WHEN THERE'S NOTHING TO LAUGH AT!
They don't spontaneously generate!
I'm not an actor, you know!
IF YOU WANT ME TO SMILE, DO SOMETHING TO MAKE ME CRACK ONE! OR ELSE JUST SAY, "A FAKE SMILE IS JUST FINE," OKAY?
WELL, I'M NOT ACTUALLY THAT MAD ABOUT IT.
I'VE HAD SIMILAR EXPERIENCES.
I'll forget by morning!
Just a mini-shock!
EXAMPLE OF SOMETHING THAT CAME AS A SHOCK (1): ONCE, LONG AGO, I WORKED HARD TO DRESS UP FOR A PUBLISHER'S PARTY, WHEN A MENTOR SAID:
WHY AREN'T YOU DRESSED UP?
...
IF YOU WORE NICE CLOTHES, YOU'D LOOK SO MUCH BETTER!
She's super-nice, so her words felt extra harsh
EXAMPLE OF SOMETHING THAT CAME AS A SHOCK (2): A DRINKING PARTY AT A NEARBY FRIEND'S HOME. I'D CHECKED MYSELF OVER BEFORE LEAVING MY HOUSE, BUT...
HEY MAN, WILL YOU AT LEAST SHAVE?
HA HA HA
I DID SHAVE!
I talked back this time
THIS IS THE BEST I CAN DO!
AH, I WANT TO FORGET IT.
LET'S SLEEP, LET'S SLEEP.
UPSIE よいしょ
WELL, SEE YOU NEXT VOLUME!
PLEASE WATCH THE ANIME!
Check it out online!

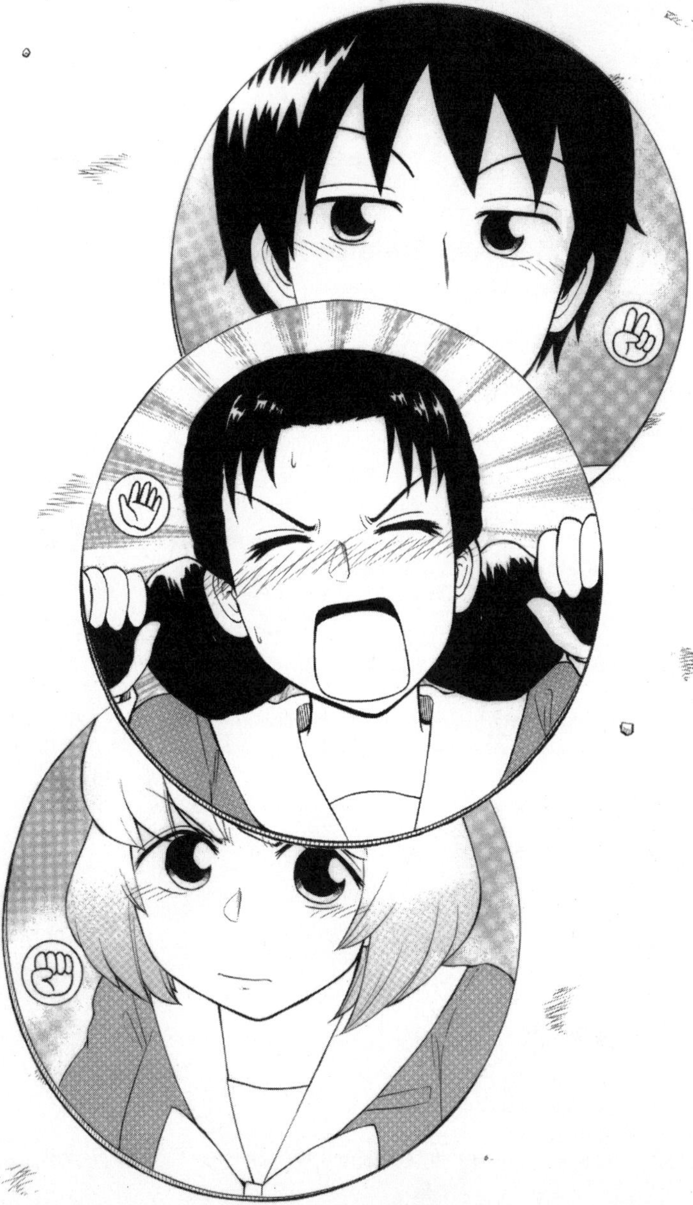

My Neighbor Seki, volume 5
Tonari no Seki-kun
A Vertical Comics Edition

Translation: Mari Morimoto
Production: Risa Cho
         Anthony Quintessenza

© Takuma Morishige 2014
Edited by MEDIA FACTORY
First published in Japan in 2014 by KADOKAWA CORPORATION, Tokyo.
English translation rights reserved by Vertical, Inc.
Under the license from KADOKAWA CORPORATION, Tokyo.

Translation provided by Vertical Comics, 2015
Published by Vertical Comics, an imprint of Vertical, Inc., New York

Originally published in Japanese as *Tonari no Seki-kun 5* by MEDIA FACTORY.
Tonari no Seki-kun first serialized in *Gekkan Comic Flapper*, MEDIA FACTORY, 2010-

This is a work of fiction.

ISBN: 978-1-941220-89-4

Manufactured in the United States of America

First Edition

Vertical, Inc.
451 Park Avenue South
7th Floor
New York, NY 10016
www.vertical-comics.com

Vertical books are distributed through Penguin-Random House Publisher Services.